Era of the Bat

Six Abstract and Political Plays

Era of the Bat: Six Abstract and Political Plays

The Lontar Foundation
Jl. Danau Laut Tawar, Blok A/53
Bendungan Hilir, Tanah Abang,
Jakarta 10210, Indonesia
www.lontar.org

Design by DesignLab, layout by Cyprianus Jaya Naipun
Cover artwork *Cremation* by Ikranagara

ISBN 978-623-7150-22-0

Era of the Bat

Six Abstract and Political Plays

by

Ikranagara

Translated by

Cobina Gillitt and Kay Ikranagara

with an introduction by

Cobina Gillitt

LONTAR

Jakarta, Indonesia

Contents

Introduction

The plays in this collection by Ikranagara were written and performed by his theater company Teater Saja between 1975 and 1997 during Indonesia's New Order era (1966–1998) when freedom of speech was severely curtailed under the autocratic rule of President Soeharto. The New Order regime was plagued by corruption, collusion, and nepotism with widespread allegations of government officials engaging in illicit activities for personal gain.

Ikranagara's body of work, represented by the plays in this collection, is part of a larger question he had been grappling with from his earliest forays into the art form. In his 1980 essay "Konsep Kerja 'Teater Saja'" (Teater Saja's Work Concept), Ikranagara posed a question that informed all his work: "What can be produced from having a corporeal self as well as a spiritual one?" Taken in aggregate, Ikranagara's plays comprise an ongoing dialogue on the purpose and usefulness of the arts and artists in the face of a corrupt and repressive authoritarian regime that stifles creativity while also renewing the original purpose of theater in Indonesia. He wanted to find a place where he did not have to wear a mask but instead live and express himself honestly and authentically. Obviously, given the political reality in Indonesia at the time, that was impossible. He explains in that essay:

> Daily life has caused us to no longer be honest or open. We must hide often, or in other words, we change from wearing one mask to another depending on the situation and conditions. We have mastered this with direct or indirect training by those closest to us, such as our families, either openly or covertly,

> willingly or through coercion. Also, sometimes we have to change the script from one to another depending on whom we are dealing with. We must be able to restrain ourselves as much as possible in order to be wise. Unfortunately, we have to be tactical in order to survive or to rescue others. In short, real authenticity or honesty is not actually possible. Everything must be processed.

When Ikranagara began working with Teater Saja, he rarely began with a written script. In a 1993 essay "The Making of Indonesian Theatre: From Globalization to Pluralistic Interaction," he explains that he prefers to focus on what he terms "direct playwriting" (writing directly from the stage, inspired by his actors' improvisations) versus "distant play writing" (writing while outside the theater). For example, in 1974, the year before Ikranagara founded Teater Saja, he had been an artist-in-residence at the University of California, Davis. While there, he led a workshop with students that culminated in the performance of *A-bim-pom-pong* upon which his play *Mask 1* is based. In his introduction to *Mask 1*, Ikranagara explains how his work with students didn't start with a pre-written script. Instead, they began with a free exploration of body and gesture without regard to a particular narrative or realistic flow. These "bits" improvised by the students were then codified and text was added. For Ikranagara, this way of creating theater represented a move from closet (literary) drama, characterized by realism and naturalism, to (theatrical) performance, characterized by spectacle, juxtaposition, experimentation, and intertextuality—in other words, a theatricality communicated through a language of the stage rather than as a literary form. In his 1980 essay, he calls it "concrete poetry" where "among all the theatrical elements no one element was dominant throughout the performance." He wanted to avoid realism, particularly realism and naturalism found in Western theater, because for him "the stage is a place for a theatrical reality" and bringing in a set or scenario based on everyday life "means we have destroyed the actual reality of the stage." In his 1993 essay, Ikranagara elaborates that his plays created from direct playwriting "need more than just their written scripts" in order to "describe" and "appreciate" them. Instead,

> They need description of the visual elements of *mise en scène* and acting too, besides reference to the traditional theaters that were involved in their creative process. To describe them in written scripts was not a simple task, if possible at all.

To help his actors and the readers of his plays, Ikranagara included drawings and sketches in the working scripts in addition to copious stage directions in order to convey the *mise en scène* of the final performance, a large part of which had been originally improvised during rehearsals. The drawings included in this collection were all drawn by the playwright.

To write about Ikranagara's work, one must first acknowledge the indispensable role that the Jakarta Arts Center, Taman Ismail Marzuki (TIM), contributed to Ikranagara's "abstract and political" plays and productions. TIM was inaugurated by Jakarta Governor Ali Sadikin on November 10, 1968 as part of the New Order's focus on national development that included identifying, promoting, and presenting the pinnacles of performing and fine art forms from across the archipelago. Sadikin recognized the importance of promoting arts and culture in Jakarta and sought to provide a space where artists and intellectuals could thrive without the New Order government's repressive restrictions. Sadikin safeguarded the role of artistic freedom during a time when speaking out against government policies and social initiatives, criticizing authorities or their families, or depicting any Indonesian reality that wasn't positive or flattering, often led to arrests, blacklisting, and censorship. Under Sadikin's protection, theater artists at TIM were able to create their art in a singular forum exempt from governmental intervention and censorship. Not only could artists experiment with form, but also with content. Although short of complete freedom of expression, there was a fair amount of latitude given to artists addressing sensitive social and political issues that weren't tolerated elsewhere. There was a great sense of playfulness and security for artists working at TIM during its first ten years from 1968 to 1978. At a time when news was strictly censored under Soeharto, theater artists experimented with ways to skirt censorship and have their plays staged for the public.

Because TIM was founded to present international productions as well as to showcase the high points of the arts and cultural traditions from across the archipelago, home to some 850 distinct languages and ethnicities, the modern theater playwright-directors presenting their work at TIM were exposed to foreign experimental theater as well as an array of traditional and regional theater genres that either reminded them of the performances they had witnessed as children or introduced them to new ways of storytelling and staging from local cultures they would not otherwise have experienced. As a result, modern theater playwright-directors, like Ikranagara, began to experiment with regional theater aesthetics and narrative structures, such as traditional forms of folk storytelling which often mingle the fantastic with the ordinary and present archetypal characters that do not develop throughout the course of the drama. They also began to include *dalang* or narrator characters, outspoken servant/clown characters, and settings in mythical and imaginary places.

Ikranagara and other playwright-directors discovered that a combination of borrowing from and hybridizing traditional theater forms and aesthetics with the brutal absurdities of living in a censored and repressive society was the path to getting their theater produced and not shut down by the authorities—at least, for the most part. However, this early freedom within TIM came to an abrupt end in 1978 after a disturbance during a reading of protest poetry by the charismatic, controversial, and outspoken playwright-director and poet Rendra. This was compounded by tensions in several major cities between university students and the military over the publication of the "White Book," a student-written critique of the government calling for Soeharto's replacement. Furthermore, Sadikin, the artists' greatest ally, was no longer in office, having been forced out the previous year by the Soeharto administration, who saw his growing popularity and increasing power as a threat. These events culminated in the creation of a censorship board at TIM, signaling the end of an era. While innovative theater experiments continued, there was a perceptual shift brought on by having to comply with censors For artists working at TIM, their safe haven was breeched and a sense of playfulness was replaced with a more determined urgency to get their productions mounted despite (and to spite) the censors.

The six plays by Ikranagara in this collection were written between 1974 and 1982 and performed at TIM between 1976 and1997. They are ordered chronologically by the date they were performed rather than written. The translations are from Teater Saja's actual performance scripts, not the versions of the plays submitted to the censors starting in 1978. Only two of the plays in this collection, *Rang Gni* and *Shhh…!!!* were written and performed before the establishment of the censorship board. Even so, Ikranagara had to be careful to make his social and political critiques obliquely so that the authorities wouldn't swoop in and close down the production. After the censorship board was put into place, playwrights, including Ikranagara, would often submit scripts for approval but then perform "off script," testing to see how far they could go without being shut down.

The leading playwright-directors mounting their plays at TIM during the New Order, including Rendra, Arifin C Noer, Putu Wijaya, as well as Ikranagara among others, were part of what can be described as a resistance movement. The shared goal of these artists was two-fold: to be able to freely create art in a repressive regime that censored anything deemed critical of the State or that portrayed anything about Indonesia in a negative light, and to simultaneously develop a modern theater practice that was distinctly "Indonesian" rather than something derivative of western-style theater. Their two-fold goal was intricately connected because, in addition to its ritual and entertainment functions, Indonesian theater has conventionally played an important pedagogical role. By modeling morality and proper behavior through the depiction of actions, behaviors, and fates of good and evil characters in local legends, historical tales, and the great epics *Mahabharata* and *Ramayana*, various traditional theater genres—such as *wayang kulit* (shadow puppet theater) and *topeng* (masked dance-drama)—have been vital for preserving and disseminating local, regional, and national interests of the ruling classes and religious leaders. At the same time, theater performances have also provided an outlet for local critique of the prevailing ruling class through the shenanigans and dialogue of the so-called clown characters, particularly in Balinese and Javanese shadow plays and masked dance-dramas. These clowns are the loyal servants who serve either the good or evil realms. The *dalang* (puppeteer or narrator) uses off-color humor and hilarious antics when playing the servant characters in order to question or challenge contemporary social and political issues, even when the story being performed is set in the past. The servant/clown characters speak the same language as the audience, literally and figuratively, while the righteous kings and evil ogres speak in old forms of Javanese or Sanskrit that are not understood by the general populace. It is up to the servant characters to translate the words of warring leaders into the local language or dialect for the audience, which the *dalang* does with a fair amount of editorializing.

Ikranagara is present in all plays he authored—as the playwright giving voice to all the characters, but also represented by one specific character or a combination of characters in each play that Ikranagara performed in productions at TIM. He makes his voice and desires unmistakable through his stand-in characters, such as the Dalang in *Shhh…!!!* In Segment III of that play, Dalang clearly explains his reasons and goals as a theater artist:

> It's because I want to live a long life that I've discovered a powerful reason to keep on living. I emphasize that reason in my work. I will continue to create stories. I draw from the wealth of our native cultures and merge them with the reality of our lives today. The pain of our nation's people deserves a place of honor. That place is in my art.

Ikranagara not only makes it evident that he's drawing from the wealth of Indonesia's native cultures (particularly Bali where he was born and raised), but that he makes use of them in their original sense, in a way that leads to opening discussion and critique of the contemporaneous social reality, even if he radically changes how they are presented. *Rang Gni* was the first script he wrote without beginning with the actors' improvisations. Addressing his question "What can be produced from having a corporeal self as well as a spiritual one?" Ikranagara saw *Rang Gni* as a means to induce a trance-like state, a method to reach a heightened spiritual level. Its origins lie in the Balinese legend of *Calon Arang*, but his intention was not to perform the ritual itself. Instead, he engaged in a complex journey with it—wrestling, absorbing, resisting, agreeing, contemplating, and even battling with it. Ultimately, the outcome was something entirely different from its source.

The resulting public productions of his plays were always different from their sources; sometimes, as he explains in his 1980 essay, "in the form of something completely new, so that the original source discipline is no longer there, but a new discipline" emerges. What was consistent was that he tried never to copy what he had experimented with before and that what resulted was always reflective of something he had "produced and had become [his] own."

The symbolism of having a *dalang* be Ikranagara's stand-in in the play immediately projects multiple layers of meaning. Commentators on Indonesian politics have often used *wayang kulit* as a metaphor. The *dalang* remains concealed behind a screen while manipulating leather puppets so that their shadows are cast on the screen, while the audience, positioned on the opposite side, can only perceive shadows but not the puppets themselves. In other words, the government is led by a hidden puppet master orchestrating a covert game, shrouded in genuine or perceived conspiracies, thereby presenting an enigmatic reality that eludes the comprehension the general population. Of course, the irony is that it has traditionally been during *wayang kulit* performances that the *dalang*, through the servant characters, has critiqued and commented upon political and social subjects. In Part Two of *Knock Knock Knock*, the poet Karoman, as Ikranagara's stand-in character, explains the ongoing relationship between the government and artists and the important role theatre plays in society:

> KAROMAN: It's the artist's destiny to forever appear suspicious to government officials!

ATMA: But it's also the unfortunate destiny of government officials to be the target of criticism and protests by artists!

KAROMAN: Of course it is! If power is not open to correction, criticism, and protest, it will become absolute and controlled by the corrupt!

When first performed, the symbols and coded references in Ikranagara's plays worked to bring the audience into a shared communal experience of the absurd with the actors during the performance. He wanted to avoid imposing his interpretation on the actors or audiences, while hoping that each would arrive at their own and bring the ensuing questions home with them to continue the discussion. However, with the passage of time, newer audiences—both Indonesian as well as those reading his plays in translation—who are unfamiliar with all the symbols and coded references, including inside jokes, won't recognize many of them and the richness of the layering of meaning in his plays. Much of Ikranagara's mastery of punning and innuendo is unfortunately lost in translation (both linguistic and temporal). Fortunately, many of the symbols can be gleaned from the context of the plays and by keeping in mind the restrictions under which the plays were written and performed. Furthermore, many of the symbols can be extrapolated to similarly absurd situations in other countries and time periods, or can be understood simply as indicative of a discordant world that doesn't follow chronological or narrative conventions. Not everything needs to be explained, nor can it be explained because it all simply exists within the absurdity of life and is open to interpretation.

Ikranagara's plays and the productions he staged with Teater Saja are representative of the shift in Indonesian theater taking place at the time that ultimately played a critical role in helping to bring about political and social change in Indonesia, culminating with Soeharto's resignation in 1998. His plays and others staged at TIM were critical theater performances that could be understood on several levels, from bizarre, meaningless entertainment to biting critiques of a society in need of fixing. The surrealistic, improvised staging, non-linear narrative, and use of nonsense words was clearly modern and a mix of varied cultural aesthetics with contemporary social issues but they didn't follow any of the conventions of realistic theater associated with modern Indonesian theater taught in the national acting academies. Instead, there were several elements that connected them to traditional performance styles. Audiences and critics had a difficult time labeling this kind of theater. Most often they were compared to plays by European playwrights such as Samuel Beckett, Eugène Ionesco, Harold Pinter, Jean Genet, and others working in the style of the Theatre of the Absurd.

While there are many similarities to European theater in Ikranagara's plays, it is important to keep in mind that his plays grow out of an Indonesian reality and are not meant to copy or be derivative of European Theatre of the Absurd. The absurdities that the post-WWII playwrights faced were not unlike the absurdity Ikranagara faced during the New Order if the etymology of "absurd" is taken into consideration: *absurdus* in Latin means out of harmony or out of tune. Therefore, the absurd is something that is discordant and incongruous with what is expected; in short, non-sensical. This definition implies that the harmonious and what is expected is a known quantity, a universal agreed-upon way things should be that has been fundamentally disrupted and replaced with a different reality.

Building upon this original meaning of absurd, Martin Esslin (1918–2002), renowned literary critic, author, and playwright, best known for popularizing the term in his book *The Theatre of the Absurd*, made an important distinction between plays that "present their sense of the irrationality of the human condition in the form of highly lucid and logically constructed reasoning" and the Theater of the Absurd plays that manifest in performance the "sense of the senselessness of the human condition and the inadequacy of the rational approach by the open abandonment of rational devices and discursive thought." In other words, in the Theatre of the Absurd, both the characters and the audience are actively immersed in the absurdity, forsaking logical reasoning, rational methods, and analytical thinking during the performance. Instead of observing and analyzing life's absurdity from a distance as existentialism does, for example, in the Theatre of the Absurd there exists only the absurd. The whole experience is meant to feel discordant to the characters and audience alike.

Ikranagara's plays fall firmly within this working definition of the Theatre of the Absurd, but from an Indonesian point of view. This point of view characterizes his plays, and other playwright-directors working in the same vein, as a uniquely Indonesian theater form. This distinctly "Indonesian" theater movement has been dubbed the "New Tradition" (*Tradisi Baru*) by Putu Wijaya. The name carries within it the very dichotomy of this resistance theater, as will become apparent in the plays included in this collection, such as *Rang Gni* and *How Could You Burn Down the Rainforest?*: the dialectic, or the state of being both this and that simultaneously, a subject that fascinated Ikranagara. New Tradition theater is at once both new and inspired by tradition, whether that be the transposing of certain traditional and folk theater genres into new situations, capturing some kind of traditional "spirit," or continuing the function of many Indonesian theater traditions as a forum for communication, dialogue, criticism, as well as the transmission of moral values. The audiences at TIM during the New Order era, primarily comprised of dissident students and the Jakarta elite, understood the coded references as social critique, coded references that more often than not eluded the censors.

Because of the restrictions on artistic freedom and free speech during the New Order, Ikranagara, who wanted to engage with these ideas, relied heavily on symbolism and abstraction to stand for that which could not be addressed directly. His first production with Teater Saja at TIM, *Rang Gni*, held immense personal significance for him, so profound that it made him question whether he had reached the end of what he could do with theater and whether the uncertainty of this also meant the end of his engagement with life itself. Ikranagara had become so absorbed in the absurdity of *Rang Gni*'s world that he was transported into a world of perpetual disharmony, a non-sensical world severed from the ordered world—albeit a shadow world controlled by an unseen puppet master—that had once helped him navigate the reality of his present.

In his 1942 essay, "The Myth of Sisyphus," French-Algerian philosopher and author Albert Camus discusses the dilemma Ikranagara faced: how can one live a meaningful life in an inharmonious world? He ruminates on the "relationship between the absurd and suicide, the exact degree to which suicide is a solution to the absurd," concluding that

> A world that can be explained even with bad reasons is a familiar world. But, on the other hand, in a universe suddenly divested of illusions and lights, man feels an alien, a stranger. His exile is without remedy since he is deprived of the memory of a lost home or the hope of a promised land. This divorce between man and his life, the actor and his setting, is properly the feeling of absurdity. All healthy men having thought of their own suicide, it can be seen, without further explanation, that there is a direct connection between this feeling and the longing for death.

Ikranagara's stand-in character in *Rang Gni*, Person, appears to have no memory of who he is or where he has been. He is left in an ending of the play in a contented dream state in a world where conflict never ends. Earlier Person almost dies before realizing that the events taking place are being controlled by others, although he is one of the only characters in the play who can act by their own volition. One ending has Person apparently accepting, for now, the world as it is rather than trying to make sense of it, to control it, or to simply lie down and die. Instead, he chooses to just experience it with time "open to possibilities," including the never-ending conflict. Earlier in the final scene, Ajero and Angreh, who have made valiant efforts to become meaningful—although neither is able to take individual initiative—contemplate suicide as the solution. Obviously, it is a choice they cannot execute, not only because they are unable to act but because, as Camus argues, once man no longer exists, the absurd disappears. The absurd only exists insofar as there is someone to experience it. Therefore, in order to live, one must accept the contradiction between a desire to understand and a world that cannot be reasonably understood. All Ajero and Angreh, as well as Rang and Gni, can experience is the void in which they are trapped, unable to break free of their endless conflicts. All they have is to hold onto the hope that someday they and the world will make sense, and more importantly, that they will matter in time.

Time, specifically the passing of time, features prominently in Ikranagara's work. Time passes... a lot of time passes but without adhering to chronology. Ikranagara sends his characters and the audience backwards and forwards in time, and has them get stuck in time or experience time compressed so that all time is experienced simultaneously. He offers up multiple possible endings to his plays, has them not end at all, or has them begin again. Keeping audiences caught up in these different constructions of time—including the time of the production itself—brings them into the absurd world along with the characters. In *Rang Gni* the sky rips apart, setting free all possibilities, including time doubling back on itself and thereby offering up three possible endings, one of which is two different endings happening simultaneously: a dialectic. It calls into question when exactly the play begins and ends, or does it continue and double back on itself with the introduction of a new Rang and a new Gni?

The final play in this collection, *How Could You Burn Down the Rainforest?*, also functions inside a dialectic, in this case a vicious cycle where the characters are doomed to repeat the entire play again, despite the fact it has been written in advance by the playwright Atma, a stand-in for Ikranagara who performed the role. In this world, despite declaring death to the dialectic, willing its change, and believing for a good chunk of time that the world has changed, the audience and characters are ultimately left with "(Not) the End" only to relive this world's absurdity ad nauseum. This vicious cycle begs a similar question that arises in *Rang Gni*: when does the performance end and life begin? Or should the question be, when does life end and the performance begin? In the absurd world of *How Could You Burn Down the Rainforest?*, Atma-Ikranagara asks in the final scene "But can a play like this actually have an end?" Despite the play's Director entering the stage and declaring the performance over, Atma-Ikranagara isn't convinced. He rejects the Director's ending as a manufactured ending by dismissing it as "not the actual end in the sense of a true ending". He declares instead that "This performance has expanded! The stage has been globalized!" and that in order to truly "*end*, we must get to *the end of the endpoint*." Naturally, the end of the endpoint is death, death for every living creature all because humans have squandered earth's greatest riches: breathable air. He calls for a time machine to go back for a do over, but realizes that humanity will simply repeat its errors and atrocities and will end up reliving it all over again.

While the logical end, played to its logical ending, ends in death, the absurd worlds of *Rang Gni*, *Shhh…!!!*, *Mask 1*, *Era of the Bat*, *Knock Knock Knock*, and *How Could You Brun Down the Rainforest?* all end ready to begin again. As surely as each time you read each play in this collection, exactly the same things will happen. If all the world's a stage, then was Ikranagara correct to be questioning whether he was done with life, given that one must accept the contradiction between a desire to understand and a world that cannot be reasonably understood?

It was a trip to London after the production of *Rang Gni* that provided Ikranagara with an answer to his conundrum. It is often said that one needs to go out in order to see in. Being in London allowed Ikranagara to see Indonesia more clearly. This led to a shift from a solipsistic focus to an urge to become actively involved with life in Indonesia by communicating honestly through his art. The result was *Shhh...!!!*, the second play in this collection, using Bali as a metaphor for the nation as a whole. Ikranagara uses several traditional Balinese aesthetics in *Shhh...!!!* but in new and unconventional ways. He names his main character after a negative character from the *wayang kulit* repertoire, a figure who is known for corruption, misuse of power, and for silencing his enemies. His sidekick is one of the traditional servant characters aligned with the "bad side." He also again uses a shadow screen, as he had used the scrim in *Rang Gni,* where shadows are cast using back lighting as in a traditional *wayang kulit* performance. In *Shhh…!!!*, the shadow puppet screen is the sole set piece besides raffia ropes hanging down like banyan tree roots dangling from their branches. (The banyan tree was the symbol of Golkar, Soeharto's ruling party.) Rather than having the narrative performed by characters behind the screen as in *Rang Gni*, the screen in *Shhh…!!!* is used unconventionally. For example, in the second scene of Act II, the reporter and two of the characters appear as shadows on the screen, reciting and enacting what the servant/clown is reading in the newspaper. As Ikranagara explains in his 1980 essay, reading the newspaper is "the translation of the theatrical reality," not the content of what he wanted to communicate, which was "the depiction of our national situation presented in *Shhh…!!!*." Unconventional and innovative use of shadows and shadow screens also figure prominently in *Era of the Bat*, *Knock Knock Knock*, and *How Could You Burn Down the Rainforest?*. During times when there is no freedom of expression, the split between the theatrical reality and what the playwright intends to communicate proves to be a successful strategy to bypass censors as long as the audience is aware of or can glean the meaning of the symbols and abstraction to reach the political commentary.

Another reason Ikranagara used traditional Balinese aesthetics and forms was, as stated above, part of the New Tradition theater movement that consciously connected modern Indonesian theater with Indonesian theatrical traditions as an ongoing art form unsullied by outside Western influence. In addition, using traditional theater aesthetics from different regions of Indonesia that conventionally include moments of critique and questioning allowed theater productions to appear less threatening to the New Order censors because it looked familiar and benign. For example, writing and performing *Era of the Bat* in the form of Balinese solo masked-dance drama (*topeng pajegan*) wouldn't raise any issues by a cursory look at it, since Ikranagara had studied the stylized dance movements and vocal techniques used in Balinese masked-dance performance. Although he didn't follow all the traditional rules because he was creating and revising, his performance of *Era of the Bat* could be taken for a traditional, non-threatening performance if not given too much scrutiny. Besides Balinese masked-dance, Ikranagara also learned how puppeteers manipulated their puppets and how to produce the voices of the different characters found in the traditional wayang repertoire. He also studied *arja*, a traditional Balinese theatrical form that incorporates singing and dance. Overall, Ikranagara found that the use of traditional Balinese genres and aesthetics helped meet his goal of having spectators enjoy the productions of his plays on different levels by each forming a unique interpretation based on a combination of the absurd theatrical reality presented on stage with what was currently happening politically in Indonesia at the time.

Cobina Gillitt

Works Cited

Camus, Albert, and Justin O'Brien. *The Myth of Sisyphus, and Other Essays* (New York, New York: Vintage Books, 1991)

Esslin, Martin. *The Theatre of the Absurd* (Albany, New York: Anchor Books, 1961)

Ikranagara. "Konsep Kerja 'Teater Saja,'' in *Pertemuan Teater 80* (Jakarta: Dewan Kesenian Jakarta, 1980)

Ikranagara. "The Making of Indonesian Theatre: From Globalization to Pluralistic Interaction," in *Tenggara: Journal of Southeast Asian Literature* (vol. 12, 1993)

Rang Gni

Production Notes

Rang Gni was first performed October 18–22, 1976 at the Jakarta Arts Center (Taman Ismail Marzuki) in the Arena Theater. Direction and design by Ikranagara. Performed by his theater company, Teater Saja.

The original cast, in alphabetical order by first name, and the roles they played is as follows: Aji Gofur (Rang), Anton Angkaw (Ajero), Bulan Surawidjaja (Child), Desi Ingkiriwang (Chorus), Ikranagara (Person), Innosanto Nagara (Child), M. Yusuf Kalana (Angreh), Suprayitno (Banas), Wienda Daniel (Gni), and Yudi Tampubolon (Chorus).

The play is divided into two parts separated by a short intermission. Segments I, II, and III make up the first part, while Segment IV makes up the second part. In the original 1976 production, at the end of Segment IV, Scene 3 when Person is slumped over and appears dead while Angreh chants "Ong" and Ajero chants "Eeee," the lights went to black and the audience was left in silence in the dark. After a short pause (but not an intermission), the Director entered and recited a speech to the audience. The decision to include the Director's speech is up to each production based on criteria enumerated below in the script.

Characters

GNI, a woman

RANG, a man

BANAS, a tall burly man

AJERO, a guard

ANGREH, a guard

CHORUS of women

PERSON

CHILD

Setting

There is a sizable crater in the center of the performance space, perhaps created by encircling platforms of increasing height. The stage is divided into three areas. One belongs to Gni and Angreh. The second is that of Rang and Ajero. The third space is the crater itself. A scrim hangs on Gni and Angreh's side of the stage.

Segment I
Us. Here. Now.

1.

The stage is dark. RANG, GNI, AJERO, ANGREH, *and* BANAS *are onstage.*

AJERO *and* ANGREH *have covered their heads with their sarongs to form hoods. They stand as still as statues on the highest platforms on opposite sides of the stage, facing each other.* GNI *stands facing the scrim, holding a flashlight in each hand in the same area as* ANGREH. AJERO *stands in the same area as* RANG *on the opposite side of the stage.* RANG, *also holding two flashlights, stands in front of and faces* AJERO.

BANAS *is hidden inside a rolled up woven bamboo mat on the ground near where* AJERO *is standing.*

RANG *and* GNI *are unaware of each other's presence because they are facing in opposite directions.* RANG *and* GNI *turn on their flashlights. They closely observe their immediate surroundings. Thoroughly. Carefully. With curiosity. Or with suspicion. Sometimes they are surprised by something their flashlights reveal.*

Time passes.

Their flashlights suddenly catch each other in their beams: GNI'*s light reveals* RANG *and* RANG*'s flashlight reveals* GNI. *Startled, they quickly step out of the beams of light to hide. With trepidation, they turn off their flashlights. They grope around in the dark, trying to see.*

After a short time, they turn on their flashlights again to search for where the other is hiding. Their flashlights illuminate the space. They both try to hide from the light, especially their faces. They rush about apprehensively.

Time passes.

GNI *circles around and suddenly stops. She lets* RANG *train his flashlight on her but still hides her face by crouching down and stooping over.* RANG *takes the initiative and approaches* GNI. *He walks around her using his flashlight to figure out who she actually is.*

GNI: Why must you know who I am?

RANG: Because it's dark! And why is it me?

GNI: I'd like to know!

RANG: I'd like to know too!

GNI: Ah. Just forget it! Turn off your light.

(RANG *points his flashlight toward the scrim. He studies it carefully. Seeing this,* GNI, *who has been lying half prone, stands up, turns on her flashlight, and looks around for a new spot.* GNI *walks toward her new spot.* RANG *focuses his flashlight on her again.*)

RANG: Hold on!

(GNI *stops and hides her face.* GNI *squats again as* RANG *approaches.*)

GNI: What?

(RANG *circles back around.*)

RANG: Who are you, actually?

GNI: That doesn't matter here.

RANG: Man or woman?

GNI: Yawn!

RANG: Who are you?

GNI: Be quiet!

RANG: I'm a man!

GNI: I know!

RANG: My name is Rang!

GNI: My name is Gni!

RANG: Gni?

GNI: Can't you be quiet?

RANG: You.... A woman?

GNI: Turn off your flashlight!

(RANG *turns his flashlight back toward the scrim.* GNI *contemplates.*)

GNI: So here is where we are now.

(GNI *shines her flashlight upwards, perhaps to the sky.*)

(*Amused, she yells loudly*) Now!

(*Beat.*)

(GNI, *amused, yells loudly*) Here!

(*Beat.*)

(GNI *resumes contemplating*) Yes... Yes!... Huh? Aha! Yes...

RANG: Thinking?

(GNI *looks at* RANG.)

RANG: What?

GNI: You really want to know?

RANG: Not really.

GNI: Us. Here. Now.

RANG: What?

GNI: I've answered everything.

RANG: You've answered everything. Yup.

GNI: I know you couldn't care less.

(RANG *laughs.*)

(*Amused*) I admire your enthusiasm!

(RANG *laughs.* GNI *chuckles.*)

RANG: I'm fond of it too.

(*They delight. They shine their flashlights on each other.*)

RANG: Gni?

GNI: Rang?

(*They approach each other, keeping their flashlights focused on the other, from bottom to top and from top to bottom. As they get closer, they look like two identical halves of a statue moving into place to complete each other. They are happy. They call out each other's names.*

Time passes.

They are content. They feel renewed.)

RANG: Our humors blend and balance!

GNI: Clarity of mind!

RANG: Ah...! We've met before!

GNI: When?

RANG: Why are the details important?

GNI: Time! I'm the only one who cares!

RANG: What?

GNI: Forget it!

RANG: Isn't it enough that here, now, we know each other? Doesn't matter to us anymore when we met!

GNI: It's not that!

RANG: Ah! Come on! Let's continue!

GNI: Continue?

RANG: With all of it. We're already on our way!!

GNI: But to where?

RANG: What do you mean, "to where"?

GNI: We. Can't. Go anywhere!

RANG: (*Looks around*) Our place is here now.

GNI: (*Approvingly*) You're beginning to get it now.

RANG: We agree!

GNI: We can continue!

(RANG *warmly hugs* GNI.)

RANG: (*Delighted*) Agreed? One for all, all for one?

(GNI *pulls away from his embrace. She doesn't like it.*)

RANG: Gni?!

GNI: You're always in such a hurry!

RANG: Don't you know? We can't slack off here!

GNI: (*Curtly*) Says what devil?

RANG: We have to hurry! Be lively! Chop-chop!

GNI: Op op hop non-stop?

(RANG *laughs.* GNI *chuckles.*)

RANG: Op, op, hop, pop, poop. Poot! Like a fart!

(*They both burst out laughing. A dim ray of light illuminates the large crater centerstage. Objects in the crater reflect the light back out.* GNI *is first to notice the light.*)

GNI: Shh!

(*Now* RANG *notices the light. As if listening to an official formal speech, they solemnly observe the light as it gradually becomes brighter. A type of ceremony. They put their flashlights down on the edge of the crater. When the light reaches its zenith,* RANG *and* GNI *spontaneously and respectfully applaud, as if at the end of an uplifting oratory.*

Silence.

Time passes.)

2.

RANG *and* GNI *walk solemnly into the crater. They appear refreshed and content. They embrace warmly.*

Silence.

Time passes.

GNI: Out of the darkness comes light![1]

RANG: From a kitchen of gloom to a kitchen of brilliance!

GNI: Ugh. I don't want a kitchen!

RANG: But I could starve to death!

GNI: I don't do kitchen stuff!

RANG: A house then!

GNI: Nope!

RANG: Then, how about just a bed?

GNI: You're so superficial! Single-minded!

RANG: So what's the connection that binds us together?

(GNI *thinks for a moment.*)

GNI: What's the matter with us? Here? Now?

RANG: Our problem is you're a woman and I'm a man!

GNI: (*Cynically*) Oh? Is that it? Excellent! (*Laughs derisively*)

RANG: What if it's love?

GNI: Now it's clear who you really are! You're nothing more than muscle and meat—a meathead dick! Hah!

RANG: Assumptions. Assumptions. All assumptions. The same assumptions with which you arrived! Who are you really?

GNI: That same question again and nothing else! Tiresome!

(GNI *exits the crater inquisitively. From the edge, she faces* RANG. *Then she circles around broadcasting her annoyance.*)

I've already answered several times, but you just keep asking questions, questions over and over, and that question again and again, even though you know that my answer will be the same, the same answer again and again, meanwhile you couldn't care less about my explanation, because no matter what I say, you'll judge me based on your own conclusions, the same ones again and again. Hopeless! Hopeless!

(*Silence.*

Time passes.

RANG *becomes agitated. He can't see where* GNI *is, so he turns on his flashlight to look for her.*)

RANG: Gni?

(*Beat.*)

GNI: Turn off your flashlight!

(RANG *turns off his flashlight.*

Silence.

Time passes.)

RANG: You can't stay out there!

GNI: Introspection is important!

RANG: We agree!

(*Beat.*)

RANG: Gni?

(GNI *steps back into the crater.* RANG *relaxes. He puts his flashlight back down at the crater's edge.*)

GNI: Weird! I can get angry too!

RANG: That means we can continue.

GNI: We agree.

RANG: I think we always agree. It's just that, what else is there other than love that keeps us eternally connected?

GNI: (*Frustrated*) Why must it be love? Why must it be forever? Besides, we know that nothing can make us last forever! A connection? And what else do you want to last forever? Meaningless! Meaningless! A big zero! Bah! Love too! And a bed? And a house?

(*She exits the crater.*)

And all of this? Why must there be a connection? Because without all of it you'd starve. You'd be lonely. You'd feel neglected. You'd lose your grip. You'd die in a frenzy. Right? Is that it? Right? See! You are alone in that light!

(*Angrily,* GNI *moves away from the crater toward the scrim.*)

RANG: Gni!

GNI: You're selfish! You're greedy! You're vulgar! You're pushy! You're petty! You're dirty! You're rotten!

RANG: (*Harshly, cutting her off*) Gni!! That's no longer introspection! That's character assassination! That's heartless criticism! Gni!!!

(RANG *jumps out of the crater. He searches for* GNI *with his flashlight, hunting her down until she's discovered.* GNI *rushes toward the scrim.*)

3.

GNI *goes behind the scrim.* RANG *doesn't follow her. He suddenly stops, facing the scrim. At that moment, flickering lights, like twinkling stars, are projected from behind onto the scrim.*

RANG: (*Warily*) Gni...?

(*No answer.* RANG *approaches the scrim with caution. He reaches out to touch the scrim with his hand. At that moment,* ANGREH *growls fiercely and furiously.* ANGREH *can be seen moving in the sarong he's wearing as a hood.* RANG, *startled by* ANGREH'*s growls, backs up. Oppressive silence.*

Meanwhile, the flickering lights move slowly across the scrim.)

RANG: (*Whispering*) Gni...?

(*Still no answer.* RANG *approaches the scrim again, keeping his eyes on* ANGREH. *Again,* ANGREH *growls when* RANG *touches the scrim.* RANG *backs away. Oppressive silence.*

Time passes.

RANG *steps away from the scrim. He looks around for something nearby with his flashlight. He discovers the rolled up mat and carefully makes his way over to it. He stares at the rolled up mat. Reflects. He caresses the mat. Meditatively. He carefully unrolls the mat. Once unrolled,* RANG *discovers* BANAS *inside.* BANAS*, a tall, burly man, lies on his back, as if asleep.* RANG *solemnly examines* BANAS *from head to toe with his flashlight.* BANAS *wears only a loincloth. A large rope is wrapped around his body, arms, and legs. Gradually,* BANAS *wakes up. He appears upbeat, ready to laugh with pleasure. His body glistens.* BANAS *stands up slowly. His bright eyes widen as he looks around.*)

BANAS: A male lizard contemplates the daybreak panorama
Knows when the fogs lifts
Probably true
Once, there was a couple who exited the gates of heaven
Descended from the heights
Toward the valleys
The fields
The forests
The rivers
The beaches
The cities
All of a sudden: a room!
Woman
Part of heaven
Who was carried out
Now in his arms
Their two naked bodies sweat from passionate lust
The male lizard's back also sweats
Startled, he suddenly
Darts off, quickly
To hunt females in the underbrush!

(BANAS *runs out of breath. He looks at the scrim eagerly. He walks toward it but* RANG *blocks his way. They stand face to face. They stare at each other.*)

RANG: Not her! No! Find someone else!

(*But* BANAS *is determined to get to the scrim. He collides with* RANG. ANGREH *and* AJERO *growl loudly, then descend from their respective spots on the top level platform to find out what's happening below. They prepare to attack* BANAS. *Anticipating bad behavior,* BANAS *quickly exits.* ANGREH *and* AJERO *angrily capture* RANG.)

ANGREH: You're gonna feel the consequences of making your decision based on lust!

AJERO: Your lust! Control it!

(AJERO *and* ANGREH *push* RANG *into the crater.* BANAS *laughs far offstage.* AJERO *and* ANGREH *angrily exit, rushing toward the laughter.* RANG *wipes his face with his hands and fixes his hair. He stands absolutely still, erect like a statue, meditating.*

The light on the crater dims a little, but doesn't go out. Meanwhile, a different light emanates from behind the scrim, in addition to the little flickering lights. A colored light. Maybe blue. Or green. Little by little, the flickering lights begin to move more quickly. GNI *can be dimly seen.*

Silence.

Time passes.)

4.

GNI, *dimly lit behind the scrim, briefly walks to and fro. Then she is still again.*

GNI: Rang?

RANG: (*Remains meditating*) What?

GNI: I am busy.

RANG: I won't bother you.

GNI: You begin to understand now.

RANG: We always agree.

(*Beat.*)

RANG: Gni?

GNI: What?

RANG: Am I bothering you?

GNI: What?

RANG: Never mind.

(*Beat.*)

RANG: Gni?

GNI: What?

RANG: Come to a conclusion!

GNI: For whom?

RANG: For us!

GNI: About what?

RANG: About us!

GNI: It turns out every conclusion is shrouded in a thick fog of uncertainty!

RANG: That doesn't matter for the time being!

(*Beat.*)

RANG: Gni?

(*Silence.*

Time passes.

The flickering lights move faster. The light on the crater grows brighter and dimmer.)

GNI: But… a conclusion! A conclusion? Yes! Every conclusion is always followed by a series of questions as thick as fog. This fog is a fog of endless doubt, giving birth to questions and more questions, so that conclusions themselves are the seeds that give birth to our doubt.

(*Beat.*)

Or… because conclusions are born to pile on doubt, so that conclusions are no different than kindling feeding the embers of doubt, enflaming questions born as infant forest ogres that quickly grow and rapidly become ferociously greedy, ready to devour every piece of kindling, along with everything else in their path, so that we also see our eventual future, in the end all of this is no different than black ash residue left after a fire, motionless, quietly quiet, silently silent, empty!

(*Beat.*)

Or… more than that, shaken by a sudden earthquake, the earth splits open and swallows up everything on its surface. A landslide covers everything. All of it, all of it. Earth is bare; the planet deserted!

(*Beat.*)

Or… easily blown away by a tempest, soaring into the sky and vanishing without a trace, our state of impermanence, our gut-wrenching fears, our unreasonable feelings of indifference, because there's really no reason to care about that which we don't know with certainty, there's no reason to care, only hands frantically grabbing for that which drifts into the boundless empty void, veins becoming more obvious with age, followed by wrinkles and rheumatism, curiosity no longer manageable, for whatever reason, for whatever need, fingers freely impulsive, veins freely crawling like worms over every cloud encountered, while fingernails frantically claw at the imagined sky, nothing idle, everything activated, buzzing, disorderly, our days filled with hustle and bustle, growing more and more frantic, more and more jumbled, we don't know what we're doing anymore, we don't know anything anymore, but what is clear is that we haven't produced even a single scrawl, as empty as the universe is big, apparently time never gave us a chance, apparently we've been mercilessly rejected, totally without mercy, without mercy, without mercy...

(*After all this anguish and agony,* GNI *moans and begins screaming uncontrollably from behind the scrim. Meanwhile,* RANG *has been shaking the whole time as if he has malaria.*)

Mercy... Mercy... Mercy...!

(AJERO *and* ANGREH *enter hesitantly.*)

AJERO: What's going on?

ANGREH: Get a sedative!

AJERO: Yes! That's our duty!

ANGREH: Duty!

AJERO: Duty!

(*The flickering lights stop moving across the scrim. The light on the crater stops getting brighter and dimmer.* ANGREH *leads* GNI *to the front of the scrim and places her in front of where* ANGREH *usually stands.* AJERO *leads* RANG *out of the crater and places him in front of where* AJERO *usually stands.* ANGREH *calms* GNI, AJERO *calms* RANG. *Both relax. After giving flashlights to* RANG *and* GNI, AJERO *and* ANGREH *return to the places they were standing at the beginning of the play.*

Dim spotlights up on AJERO *and* ANGREH. *They slowly remove the sarongs that have been covering their heads. They freeze in place, like statues.* RANG *and* GNI *turn on their flashlights.* GNI *focuses on* ANGREH. RANG *focuses on* AJERO. *Solemnly.*

Time passes.

All lights out, including the flashlights.

Blackout.)

Segment II
100 Horses

1.

The stage is dark. AJERO *and* ANGREH *stand in their places. Their sarongs no longer cover their heads.*

RANG *and* GNI *squat facing each other, but they are far apart.* RANG *is near* AJERO *and* GNI *is near* ANGREH. *Silence.*

RANG *and* GNI *aim their flashlights at each other's faces. They remain like this for a while, silent, not moving. After a bit, they slowly stand up straight. Keeping their flashlight beams focused on each other's faces,* RANG *and* GNI *look around, searchingly. After a short time, they use their flashlights to search for something until they find it: the mat in which* BANAS *had been rolled up.*

The mat lies open on the ground. They walk toward it cautiously and silently. When they get close to the mat, they examine it. Thoroughly.

Time passes.

They put their flashlights on the mat and carefully lift it. Their flashlights remain lit as they carry the mat like a stretcher and place it down carefully inside the crater. Silence.

Time passes.

Lights up on the crater. RANG *laughs gleefully.* GNI *grabs her flashlight and examines* RANG *all over with it.* RANG, *still happy, grabs his flashlight and does the same to* GNI. *Because they are so close to each other, and because they are shining their flashlights on each other, from top to bottom and bottom to top, they seem like two complimentary moving halves of a statue. They're happy. They call out each other's names. Their movements this time create a writhing dance interspersed with short bouts of laughter.*

Time passes.

GNI: Wanna hear?

RANG: What?

(*They stop moving. They stare at each other. Their faces appear bright and fresh in the light after stepping back into the crater and standing in it.*)

What?

GNI: A conclusion!

RANG: I figured!

GNI: Don't be cynical!

RANG: For us?

GNI: For us!

RANG: About us?

GNI About us!

RANG: What?

GNI: You see my face?

RANG: You look happy!

GNI: You look happy too!

RANG: Both of us are happy!

GNI: Us. Happy. Here.

RANG: If we continue, I'll end up dancing!

GNI: I'll end up singing!

RANG: We can continue!

GNI: Our happiness! That's the connection that binds us together!

RANG: A happy conclusion!

GNI: Music!

RANG: Dance!

(AJERO *and* ANGREH *play upbeat music. It could be dangdut-style popular dance music. Perhaps* ANGREH *plays the harmonica and perhaps* AJERO *plays a drum.* RANG *and* GNI *dance. Their flashlights in their hands send beams of lights all throughout the space.*)

RANG: Yeehoo…!

GNI: (*Singing*) We rejoice together, forgetting sadness…

GNI and RANG: Hey! Hey! Hey!

GNI: And sorrow!

RANG: Yeehoo!

(BANAS *enters along with a* CHORUS *of women wearing translucent clothing. They move to the rhythm of the song. They sway their way across the stage. They join in, happily singing* GNI*'s song. Lights up on additional parts of the stage, especially around the edge of the crater. They encircle the crater where* RANG *and* GNI *continue to dance and sing.*)

RANG: We are deer in the forest/

BANAS and CHORUS: We are deer in the forest/

GNI: We are fog in the valley/

BANAS and CHORUS: We are fog in the valley/

RANG: We are birds on the boughs/

BANAS and CHORUS: We are birds on the boughs/

GNI: We are clouds in the sky/

BANAS and CHORUS:	We are clouds in the sky/
RANG:	We are rocks on the beach/
BANAS and CHORUS:	We are rocks on the beach/
GNI:	We are ambience in the air/
BANAS and CHORUS:	We are ambience in the air/
RANG:	We are eels in the mud/
BANAS and CHORUS:	We are eels in the mud/
GNI:	We are currents in the river/
BANAS and CHORUS:	We are currents in the river/
RANG:	We are fish in the pond/
BANAS and CHORUS:	We are fish in the pond/
GNI:	We are hues of the light/
BANAS and CHORUS:	We are hues of the light/

(BANAS *and the* CHORUS *enter the crater, while* RANG *and* GNI *leave it.* RANG *goes to where* AJERO *is standing and* GNI *goes to where* ANGREH *is standing.* AJERO *and* ANGREH *continue to play lively music.* BANAS *and the* CHORUS *dance wildly.*

Music stops all of a sudden. Silence everywhere. BANAS *and the* CHORUS *are stunned. They look at each other, questioning in silence. They look around, searchingly. All at once, the* CHORUS *looks at* BANAS. *One of them looks ready to hug him, her face expressing joy or passion.* BANAS *backs away, but she continues facing him and advances toward him.*

BANAS *exits the crater. The* CHORUS *follows him.* BANAS *backs away, smiling.*

The CHORUS *member in front is pushed back by one of the others. The new one in front pursues* BANAS *with slow but sure steps, while also smiling.*

BANAS *retreats across the stage. The* CHORUS *continues to chase him, slowly but surely, pushing each other out of the way to get to the front.*

Time passes.

One of the CHORUS *manages to catch* BANAS, *but he violently escapes her grasp. The others in the* CHORUS *join in the melee. The commotion only lasts a moment because* BANAS *succeeds in breaking free and exits swiftly from the stage, laughing.*)

CHORUS: Damn it!

CHORUS: Now, he's playing hard to get!

CHORUS: He's bored with us!

CHORUS: We're being too obvious!

CHORUS: We're too cheap!

CHORUS: Where'd he go?

(*They look for* BANAS. *They call his name.*)

CHORUS: Ugh! Just let him go! I'm bored!

CHORUS: No cheating!

CHORUS: Let's all be bored together, shall we?

CHORUS: You want him all to yourself, huh?

CHORUS: Where'd he go?

CHORUS: Let's get outta here!

(CHORUS *exits.*)

RANG: It's because I'm blood in veins!

GNI: I'm the throb of the heart!

RANG: (*Descending from where* AJERO *is standing*) I'm nerves in the backbone!

GNI: (*Descending from where* ANGREH *is standing*) I'm words in a sentence!

RANG: (*Steps closer to* GNI) I'm paper in books!

GNI: (*Steps closer to* RANG) I'm the seed of every thought!

RANG: I'm muscles in the body!

GNI: I'm the spirit of the body!

RANG: I'm space in time!

GNI: I'm time in space!

RANG: (*Cuts in*) Space in time!

GNI: Time in space!

RANG: (*Cuts in faster*) Space in time!

GNI: (*Cuts in faster*) Time in space!

(*Their responses become faster and faster. Time passes quickly.*)

RANG: Space!

GNI: Time!

RANG: Space!

GNI: Time!

(*Their exchange gets even faster.*)

GNI: (*Abruptly*) Hush!

(*Sudden silence.* GNI *sits on the mat at edge of the crater.* RANG *just observes her.*)

GNI: T_I_M_E!

(RANG *sits in front of* GNI.)

RANG: S_P_A_C_E!

GNI: Time!

RANG: Space!

GNI: Time!

RANG: Space!

(*Sometimes they respond quickly in a high voice. Sometimes in a low voice. Sometimes faintly. Or suddenly one of them yells loudly followed by a moment of silence, and then followed by a different voice repeating quickly but faintly. They try several other variations so that it sounds like music using their voices and responses. They become so enthralled that they seemingly cannot escape the music they are creating. They don't know when or how to stop.*)

2.

Their melodic exchange eventually becomes a single tone so that it sounds like someone performing dhikr, or chanting a mantra. They seem to be falling into a trance.

Time passes.

Suddenly BANAS *jumps onstage, then stands up straight and stares directly at* GNI.

BANAS: (*Bellows*) Gni…!

(BANAS *roars with laughter.* GNI *and* RANG *awaken from their trance. They see* BANAS *who takes a step at a time in* GNI*'s direction.* RANG *is leery and somewhat irritated.*)

RANG: Banas!

BANAS: But we're buddies, Rang!

(BANAS *chortles.*)

RANG: No, Banas! Not her! Someone else!

BANAS: I need Gni here now.

GNI: (*To* BANAS) What for?

RANG: Let me handle him, Gni. Just be quiet.

GNI: Since when do you have the right to tell me what to do?

RANG: Gni?!

(BANAS *sniggers.*)

RANG: (*To* GNI *while pointing at* BANAS) You see yourself, he's a savage!

(BANAS *roars with laughter.*)

GNI: You're both the same. Just muscle and meat—meathead dicks!

BANAS: But, Gni, I'm a poetry-writing meathead dick!

RANG: (*Scornfully*) Poetry!

BANAS: Gni, I need you to finish the poem I'm in the process of writing. Listen to how it begins…

(*Beat.*)

One hundred horses
Unite
Impatient
Neighing

RANG: (*To* GNI) You hear? He's a horse! A savage horse!

BANAS: Don't be reckless, pal!

RANG: Pal, you're the one being reckless! Pal, feral forest dwellers are uncivilized! Savages! Brutes! You horse!

BANAS: And you? What are you? Cultured? Hah! Civilized? What civilization is that?

Take off your mask! Go on! Take it off! Then you'll see for yourself you are nothing more than a reflection of me! Strip off all your clothes! Probably dozens of cases of gonorrhea and syphilis in your crotch.

RANG: Beast!

BANAS: Hypocrite!

(RANG *and* BANAS *prepare to fight. They glare at each other, breathing heavily. Eventually, they pounce on each other.* GNI *watches, spits, and begins to exit the stage.*)

ANGREH and AJERO: Gni!

(GNI *stops at the edge of the stage. She looks at* ANGREH, *then at* AJERO.)

GNI: What do you all think I am? An object? A thing up for grabs? You're nothing more than feral horses!

(GNI *spits and resolutely exits.* AJERO *and* ANGREH *call loudly for* GNI *as they descend from where they had been standing. The brawlers stop mostly because* RANG *doesn't want to continue. His face shows his frustration and annoyance.* BANAS *stands up straight, but his face doesn't show any frustration; instead he's upbeat and passionate.*)

RANG: (*To* AJERO *and* ANGREH) I can't continue!

ANGREH: All because of your lustful behavior! You can't control yourself! It's shameful!

AJERO: Shameful!

(*Disillusioned,* RANG *begins to exit.*)

AJERO: Hey! Where you going?

RANG: I can't continue without Gni!

(RANG *exits.* AJERO *and* ANGREH *glare at* BANAS. BANAS *just smiles back.*)

BANAS: We can continue!

AJERO: Ha! You!

ANGREH: We'll take care of you later.

(BANAS *responds with a laugh.* AJERO *and* ANGREH *move in close together. They confer in whispers. After a moment they move apart.*)

ANGREH: So, you take care of Rang.

AJERO: You take care of Gni.

BANAS: I take care of Gni! I need Gni to finish my poetry!

(AJERO *and* ANGREH *ignore him and exit.*)

Hey! Listen to my poetry! Gni!

(*He keeps his ears open while his eyes explore his surroundings. He recites his poem loudly.*)

One hundred horses
Unite
    Impatient
        Neighing

        The night sky expansive as a net!
                        Full moon

    Whole
    Her body naked
    Caressed by grasses in the fields
    Tossed by waves on the nearby shore
    The night sky as expansive as a net
        The clear lake
        —the hunted—
        Hides

Under the belly of the full moon

(*Offstage, the* CHORUS *calls* BANAS'*s name over and over.* BANAS *is silent. Listens.*)

BANAS: Damn it! Them again! My poetry comes to a standstill because of them! Damn it! Gni…!

(*He listens for a moment.*)

I must be able to finish my poetry! I must have you! Gni...! Don't stay out there for so long! I can't stand it here for much longer! Here is where I can finish and let my poetry flow! Gni…!

3.

The CHORUS *calls* BANAS*'s name over and over from far offstage.* BANAS *listens carefully each time his name is called until the calls stop. Once they stop,* BANAS *curses and anxiously seeks a place to hide. This scenario repeats several times.*

Time passes.

Eventually, BANAS *tries to hide in the crater. He uses the mat in which he had been rolled up and* ANGREH'*s and* AJERO'*s discarded sarongs until he's well hidden in the crater.*

The CHORUS *begins calling his name again from offstage. After the umpteenth time,* BANAS *stands up from his hiding place and listens to the voices calling his name until they stop.*

BANAS: Damn it! Damn it! I'm too much in love with hearing other people calling my name! This is insane! But why should I be angry at myself? In point of fact, this is who I am! Obviously I love hearing people say my name! (*Smiles*) Sure! I enjoy it! So what! Especially if it's a female voice.

(*He chuckles. The* CHORUS *calls his name again, but this time the voices are closer.* BANAS *listens with pleasure.*)

I love this! (*Laughing*) I love this! Love it. Love it. Truly love it! Hey! Gorgeous girls! Banas is over here! (*Laughing*) I'd be even happier if they'd call my name from here.

(BANAS *exits, laughing. Silence.*

Still offstage, the CHORUS *calls* BANAS*'s name again.* BANAS *answers from offstage alerting them where he is. This exchange lasts for a time while the stage remains empty.*

Time passes.

The CHORUS *enters. With keen eyes, they search for* BANAS *in case he's hiding onstage. They try to sniff him out. But he's nowhere to be seen.*)

CHORUS: This is too much!

CHORUS: This is making us frustrated!

CHORUS: More than frustrated! I'm so horny!

CHORUS: Do you smell something or not?

CHORUS: Yes!

CHORUS: What?

CHORUS: What smell?

CHORUS: Smell of sweat!

CHORUS: Banas's sweat?

CHORUS: Who else?

CHORUS: (*Sniffs again*) Yes! That's his sweat!

CHORUS: His sweat when he's feeling horny!

CHORUS: You think he's like us?

CHORUS: Always thinking about sex?

CHORUS: Banas is always horny!

CHORUS: What's that about, huh?

CHORUS: Full mast!

(*They laugh.*)

CHORUS: Shush!

(*She sniffs again.*)

CHORUS: Smell his sweat again?

CHORUS: Quiet! I'm investigating the source of the smell.

CHORUS: The smell of his sweat?

CHORUS: Quiet! Nobody move!

(*The* CHORUS *continues sniffing, searching for the source of the smell. One of them circles around and around until she thinks she has found a trace of* BANAS.)

CHORUS: (*While sniffing*) He's hiding here! It's definitely his sweat!

CHORUS: Close your eyes so it sharpens your sense of smell!

CHORUS: You think my eyes have been open this whole time? My feet follow the will of my nose!

(*The* CHORUS *member continues to sniff with her eyes closed. She moves toward the others who all dodge her. The* CHORUS *member pursues the others. Finally, she realizes that they are toying with her. She opens her eyes and calls them out.*)

CHORUS: Not funny.

CHORUS: You're the one who's not funny.

CHORUS: You said you could smell Banas's sweat!

(*In the end, they all laugh.*

Time passes.

The CHORUS *begins to call* BANAS*'s name again. Repeatedly. Loudly. Then in unison.*

Time passes.)

CHORUS: Enough! Enough! Enough already!

CHORUS: We're beat!

CHORUS: Seriously, his name is the only one we've called.

CHORUS: Exactly! There is more than one Banas here!

(*They are referring the audience. The* CHORUS *proceeds to mingle with the audience, asking random spectators, men and women, for their names. They substitute the audience members' names for* BANAS. *They call out the spectators' names, over and over.*

Time passes.

Eventually, the CHORUS *members exit one by one.*

The stage is empty. The lights dim until they go out. The stage is dark.

Silence.)

Segment III
The Mortuary Stretcher

1.

The stage is empty. Dark. Silence. AJERO *enters from one side;* ANGREH *enters from the other. They carry flashlights. They meet.*

AJERO: Located?

ANGREH: Yes! What about Rang?

AJERO: All set! Gni ready?

ANGREH: Not yet! Rang ready?

AJERO: Almost!

(*They laugh happily. All of a sudden, a faint and sad sound is heard in the distance.* AJERO *and* ANGREH *hear the sound and listen for a moment.*)

AJERO: Time to return to our respective duties.

ANGREH: Yes, our duty!

AJERO: Duty calls!

(AJERO *and* ANGREH *move apart and quickly exit. The stage is empty again. Dark again. The sound floating in from the distance is the* CHORUS *still searching for* BANAS. *Their voices get closer.*

Time passes.

The CHORUS *enters. They no longer wear translucent clothing but long black veils that fully cover their bodies. They carry a mortuary stretcher, the kind usually used for a casket or a corpse. But there is no casket or coffin. Instead, a white shroud is draped over the stretcher, hanging limply off the sides. Each* CHORUS *member carries a torch. The* CHORUS *walks slowly, one by one, as if in mourning. Their voices are faint and mournful as they chant.*)

CHORUS: It gets so black here. The horizon and the sky merge in darkness. Desire has long been depleted. There's not even anything left to talk about.

CHORUS: In fact, it's like the encounter never happened here. Being with them is a waste of time. It's pointless.

(*They put the stretcher on the stage.*)

CHORUS: ...Or each walks alone on the surface of the sea, reaching separately for the horizon.

(*Beat.*)

CHORUS: ...Or are they actually intimately fused here because the small waves ripple and merge into the sea and the horizon and the sky and the dark?

(*They look about anxiously. They attach their torches to the stretcher. Then they step back apprehensively and walk.*)

CHORUS: Night can actually be this pitch black.

CHORUS: The desolation of a lonely wind that reeks of corpses.

CHORUS: Be careful

CHORUS: Be careful

CHORUS: Be careful

(CHORUS *exits. Silence.*

Time passes.

RANG *enters followed by* AJERO *who holds a pole that has several flashlights hanging on a rope tied to the end of it.* AJERO *makes sure the flashlights shine on* RANG. *Likewise,* RANG *pays attention to his steps and position in order to stay in the flashlight beams.* RANG *stops in his usual place.* AJERO *continues to his usual spot. After* AJERO *is in place,* RANG *faces* AJERO. *He keeps his eyes fixed on him.*

Time passes.

ANGREH *enters nervously. He notices* RANG *but crosses directly to* AJERO.)

AJERO: Rang is ready.

ANGREH: But Gni isn't!

AJERO: The important thing is that Gni is willing to continue!

ANGREH: More importantly, Gni must take part in the planning as well as the act!

AJERO: Rang on his own is enough!

ANGREH: But it won't work!

AJERO: Do your duty first! My job is done! This is not my fault!

(ANGREH *can't find the words to answer* AJERO. AJERO *moves the pole.* RANG *moves accordingly in order to remain in flashlights' beams of light.* ANGREH *turns to exit.*)

ANGREH: It won't work!

(ANGREH *exits.* AJERO *and* RANG *are left onstage.* RANG *becomes restless from waiting. His eyes begin to wander, looking for where* BANAS *might reappear.*

Time passes.)

AJERO: Don't worry! Banas will definitely come. You must save your strength. Banas doesn't mess around. But don't worry. You'll subdue him and roll him back up in his original packaging. Be calm. Save your strength!

(*Silence.*

Time passes.

BANAS *doesn't arrive.* ANGREH *enters.*)

ANGREH: This won't work!

AJERO: You're just interfering.

ANGREH: Gni is ready!

AJERO: Bravo!

ANGREH: But she'll only do it if she's one who takes care of Banas!

AJERO: What?!

ANGREH: What I've been telling you! Gni wants to take part and that means taking part on her own, without you, without Rang! We're both ready. You guys need to get out of the way!

AJERO: (*Growling*) Angreh!

(*Perplexed,* ANGREH *exits.* AJERO *moves his pole.* RANG *moves to remain in the beams of light from the flashlights.* RANG *ends up on top of the stretcher.*)

RANG: Here?

AJERO: Don't ask too many questions. Sit down. Meditate.

(RANG *obeys.*)

AJERO: You're my superhero. You'll easily defeat the monster. Trust me.

(RANG *meditates. Silence.*

Time passes. Silence.

Time passes. Silence.

Time passes. Silence.

Nothing changes for a long time. ANGREH *re-enters, flummoxed.*)

ANGREH: Use your heads! This won't work! It can't go on like this! Banas won't come! Use your heads! Banas wants Gni, right? See! As long as Gni isn't here, Banas won't show up! Is that too hard to understand? You're impossible! Beat it! Quickly! Don't dawdle!

(GNI *enters.*)

GNI: Leave the matter of Banas to us!

ANGREH: Outta here! Make it fast!

(BANAS *calls* GNI*'s name from far away.*)

AJERO: There! It's him!

RANG: He's coming! I can't wait!

ANGREH: Fool! Banas is coming for Gni!

AJERO: What nonsense. He's coming. He's on his way here. This is how it is now! Get out of the way!

ANGREH: Gni! Go!

(GNI *obeys and exits the stage.*)

Wait here for Banas until the end of times then! Banas won't come!

(ANGREH *exits.* AJERO *and* RANG *wait and wait and wait.* BANAS *doesn't come. His voice no longer calls out* GNI*'s name.*

Time passes.

ANGREH *re-enters.*)

Well?

(*Beat.*)

Still don't believe me?

AJERO: It's hard for me to believe even if Rang and I end up leaving here. It's because we trust in our own experience!

ANGREH: And so?

(AJERO *and* RANG *exit.*)

2.

ANGREH *calls* GNI. GNI *appears. She looks all about.*

ANGREH: They're gone.

GNI: I know.

ANGREH: Get ready.

(GNI *is surprised to see the stretcher.*)

GNI: But it smells like dead bodies here…

ANGREH: That stretcher?

GNI: How did it get here?

ANGREH: It is odd.

GNI: Who brought it here?

ANGREH: Those women.

GNI: But for what? For whom?

ANGREH: For a corpse, of course.

GNI: There's been a death?

ANGREH: Yes.

GNI: Whose?

ANGREH: I don't know!

GNI: But where's the body?

ANGREH: You think there's a body?

GNI: So you don't know either?

ANGREH: All I know is that death happens—but not who died, or where the body is, or when the death occurred, or why.

GNI: Death!

ANGREH: Yes, if it's not for us, then it must be for someone else. If it's not for someone else, it could be for either one of us.

GNI: Huh

ANGREH: If not now, it definitely will in the future. If not in the future, then it happened already.

GNI: Time…!

(ANGREH *suddenly hurries toward the stretcher. He readies himself to pick it up.*)

ANGREH: Come on!

(GNI *goes to pick up the stretcher.*)

GNI: Why? Where to?

ANGREH: Over there!

GNI: I also feel It should be moved over there. But why?

ANGREH: I don't know! Do you have a reason?

GNI: Not really.

ANGREH: But you also feel we should take it over there?

GNI: Yes!

ANGREH: We agree!

GNI: How bizarre!

ANGREH: Come on!

(*All of a sudden,* BANAS *is heard in the distance calling* GNI*'s name repeatedly.*)

ANGREH: Put out the torches!

(*They extinguish the torches. Blackout. They get to work in the darkness. They carry the stretcher behind the scrim along with the torches.*

Time passes.

BANAS *enters. He calls out* GNI*'s name in the dark. He searches for* GNI *in several different places.*

Time passes.

The torches behind the scrim rekindle. The mortuary stretcher appears to be floating in silhouette on the scrim. BANAS *observes the scene from afar. All he can see is the silhouette or shadow of the mortuary stretcher on the scrim.* GNI *and* RANG *cannot be seen, even in silhouette or as shadows.*)

BANAS: (*Surprised, suspicious, worried*) A burial?

(ANGREH *laughs from behind the scrim.* BANAS *startles and appears fearful.*)

Hey! Who are you behind those shadows? A corpse?

(ANGREH *responds with an even louder laugh.* BANAS *seems confused and uneasy. From behind the scrim,* GNI*'s sweetly sings a melody, her voice sensual, so warm, so soft.*

BANAS *listens carefully. Eventually, he recognizes her voice, and his suspicions, worries, and anxiety subside. He appears joyful and hopeful again. He is exuberant.* BANAS *moves toward the scrim. Once he is in front of the scrim and close to it,* ANGREH *growls fiercely.* BANAS *stops in his tracks.* ANGREH*'s growls more savagely! Meanwhile, something moves wildly behind the scrim.*

Sounds of a struggle. A scream. Wild laughter. Banging. ANGREH*'s laughter fills the air.*)

ANGREH: (*Fierce and wild*) One hundred horses
Unite
Neighing…

(ANGREH *continues to growls viciously. The sounds of a struggle resume behind the scrim.* BANAS *fills the air with bloodcurdling screams.*)

BANAS: (*Shrilly*) The night sky expansive as a net!

(ANGREH *continues to growl savagely.* BANAS *also gets unruly.*

Time passes.

The commotion behind the scrim abruptly stops. It's quickly followed by GNI*'s singing again.* BANAS *is quieted by this.* GNI*'s voice swells and fills the air. Her voice smooth and melodious.*)

GNI: Full moon
Whole
Her body naked
Caressed by grasses in the fields
Tossed by waves on the nearby shore

(BANAS *goes wild.*)

BANAS: The night sky expansive as a net!

GNI: The clear lake
—the hunted—
Hides
Under the belly of the full moon

(BANAS *eagerly shoves his way behind the scrim.* BANAS *is now seen in silhouette as a shadow on the scrim. At the same time,* GNI*'s silhouette appears.* BANAS *and* GNI *face each other.*

Meanwhile, ANGREH *growls are interspersed with his thunderous laughter.*)

ANGREH: One hundred horses
Unite
Impatiently
Neighing
Kicking up the grass on the plains
Splashing into the waves on the nearby shore…

(*Meanwhile, behind the scrim, a passionate love scene takes place between* GNI *and* BANAS. *They express everything, explicitly, holding nothing back.*)

The night sky is ripped apart like a frayed net!
Even time is open to possibilities!

(BANAS *and* GNI *are on the verge of climaxing. Their panting gets louder and louder.*)

ANGREH: Under the belly
of the full moon,
one hundred horses—
free and full of desire,
devouring, devouring,
devouring, devouring,
devouring....
Clear lake water.

(BANAS *reaches the height of ecstasy. Orgasms.*)

BANAS: It's happening! I'm coming!
Now, this is a climax! Gni!
Gni!

(BANAS *achieves orgasmic release.*)

(*Meanwhile,* AJERO *and* RANG *enter. They witness everything from afar.* RANG *moves about anxiously while* AJERO *remains restrained and calm.*)

AJERO: (*To* RANG) Close your eyes if you can't bear to watch! This is insane! Crazy! This has nothing to do with what we planned! (*To* ANGREH) Traitor!

(*But* ANGREH *and* GNI *appear not to care, or not to hear*

AJERO, *or don't know what's happening on the other side of the scrim.*)

AJERO: (*Growls*) Angreh! Stop!

(*Enter the* CHORUS, *wearing black headscarves, murmuring and holding small lanterns with flickering candles.*)

CHORUS: (*Murmurs*) This silence is the soundless waft of corpses.

CHORUS: (*Murmurs*) Beware…

(*While continuing to murmur these words, the* CHORUS *walks across the stage as if in mourning.* AJERO *and* RANG *back away to* AJERO*'s original spot on the highest level.* BANAS, *exhausted, appears as if he were drunk, drunk with happiness. His breathing sounds like he's singing a simple melody punctuated by chuckles.* GNI *watches him. She looks worried that* BANAS *might trip and fall.*)

GNI: Angreh?

ANGREH: Is he gratified?

GNI: It appears so…. Yes!

BANAS: Yes, yes, yes! I reached the pinnacle!

GNI: Angreh?

ANGREH: Is he running out of steam?

GNI: Yeah

ANGREH: Don't I know it. Still, he did climax. Life can lead to gratification.

BANAS: Gratification and happiness.

ANGREH: See! What more are you waiting for, Gni? What don't you understand?

GNI: But how?

ANGREH: Life can lead to gratification and happiness!

GNI: I get that! But how?

ANGREH: Don't ask me. You know I've never accomplished anything. But you've always been able to take action! To act! This is your one dream—the only one you have!

GNI: But I don't know when is the time is right!

ANGREH: (*Roars*) Now!

(ANGREH *growls fiercely.* GNI *becomes animated as if motivated and re-energized by* ANGREH *to take action and take* BANAS*'s life. To kill him! Meanwhile, the* CHORUS *exits.*

AJERO *and* RANG *witness the murder and are astounded. RANG is especially enraged and tries to rush toward the skirmish, but* AJERO *holds him back.* BANAS *is beyond help. He dies at the hands of* GNI. RANG *tries to break free from* AJERO. *While* AJERO *and* RANG *wrestle,* ANGREH *gives orders to* GNI.)

ANGREH: Slaughter! Slaughter! Slaughter!
Crush! Crush!
Eat! Guzzle! Chew! Swallow! Finish him off!
Slaughter! Slaughter! Slaughter!
Until there's nothing left!
Create empty space. Create void. Leave no trace!
Slaughter! Slaughter! Slaughter!
Show no mercy. Give him no chance. Annihilate him!
There's not much time. Eliminate everything. Show no mercy.
Slaughter! Slaughter! Slaughter!
Time's running out. Leave no trace.
Perfect your emptied space. Perfect your void. Perfect what is yours.
Your opportunity. Your share. Your actions. Your potential.
Slaughter! Slaughter! Slaughter!

(GNI *enthusiastically carries out* ANGREH'*s orders. Meanwhile,* RANG *manages to escape from* AJERO. *He hurries toward the scrim. When he sees what GNI has been doing, he freezes, aghast, and remains standing in front of the scrim. His soul has been crushed. He can't bear what he sees and screams like a lunatic.*

AJERO *rushes over to* RANG *who's hysterical. When* AJERO *reaches out to touch* RANG, *intending to calm him,* RANG *startles and screams even more. He goes berserk.* AJERO *chases and tries to catch* RANG, *wanting to soothe him. Instead,* RANG *becomes even more panicked and fights him off.* RANG *falls, flails like a chicken with its head cut off, or like a worm squirming in hot ashes.* AJERO *tries again and again to calm* RANG *who keeps resisting.* AJERO *yells several times at* RANG *to calm down and be quiet, but to no avail. Meanwhile,* ANGREH *continues to give orders to* GNI, *who obeys him.*

Ultimately, RANG *begins to lose strength. He starts speaking gibberish. With difficulty,* AJERO *drags him to his spot on the upper level and makes him lie down.* RANG *keeps spouting nonsense while becoming progressively weaker.* AJERO *ponders, standing in place. He stares keenly at the scrim.* ANGREH *and* GNI *continue on as before.*)

AJERO: (*Growls loudly*) Angreh!

(GNI *stops what she's doing.*)

You have rendered the reason for our presence to become suspect, to become despicable.

ANGREH: You know very well what you just said is not true. On the contrary, meaning is now clarified or perfected—completed.

AJERO: What nonsense are you spouting!

ANGREH: I speak the truth!

GNI: On the contrary, it's your babble that's pure nonsense, Ajero!

(ANGREH *laughs, together with* GNI.)

AJERO: Angreh!

(*Hearing* AJERO*'s loud growls,* ANGREH *and* GNI *fall silent.* ANGREH *quicky extinguishes the torches. Blackout. Silence.*

Time passes.)

Segment IV
Jailangkung—Spirit Puppet Divination

1.

The stage is empty. The crater is illuminated.

PERSON[2] *enters with faltering steps. His clothes are in tatters, with scorch marks, blood stains, and mud. His body is covered with injuries. There is an open wound. There is a bandaged wound. He looks like he's suffering and in pain. He drags a bundle and has another on his back. He heads toward the crater. He rests in the crater. His eyes dart suspiciously across the stage. He places his bundles on the edge of the crater. They aren't properly closed, but are half open so that some of their contents is visible. They are full of broken objects. There's a broken doll. There are broken household appliances, damaged vehicles, and other things, all damaged or broken. All the objects are in miniature, things usually for small children to play with. Silence.*

Time passes.

PERSON *cleans up the crater. He is noticeably crying. After the crater is clean, he opens the bundles. He sobs loudly when he sees the broken objects. His favorite things, and all are broken. He cleans each object, one by one, and puts it down lovingly at the bottom of the crater, wrapped in shreds of cloth, as if they were shrouded corpses.*

Time passes.

Once all the objects are laid out in at the bottom of the crater, he covers everything with the cloth from the empty bundles, the mat, and whatever else he finds onstage, until all the objects are buried. Silence.

Time passes.

All of a sudden, PERSON *is startled, becomes frightened and anxious. He hides in the crater, covering himself with the mat.*

2.

AJERO *enters from one side of the stage while ANGREH enters from the other. They each have a torch in hand. They stare at each other. Silence.*

Time passes.

AJERO: You must hand over Gni to me as a sacrifice. Deliver Gni to me!

ANGREH: Never! You are the one who must hand over Rang to me as a sacrifice. Give Rang to me!

AJERO: You misled Gni!

ANGREH: You misled Rang!

AJERO: Gni was misguided!

ANGREH: Rang was misguided!

AJERO: Angreh…!

ANGREH: Ajero…!

(*Beat.*)

AJERO: Gni started it all!

ANGREH: When she obliterated Banas?

AJERO: Banas was killed! Banas was slaughtered mercilessly. Banas was completely destroyed.

ANGREH: But you forget how many other Banases Rang has killed, slaughtered, and destroyed.

AJERO: Because those other Banases were members of Gni's squad.

ANGREH: Oh... the heroic theory? (*Laughing cynically*) Gni has also destroyed other Banases who were Rang followers. Gni is also a hero.

AJERO: Depends on whose point of view you take!

ANGREH: It works from my point of view!

AJERO: Only my point of view is legit!

ANGREH: What nonsense! Just remember who released Banas in the first place. Rang! Rang is the one who must be punished. Rang must be handed over to me as a sacrifice. Deliver Rang to me!

AJERO: So much blood has been spilled. Are you still not satisfied?

ANGREH: Rang's hands are also covered with blood

AJERO: But that's the blood of Gni's followers!

ANGREH: The blood on Gni's hands is the blood of Gni's enemies!

AJERO: You misled Gni!

ANGREH: You misled Rang!

AJERO: You!

ANGREH: You!

AJERO: Misled!

ANGREH: Misled!

AJERO: Misled!

ANGREH: You!

AJERO: You!

ANGREH: Ajero!

AJERO: Angreh!

(*Beat.*)

We've gotten ourselves in a jam!

ANGREH: Deadlocked.

AJERO: Deadlocked.

ANGREH: The key doesn't work.

AJERO: The hole is clogged.

ANGREH: The only key is this reality. Rang has blood on his hands.

AJERO: Gni has blood on her hands.

ANGREH: Who's at fault?

AJERO: Are you accusing us of being at fault?

ANGREH: Could it be our fault?

AJERO: Impossible!

ANGREH: We aren't capable.

AJERO: We have no tactical imagination.

ANGREH: But they were our *jailangkung*.

AJERO: So if a spirit divination puppet does something evil, are we at fault if we were part of it?

ANGREH: The *jailangkung* is at fault!

AJERO: Why does it have fangs?

ANGREH: The *jailangkung* is at fault!

AJERO: We agree!

ANGREH: Rang and Gni are more than *jailangkung*. They have abilities.

AJERO: The ability to do evil.

ANGREH: The ability to do many things.

AJERO: Yes, many things, when they submit to their own will.

ANGREH: So what's the problem between us? Besides flowing blood, screams of pain, a soul severed from its body. The wreckage, all the rubble.... Disastrous for them, but the opposite for us. It's amazing to see our ideas and plans become reality on earth beneath the heavens above.

AJERO: Rang and Gni need us more and more every day.

ANGREH: What we did was a great success. To hell with all the rubble and wreckage. The greater the disaster, the greater our significance, and the greater our value in the eyes of Rang and Gni. What else is there to discuss?

AJERO: The demand for a scapegoat grows stronger. That's the problem. Now Rang demands that Gni be sacrificed

ANGREH: That's your demand!

AJERO: You've also demanded Rang be sacrificed for you!

ANGREH: Yes! Give Rang to me!

AJERO: No way! Hand over Gni!

ANGREH: Hand over Rang!

AJERO: Hand over Gni!

ANGREH: Rang!

AJERO: Gni!

(*Beat.*)

AJERO: Jammed!

ANGREH: Deadlocked!

AJERO: That means one of us has to give up!

ANGREH: Who?

AJERO: You already know my answer!

ANGREH: You also know my answer!

AJERO: Jammed again!

ANGREH: Our fatal flaw.

AJERO: Put your desires aside!

ANGREH: You know that's impossible.

AJERO: Will this conflict never end?

ANGREH: Are you recommending we kill ourselves?

AJERO: You should give up!

ANGREH: You just give up!

AJERO: Hand over Gni to me!

ANGREH: Hand over Rang to me!

AJERO: Gni!

ANGREH: Rang!

AJERO: Gni!

ANGREH: Rang!

(*Beat.*)

AJERO: Jammed!

ANGREH: Deadlocked!

(*Beat.*)

ANGREH: If we let Rang and Gni continue to fight–

AJERO: You know they're equally tough–

ANGREH: They'll both run out of energy–

AJERO: They'll both collapse.

ANGREH: Their energy gone.

AJERO: They'll lose their abilities.

ANGREH: They will be reduced to nothing.

AJERO: Nothing…

ANGREH: Nothing...

(*Beat.*)

ANGREH: (*Aghast*) But others will come after Rang and Gni!

AJERO: (*Cynically*) How many eons will that be?

ANGREH: Yeah, how many eons?

AJERO: It took a fairly long time to get to Rang and Gni. We waited ages for them.

ANGREH: Why must it be evolution? Why not revolution?

AJERO: Or…?

ANGREH: Time…!

AJERO: Death…!

ANGREH: A threat…

AJERO: Rang and Gni?

ANGREH: A threat?

AJERO: It's a possibility!

ANGREH: Stop talking!

AJERO: But it's reality!

ANGREH: Shut up!

AJERO: Once they realize—

ANGREH: Stop!

AJERO: Once they know that we used them as *jailangkung*, once they know they have the ability to act, once they dream of those actions—

ANGREH: Stop!

AJERO: Once they come to that realization—

ANGREH: Quiet!

AJERO: —that will be the moment they'll have a will of their own. That moment will arrive soon!

(*Beat.*)

The moment we no longer mean anything to them. The moment they kick us out...!

ANGREH: (*Horrified*) Ajero!

(ANGREH *groans. Silence.*)

3.

PERSON *comes out of hiding.* AJERO *and* ANGREH *are very surprised.*

ANGREH: Hey! There's another person!

AJERO: He must have overheard what we were saying!

PERSON: It turns out you two are the ringleaders!

ANGREH: Hey now! He's misunderstood our conversation.

AJERO: Hey! Who are you?

PERSON: I am my own person. I'm no *jailangkung*!

ANGREH: Wah! He's dangerous!

AJERO: Where's Rang?

ANGREH: Yeah! Where's Gni?

AJERO: Rang!

(*Beat.*)

ANGREH: Gni!

(*Silence.*

AJERO *and* ANGREH *keep calling, but their voices grow weaker and more desperate. The silence swallows each call, one by one, as they get weaker until only quiet remains. Silence.*

Time passes.

AJERO *and* ANGREH *watch as* PERSON *tries to crawl out of the crater but he's too exhausted and weak.*)

ANGREH: He's lost too much blood.

AJERO: Who is he?

ANGREH: He's already answered that.

AJERO: A follower of Rang or Gni?

ANGREH: Ha! Rang is the one who hurt you, right?

AJERO: No! Obviously he's been wounded by Gni!

ANGREH: Rang! Rang is evil!

AJERO: It must've been Gni who hurt you!

ANGREH: Say Rang!

AJERO: Say Gni!

ANGREH: Rang!

AJERO: Gni!

(PERSON, *who has not yet been able to make it out of the crater, is disoriented by* AJERO *and* ANGREH *quarreling.* AJERO *and* ANGREH *swarm around him like flies over a carcass. Finally,* PERSON *groans loudly, unable to bear it any longer. Silence.*)

AJERO: There's no way this person could be dangerous—

ANGREH: Even though he has a will of his own.

AJERO: He's run out of energy.

ANGREH: Best if he just died.

AJERO: Death…

ANGREH: Death…

AJERO: But where's Rang?

ANGREH: Yeah! Where's Gni?

(*They look for* RANG *and* GNI *everywhere onstage, but find nothing. They look at the contents of the crater.*)

ANGREH: Crater

AJERO: Wound

ANGREH: Broken

AJERO: Wreckage

ANGREK: Burnt

AJERO: Wound

ANGREH: Corpse

AJERO: Blood

ANGREH: Death…

AJERO: Death…

(*While still murmuring "Death,"* AJERO *and* ANGREH *back away carefully from the crater with frightened and suspicious faces. They look at* PERSON *still slumped at the edge of the crater. Their murmurs grow fainter, their steps grow fewer. Once they are far enough away from the crater, they stop. Silence.*)

AJERO: Is it time, Angreh?

ANGREH: Don't continue!

AJERO: Is the time now, Angreh?

ANGREH: Don't continue!

(ANGREH *nervously covers both eyes with his hands.*)

AJERO: With eyes closed everything becomes clearer. Your efforts are useless. We can't deny the obvious.

(ANGREH *nervously sticks his fingers into his ears so he can't hear* AJERO.)

(*Laughing loudly*) It's hopeless! Useless!

(AJERO *continues to laugh. Annoyed,* ANGREH *opens his eyes and unplugs his ears. He looks at* AJERO *angrily.* AJERO *continues to laugh.*)

ANGREH: You can still laugh in a situation like this?

(AJERO *suddenly stops laughing.*)

AJERO: What do you see? What do you hear?

ANGREH: I see pure void! I hear pure silence!

(AJERO *is agape upon hearing* ANGREH*'s pronouncement.* ANGREH *freezes in place after his statement. Silence.*

Time passes.)

AJERO: The silent void. Here. Now.

ANGREH: Oooonnnnggggg...

AJERO: Eeeeeeeeeeeeeeee...

(*As if intoning a monotonous mantra,* ANGREH *continues to make a prolonged "Ong..." sound while* AJERO *makes a prolonged "Eee...." sound as they walk slowly toward their places they were at the beginning of the play. After hooding themselves with their sarongs, they stand stiffly, like swathed statues, in their respective spots. They continue their chant as if it will last forever.* PERSON *has not moved. Slumped over. As if dead.*

Time passes.

Blackout.)

Director/Stage Manager Speech

The decision to include the following speech and/or the remainder of the script is up to the director of each production based on the following criteria:

- If you feel the play has reached its conclusion, stop here and actors should take their curtain call. The remainder of the script should not be performed.
- If you don't consider this a natural ending point, do not perform following speech and proceed directly to Scene 4 beginning with CHILD's entrance.
- Only productions exploring the dialectical nature of the play should include this following interruption by the play's Director or Stage Manager and then continue with the remainder of the play as written.

After what feels like a long time, houselights rise to half. The play's DIRECTOR *or* STAGE MANAGER *enters and delivers the following speech. Alternatively, it could be distributed in print to the audience members for them to read before the play continues.*

DIRECTOR: At this point, the play could be considered concluded. If you consider it concluded, then this is the end of our performance of *Rang Gni.* But if you don't consider it finished, then the scenes we perform next may be considered the end. It's up to you, the audience, to decide when this play ends. We invite you to come to your own conclusion. That said, if you believe that the play has ended, we hope you will be patient for a bit longer and watch the next part of the play we're about to perform. Who knows, perhaps you'll change your mind. If it doesn't change, well, at least you'll have validated your decision. And if it turns out that the conclusion is a dialectic, meaning that the end could be this one as well as the next one, that's perfectly okay. That would mean there are at least three possible conclusions each of us could reach: the first ending would be this one; the second ending would be the one we are about to perform; and the third ending would be both first and second endings at once. Once again, we sincerely hope that you are willing to remain open to another possible ending we are about to perform. Thank you!

(*House lights out as* DIRECTOR *exits.*)

4.

Lights up onstage. A small child[3] *cautiously enters on tiptoe.* CHILD *carries a partially open bag so that some of its contents are visible. There is a triangular ruler, a thick notebook, a magnifying glass, a pencil box, and a few other things.* CHILD *also carries a small canteen. Both the canteen and the bag hang from* CHILD'*s shoulder.* CHILD *has a flashlight.* CHILD *arrives at the scrim and studies it with the flashlight. Not satisfied,* CHILD *takes out the magnifying glass and examines the scrim with that, then takes out the notebook and writes something in it.*

Next, CHILD *crawls on all fours toward the crater. Bewildered to see the collapsed* PERSON, CHILD *examines him, scanning him from head to toe with the flashlight.* CHILD *holds* PERSON*'s wrist trying to find a pulse, then listens to* PERSON*'s chest for a heartbeat, then checks* PERSON*'s eyes.*

PERSON *opens his eyes. He opens his mouth as if to say something. He stretches.*

CHILD *quickly gets organized by taking out equipment and medicine from the bag.* CHILD *gets down to business! CHILD gives* PERSON *a drink.* PERSON *is now able to move. He tries to get off the ground and sit up.* CHILD *helps him.* PERSON *sits on the edge of the crater.* CHILD *takes out a pill and helps* PERSON *swallow it.* CHILD *checks* PERSON*'s mouth and throat, then gives him a spoonful of medicine from a bottle.* CHILD *examines* PERSON'*s eyes, then gives him eyedrops.* CHILD *takes out a syringe and injects it into* PERSON*'s arm.* CHILD *takes out some food from the bag and gives it to* PERSON. PERSON *eats ravenously. He drinks. Finally* PERSON *is healthy again.*

CHILD: Feeling better now?

(PERSON *nods.* ANGREH *is surprised. Suddenly his "Ong" chant stops.*)

ANGREH: Hey! Ajero!

(AJERO *stops chanting "Eee..."*)

ANGREH: I hear a child's voice!

AJERO: (*Laughs briefly*) You're dreaming!

ANGREH: Aha.... Hope!

AJERO: Evolution...!

(*Beat.*)

CHILD: Can you see now?

(PERSON *nods.*)

ANGREH: Ajero!

CHILD: Can you hear now?

(PERSON *nods.*)

AJERO: Yes! A child's voice!

CHILD: Can you talk now?

(PERSON *nods.*)

CHILD: Then talk! Don't just nod!

PERSON: Yes!

(AJERO *and* ANGREH *have removed their sarong hoods. They are astonished to see what is on the stage.*)

ANGREH: He's still alive!

AJERO: And it really is a child!

ANGREH: Is there something wrong with our eyes?

(*They open their eyes wide.*)

ANGREH: It is really him!

AJERO: He's alive! And well!

ANGREH: And it really is a child!

AJERO: Who is it? From where?

ANGREH: How should I know?

AJERO: Shh!

(*They descend from their spots while talking.* CHILD *arranges the things again.*)

PERSON: Hey kid, where did you come from?

CHILD: I don't know.

PERSON: From school?

CHILD: Have you been to school?

PERSON: Not yet!

CHILD: So then, you're ignorant, right?

PERSON: But what kind of school is your school?

CHILD: Do you want to go to school?

PERSON: Sure!

CHILD: School… what kind of school?

PERSON: Hey, watch it. Don't mock me!

CHILD: How about philosophy school, okay?

PERSON: Gee… I dunno.

CHILD: I've graduated already!

PERSON: Don't make fun of me!

CHILD: You don't believe me?

PERSON: I believe you!

CHILD: Have you ever heard a fairytale?

PERSON: What kind of fairytale?

CHILD: The kind that puts you to sleep.

PERSON: Argh, I don't want to sleep.

CHILD: You aren't well yet! You must rest. You must take medicine. You must eat lots of healthy food. You must listen to music. You must sleep now.

PERSON: What's the fairytale?

CHILD: The Tale of the People Eaters.

(AJERO *and* ANGREH *listen from a distance.*)

PERSON: Ooh! How does the story go?

CHILD: There was a tribe. They lived in the forest. They liked to eat people. Why?

PERSON: How should I know?

CHILD: Oh right, I forgot, you're ignorant.

PERSON: Stop teasing me!

CHILD: They ate people because the gods told them to! That's all!

PERSON: That's all?

CHILD: That's all.

PERSON: It's finished?

CHILD: The end!

(PERSON *laughs happily.*)

CHILD: Of course you liked it. I knew it! It's easy to entertain you!

(PERSON *and* CHILD *laugh together.*)

CHILD: Do you want another fairytale?

PERSON: Yes! But not one like that again!

CHILD: This one is different! An avant-garde tale! Listen, ok? There was an old man who was really old and he wanted to tell a story but he didn't know what he wanted to say but he still wanted to tell a story but he still couldn't but he also still wanted to tell a story but he still couldn't but he wanted to but he couldn't but he wanted to but he couldn't! The end!

PERSON: That's it?

CHILD: Don't you know the meaning of "the end"?

PERSON: I know, I know, I know! That's the whole story!

CHILD: Now you're getting smarter.

(*Suddenly* PERSON *bursts out laughing. Apparently he had been holding back his laughter for a while.*)

CHILD: Don't laugh by yourself. People will think you're a madman.

(PERSON *suddenly stops laughing.*)

PERSON: Not a madman but a mad dog!

(PERSON *bursts out laughing again.*)

CHILD: What's so funny?

(PERSON *continues laughing so hard his stomach hurts.*)

5.

PERSON *appears tired. He lies down.* CHILD *also lies down.*

Silence.

Time passes.

They sleep. AJERO *and* ANGREH *come out from hiding.*

AJERO: (*Whispers*) What do you think?

ANGREH: (*Whispers*) The kid likes to tease.

AJERO: The person blamed us.

ANGREH: If we aren't careful we'll be blamed and ridiculed.

AJERO: But the kid's still a possibility.

ANGREH: You think the kid can be manipulated?

AJERO: We don't know yet!

ANGREH: It's too risky. If the kid refuses, it won't just be a refusal. They'll make fun of us at the same time and maybe even.... Ack! I can't face it.

AJERO: So we'd have to leave this place?

ANGREH: Kill ourselves?

AJERO: It's an even more awful risk!

ANGREH: It's obvious we don't matter out there.

AJERO: But we don't matter here either. What's the difference between here and there?

ANGREH: Yeah, whatever the risk, I have to try to make this kid a Gni.

AJERO: Not happening! I must make a Rang!

ANGREH: Must become Gni!

AJERO: Must become Rang!

ANGREH: Must become Gni!

AJERO: Rang!

ANGREH: Gni!

AJERO: Rang!

ANGREH: Gni!

AJERO: Rang!

ANGREH: Gni!

(PERSON *stretches, awakened by the bickering.*)

PERSON: Will this conflict never end? Hasn't enough blood been spilled? Hasn't enough pain been inflicted? Hasn't enough time been wasted? Conflict and conflict and conflict and conflict! Stop all of this! The era of *jailangkung* is over!

(*Beat.*)

You guys haven't left yet? (*Bellows*) Hooaaahhh! What are you waiting for? Rang? Rang is gone! Gni? Gni is gone! The era of Rang-Gni has ended! Your time's up too!

(*Beat.*)

What else are you waiting for? Are you asking to be banished? Asking to be kicked out? Asking to be ridiculed? How dare you guys interfere. How dare you guys hope. How dare you guys challenge. How dare you guys insult. As if we were just clay that you can shape into whatever you want?

(*Bellows*) Hooaaahhh! Get out of this place! You no longer have any significance here! I'm not a character like Rang-Gni that you can trick to forget the agony of fulfilling your holy desires.

Hah! Holiness! Who needs your holiness? My choices and actions don't require holy blessing. Holy blessings can't erase this pain. Your hogwash doesn't work anymore. You're ruined! You're rotten! You're vile! You make me sick to my stomach. Don't wait any longer. I'm gonna throw up and smear your faces with vomit. Get out!

ANGREH: This is outrageous! Rejection is quite enough, but all the verbal insults are entirely inappropriate!

PERSON: (*Enquiringly*) Propriety? Propriety? What do you know about propriety? Was the devastation we've endured as a result of your protagonists' actions appropriate according to the standards of your holiness? (*Bellows*) Hooaaahhh!

(PERSON*'s bellows cause* AJERO *and* ANGREH *to recoil. They flinch with each bellow until finally* AJERO *and* ANGREH *leap offstage.*)

PERSON: The sky you have spread
The sky is like a torn net

Even time is now also again open to possibilities!

(CHILD *wakes up.*)

PERSON: Go back to sleep. The disruption is over.

(*But* CHILD *ignores* PERSON *who makes no effort to enforce his suggestion to sleep.* CHILD *is occupied with the notebook.* PERSON *prepares to go back to sleep.*)

I'm going to sleep. While I sleep, I'll dream about a love story that doesn't receive heaven's holy blessing. The bodies of the bride and groom are scarred by wounds from lightning strikes and tempests. Their blood has saturated the earth. How awful! But the earth is weary of being soaked with human blood. From age to age, blood keeps flowing. The earth is tired of listening to the cries of human pain and suffering. From age to age, the earth is sick of seeing the smug exploits and whims of lightning and tempests dispatching light skies and dark skies. The bride and groom lie prone on the ground. They receive blessings from the hallowed earth. The bride and groom rise up and shoot arrows toward the sky. The night sky is ripped apart like a frayed net. It's raining blood. Later on in my dream, the bride and groom will be covered in blood pouring from the sky during the festivities.

(*Laughs softly, born of a feeling of contentment.* PERSON *falls asleep.*)

CHILD: He really likes to exaggerate even it's only in a dream.

(CHILD *becomes engrossed again in the notebook. Silence.*

Time passes.

Blackout.)

THE END

Shhh...!!!

Production Notes

The play, *SSST...!!!*, translated here as *Shhh...!!!*, was first performed by Teater Saja at Taman Ismail Marzuki in Jakarta, September 28–30, 1977. The production was directed by Ikranagara and Aji Gofur. Frans Haryadi coordinated sound effects. It went on tour through Java later in the year.

The original cast, in alphabetical order by first name, and the character each cast member played are as follows: Aji Gofer (Person), Anton Angkaw (Togog), Ikranagara (Dajal), Innosanto Nagara (Intel), Iran AR (Dalang), Suprayitno (Cupak), Tigun Supangat (Gombal), Wienda Daniel (Reporter), and Yudhi Tampubolon (Dongok).

The poster for the 1977 production announced the following:

- *Shhh...!!!* contains hilarious dialogue, but those who deploy power and strength, full of suspicion and incompetence, will only grin awkwardly.
- *Shhh...!!!* interrogates creative independence, the freedom to express thoughts, feelings, and facts, freedom from poverty and ignorance, freedom from fear.
- *Shhh...!!!* features symbolic imaginative characters resulting from a fusion between the cultural treasure of the Balinese theatre form Arja and the reality of our present circumstances.
- *Shhh...!!!* is appropriate for all levels of society along with journalists, students, citizen representatives, government workers, as well as artists themselves.

Translator's Note

Indonesian pronouns are non-gendered. This translation reflects the gender of the actor who originated the role, but each could conceivably be played by male or female performers unless otherwise indicated.

Like many of Ikranagara's plays, *Shhh...!!!* uses word play and puns to create humor as well as oblique political and social critique in order to slip by the censors during the height of the New Order regime under President Soeharto. He lays out his strategy in the poster publicizing the production (see above) and through the pronouncement of Dalang in Segment III: "I draw from the wealth of our native cultures and merge them with the reality of our lives today."

Ikranagara draws from traditional Balinese and Javanese performances and merges them with the realities of the 1970s. In order for a non-Indonesian speaking audience to better appreciate the puns as they are composed in the original Indonesian script, I have chosen to translate or give approximate meanings of the names of the characters so that English-speakers get a taste of what the punning would have been like for original audiences.

For example, Doofus has a similar meaning to Dongok, the character's name in the Indonesian version. Similarly, Draggle is an approximation for the Indonesian character's name Gombal. Just as doofus and draggle aren't used as personal names, the same can be said for *dongok* and *gombal* in Indonesian.

Stickler and Toggle are "translations" of the characters Cupak and Togog respectively. The play *Cupak Gerantang* is a story often told during Balinese *wayang kulit* (shadow puppet) performances. *Cupak Gerantang* is a moralistic tale about two brothers, the greedy and unethical Cupak, who is short, fat, and crass, and his thoughtful and helpful brother Gerantang, who is handsome and refined. In *Shhh…!!!*, the Cupak character has been translated as Stickler. Togog is one of the main clown/servant characters in Javanese performance traditions who is loyal to the bad side. Togog cannot be trusted; he frequently changes allegiances to benefit his own desires. He is an opportunist who says whatever is needed to get ahead. In *Shhh…!!!*, Togog is called Toggle to reflect his character.

No changes were made to the name of the character Intel, which is the same as the Indonesian version. Reporter is a translation of the Indonesian word *wartawan*, and Dalang is the Indonesian word for master puppeteer or narrator. In the 1970s, *dalang* was used in cultural discourse to signify the person behind the scenes "running the show." The Torch Bearers are simply referred to as the chorus in the original Indonesian version. For alternative endings characters, Dajal is a personification of evil in the Islamic tradition, a type of antichrist or false prophet, and Person is simply described as paranoid.

Cobina Gillitt

Characters

DOOFUS, female

INTEL, a small child

DRAGGLE, male

TOGGLE, a tough guy. Stickler's fixer

STICKLER, the one with power

REPORTER, for the national newspaper

TORCH BEARERS, a chorus carrying torches

DALANG, a shadow puppet master

Additional characters for alternate endings:

PERSON

DAJAL

Setting

A shadow screen, like the kind used for shadow puppet performances, is placed stage right. Raffia ropes hang from above to the ground and sway like banyan tree roots dangling from the tree's branches.

Act I
The Three Confederates

1.

Lights up on the shadow screen and the tops of the hanging raffia ropes that look like hanging banyan tree roots. The remainder of the performance space is dark, save for a lit oil lamp on the ground that faintly illuminates the area around it. DOOFUS, *who is sleeping nearby, can be seen in its dim light. Total silence.*

Enter a small child who investigates the space with a flashlight. It's INTEL. DOOFUS *also becomes an object of his investigation.*

Time passes.

Far in the distance come the sounds of jingling bells and the clacking jaws of a wooden mask. INTEL *is startled and quickly hides. The sounds get closer.*

Time passes.

Eventually the source of the sounds enters onstage. It's DRAGGLE, *who's having fun dancing with a wooden mask.* DOOFUS *wakes up and grabs the oil lamp. She joins in the fun with* DRAGGLE *and plays with the light from the oil lamp. The two dance to the music they create with ankle bells they both wear and the clacking of the mask's wooden teeth.* DRAGGLE *holds the mask by its horns.*

DRAGGLE: We could be happy too!

DOOFUS: But your destitution keeps us hungry!

DRAGGLE: And you? Your ignorance keeps us stupid!

DOOFUS: You're a drag, Draggle! (*Giggles*)

DRAGGLE: And you? You're a doofus, Doof! (*Laughs*)

(*They continue mocking each other's names.*

Time passes.

They stop abruptly and stand erect on the edge of the stage.)

DOOFUS: But you can get angry!

DRAGGLE: Furious! Watch out!

(*After a time, they exit, continuing their antics. Silence returns.*

INTEL *goes back to investigating the space with his flashlight. Someone else enters. He's not a child, but a tough guy. It's* TOGGLE. *He enters behind the shadow screen so all that's visible is the shadow of his face and shoulders and that he's carrying a rifle in one hand.*)

TOGGLE: Shhh…!!!

(INTEL *quickly points his flashlight at* TOGGLE, *whose face becomes visible in the beam of light.*)

INTEL: Shhh...!!!

TOGGLE: Well?

INTEL: Secure!

TOGGLE: Secure?

INTEL: Tell Stickler!

TOGGLE: You tell him!

INTEL: What's the difference?

TOGGLE: The difference is you're Intel and I'm not.

INTEL: Just admit you're too lazy, Mr. Not.

TOGGLE: No insults! When Stickler needs force, he orders "Attack the enemy!" Who steps up? Me! Not you! We have different duties, man!

INTEL: But we help each other out, man! Now help out and tell Stickler this area has been secured. It's ready for Stickler.

TOGGLE: This time you're the one to help me. Submit your own report. Hurry up! Mr. Stickler can't wait any longer. Worried. Nervous. Pacing back and forth and so forth, especially when he hears that typewriter. The louder it gets, the more upset he gets.

INTEL: I've already reported the typewriter issue. When will decisive action be taken?

TOGGLE: The decision to take action is in Stickler's hands—our leader, the one with the power. I just carry out his orders. Period! Understand? Now do your job or I'll waste you!

(TOGGLE *threatens* INTEL *with his rifle.*)

INTEL: Don't mess around with guns!

TOGGLE: Then hurry up!

(TOGGLE *hurriedly exits.* INTEL *is irritated. He takes out his pistol, a baby colt.*)

INTEL: He thinks I don't have a gun. Even though my pistol is tiny, one shot would do him in as long as it hits him in the heart. Hey! Why am I talking to myself?

(INTEL *giggles and puts away his pistol. Exits.*

Blackout.)

2.

Lights up on the area in front of the shadow screen. STICKLER *and* TOGGLE *enter cautiously from behind the shadow screen. They are both still suspicious. They pull a wagon. Its four wheels are small and squeaky.*

STICKLER: All secure?

TOGGLE: I think it's safe.

STICKLER: I think, I think! Investigate the whole area! Where's Intel?

TOGGLE: Hmm, where did he go earlier?

STICKLER: Earlier earlier earlier! I'm asking where he is now!

TOGGLE: But what should I do first?

STICKLER: What?

TOGGLE: Investigate or find Intel?

STICKLER: Do you think you're more skilled than Intel when it comes to investigating?

TOGGLE: Investigating is Intel's job.

STICKLER: So?

TOGGLE: So what, sir?

STICKLER: So what should you do?

TOGGLE: Waiting for your orders, Mr. Stickler!

STICKLER: Damn you, you can't use your head, can you!

TOGGLE: That's right, sir!

STICKLER: Bring Intel here!

TOGGLE: Right, sir!

STICKLER: Do it!

TOGGLE: Right, sir!

(TOGGLE *promptly begins to exit.* STICKLER *is taken aback.*)

STICKLER: Toggle! Come here!

(TOGGLE *returns to face* STICKLER.)

STICKLER: Where are you going?

TOGGLE: To fetch Intel.

STICKLER: Where?

TOGGLE: (*Confused*) Where, sir?

STICKLER: You idiot!

TOGGLE: Right, sir!

STICKLER: No one at all is allowed to know Intel's location except me.

TOGGLE: Yes, sir!

STICKLER: Intel is everywhere. Here, there, anywhere. Understand?

TOGGLE: Understood, sir.

STICKLER: So, there's no reason for you to go anywhere. Understand?

TOGGLE: Understood, sir.

STICKLER: What do you understand?

TOGGLE: All of it, sir.

STICKLER: All of what?

TOGGLE: Um… uh… everything you just said, sir.

STICKLER: Then?

TOGGLE: (*Confused*) Then… then what, sir?

STICKLER: (*Annoyed*) Toggle Toggle! If you want to summon Intel, just call from here. Open your ears. Listen for the answer. He's closer to you than you are to yourself.

TOGGLE: Right, sir.

STICKLER: Call and ask for the status of this area one more time!

TOGGLE: From here, sir?

STICKLER: What did I just say?

TOGGLE: Call from here.

STICKLER: So?

TOGGLE: Yeah, call from here.

STICKLER: Can you do that?

TOGGLE: Sure, no problem!

(TOGGLE *crosses downstage, close to the audience. His eyes look penetratingly into the audience. He calls out as if he's sure* INTEL *is among the spectators.*)

TOGGLE: Intel! Is this place safe? Intel? Is it secure?

(INTEL *listens carefully. It appears* TOGGLE *hears from* INTEL. *The answer seems to satisfy him. Only* TOGGLE *can hear the answer.*)

TOGGLE: (*To* STICKLER) Intel says it's secure, sir!

STICKLER: Well, that's that then! Come here you!

(TOGGLE *returns to* STICKLER.)

STICKLER: I usually give you a special reward whenever you complete a task, but this time you did it badly. How well you do your job determines whether you get a reward or not. This time was not good!

TOGGLE: Right, sir!

STICKLER: Your mistake was when you decided to leave me. How could you leave me alone in a place that might not be safe? That shocked me and shock always comes with unforeseen consequences. It could cause my illness to relapse. It's a proven fact that illness is closely related to shock. The thing is, I'm extremely sensitive. Got it, Toggle?

TOGGLE: Yes, sir!

STICKLER: Don't leave me alone. It's against orders. It's against regulations. It's even against the law. Your blunder could be considered treason. Do you understand, Toggle?

TOGGLE: Understood, sir!

STICKLER: So, how about next time?

TOGGLE: What do you mean, Mr. Stickler?

STICKLER: Oof. You!

TOGGLE: Yes. What about next time, sir?

STICKLER: Since you made a mistake today, what about next time?

TOGGLE: Oh… that's easy to answer, sir!

STICKLER: Don't show off in my presence!

TOGGLE: Sorry, sir. I mean—

STICKLER: I mean I mean I mean!

TOGGLE: I mean… next time I won't do it again!

(STICKLER *is still aggravated. He scrutinizes* TOGGLE *from bottom up and back to front.*)

TOGGLE: Don't be angry with me, sir.

STICKLER: What right do you have to give me orders? I have a right to be angry with you. With anyone! Including angry with you! Do you understand?

TOGGLE: Right, sir!

STICKLER: Slow down! Stop trying to use your brain in a functional way.

TOGGLE: No, sir.

STICKLER: You know, Toggle, it's no good. It's bad for our relationship. Matters that require thinking are my domain. I'm the one in charge here. It's not appropriate for the likes of you to think.

TOGGLE: Right, sir!

STICKLER: Just as it wouldn't be right for me to be you.

TOGGLE: Right, sir!

STICKLER: You are my feet, my hands, my operative.

TOGGLE: Yes, sir!

STICKLER: You're merely a tool of my power. I am the only brain here. Do you understand?

TOGGLE: I fully understand.

STICKLER: Remember all my training!

TOGGLE: Right, sir!

(STICKLER *takes a pack of candy from his pocket.*)

STICKLER: In light of the training you received today, you may receive one of my special rewards.

(TOGGLE *smiles.*)

STICKLER: What is this?

TOGGLE: Candy!

STICKLER: Special and wholesome candy. You know why?

TOGGLE: Because Mr. Stickler has sucked it already!

STICKLER: Like high quality luwak coffee that's gone through a civet's digestive system before roasting!

TOGGLE: Right, sir!

STICKLER: Only I have the right to virgin candy. Here, everyone else must accept my remainders, my residue.

TOGGLE: Right, sir!

(STICKLER *gives* TOGGLE *a packet of candy.* STICKLER *opens the wagon.* TOGGLE *opens the packet of candy.* STICKLER *retrieves some small bananas and other food from the wagon.* TOGGLE *sucks on the candy.* STICKLER *eats.* INTEL *enters stealthily without making a sound. He steals the pack of candy that* TOGGLE *has put on the ground.* TOGGLE *continues to suck on the candy as he resumes his guard duty.* INTEL *quickly exits.* STICKLER *is occupied with his food.*)

3.

TOGGLE *frantically searches for his packet of candy.* STICKLER *cleans up the remainder of his food. He puts it back in the wagon.* STICKLER *observes* TOGGLE*'s behavior.*

STICKLER: Toggle!

(TOGGLE *is too busy to notice* STICKLER *calling him.*)

STICKLER: Toggle!

(TOGGLE *startles when he hears* STICKLER*'s rebuke.*)

TOGGLE: Yes, sir!

STICKLER: What are you doing?

TOGGLE: The candy is missing, sir!

STICKLER: That old song! Bonehead! You can't even take care of a reward. Enough! Forget it!

TOGGLE: Can I get a replacement, sir?

STICKLER: How lovely that would be. You should be punished for losing the reward I gave you!

TOGGLE: In that case I'll just forget it, sir.

STICKLER: That's your business. Now, listen to my orders.

TOGGLE: Right, sir!

STICKLER: I'm going to take a break. I have an important meeting tomorrow. I need to rest and strategize. You must keep me safe. You have to be on guard. You may not rest. Make a general announcement to the country that we're in a state of emergency.

TOGGLE: Right, sir!

STICKLER: We're facing a Vacuum of Power.

TOGGLE: Right, sir!

STICKLER: Being Stickler isn't easy. Many people are jealous and resentful. Danger threatens at all times, especially when I'm sleeping soundly. So you can't rest. You have to keep watch.

TOGGLE: Right, sir!

STICKLER: Now get up here!

(TOGGLE *gets on the wagon. He stands at attention, his rifle at the ready.*)

STICKLER: Now tell Intel to be on alert as well. Publicly announce to the whole country that we're in danger. Do it!

TOGGLE: (*To the audience*) Intel? Intel? Yes! It's me, Toggle! Toggle! Listen up! We're in danger! We must be on guard! Enemies threaten from all over! It's a life and death situation! Critical! Over and out.

STICKLER: Excellent! I'm going to take a break

TOGGLE: Right, sir!

(STICKLER *looks for a place to hide. He goes to sleep in a thicket of jungle-like banyan tree roots created by the hanging raffia ropes. He sleeps soundly.* TOGGLE *stands guard on top of the wagon.*)

4.

Sounds offstage. TOGGLE *is wary. He listens carefully. The sounds get closer and clearer.*

TOGGLE: What is this anyway? (*Cupping his ear*) Not the sound of a typewriter! (*Cupping his ear*) Not the sound of a gamelan orchestra! (*Cupping his ear*) What's this sound? Why is it coming here?

(TOGGLE *gets off the wagon. He hides behind it. The sounds come closer. A jingling sound.*

Time passes.

DRAGGLE *and* DOOFUS *enter. One carries the oil lamp, the other carries a wooden mask on his shoulders. The jingling comes from the bells wrapped around their ankles. They jingle with each step they take.* DRAGGLE *and* DOOFUS *don't think there's anything special or out of the ordinary about the place. They aren't suspicious of anything. They act as usual.*)

DRAGGLE: Let's just rest here, okay?

DOOFUS: Why such a weird sentence?

DRAGGLE: Weird how?

DOOFUS: I don't know but it's a weird sentence.

DRAGGLE: My sentence is weird! But why is it weird? You don't know! But what do you know?

DOOFUS: I know you're Draggle!

DRAGGLE: So what?

DOOFUS: What?

DRAGGLE: Ugh! Enough!

DOOFUS: Does that mean you're mad at me, Drag?

DRAGGLE: Huh? When am I angry?

DOOFUS: Your question is weird!

DRAGGLE: Which question?

DOOFUS: You asked me when you're angry. How would I know? The only one who would know when you're angry is you.

DRAGGLE: Oof! This is getting complicated! Enough already!

DOOFUS: But what about food?

DRAGGLE: Yes, right. How could I forget we have to eat. But how? Better to forget things like eating, drinking, and clothes.

DOOFUS: How is that possible? Don't be like that. Ah!

DRAGGLE: If this is our fate, then what? Think about it! Now, what would you eat?

DOOFUS: You're asking me again?

DRAGGLE: I'm not just asking you but anyone with ears who isn't deaf.

DOOFUS: What's deaf about my ears?

DRAGGLE: Don't go deaf, Doof.

DOOFUS: But if it's fate, then what?

DRAGGLE: It feels like fate's always to blame.

DOOFUS: But if it isn't fate, what is it?

DRAGGLE: It's your ignorance!

DOOFUS: It isn't! It's your poverty!

DRAGGLE: Your ignorance!

DOOFUS: Your poverty!

(DRAGGLE *and* DOOFUS *insult each other. They get noisy.* TOGGLE *comes out from his hiding place.*)

TOGGLE: Hey!

(DRAGGLE *and* DOOFUS *are startled. They fall silent.*)

TOGGLE: Shhh...!!! Don't make such a racket while insulting each other! This place doesn't belong to you.

DRAGGLE: Who says we've ever owned anything?

DOOFUS: Careful, Draggle. He's got a gun.

DRAGGLE: Are you going to shoot us?

DOOFUS: Whoa! That question is weird and dangerous, Drag!

TOGGLE: Shut up, both of you! You have to get out of here! There's no room for you here! Here will be an expansive, picturesque park. Here will be large hotels. Here will be factories. Here will be food markets. Here will be real estate complexes with luxurious and clean houses. There's no place for squalor and ignorance here.

DRAGGLE: Wait! Eliminate squalor and ignorance, but don't drive away the needy and ignorant!

TOGGLE: I didn't mean it that way.

DRAGGLE: We are one nation!

DOOFUS: Just with different luck!

DRAGGLE: Different odds!

TOGGLE: Shhh...!!! The main thing is this place must be clean, respectable, and beautiful. Imagine if foreigners knew you were here. That would humiliate our country! Am I right?

DRAGGLE: But what about our fate? Think about it!

TOGGLE: You want me to think about it? Impossible! You know there's only one who has a brain around here and I'm not the person who has that brain!

DOOFUS: Come on! Let's just go! He's got a gun. One wrong move and he'll destroy us!

DRAGGLE: Well! That weapon of yours!

TOGGLE: What about it?

DRAGGLE: How much does it cost?

TOGGLE: Not for sale! Some nerve, asking about the price of my gun. Do you think a beggar like you could buy a gun? Do you think a fool like you could handle a gun? Get out of here!

DRAGGLE: I just want to know how much it costs.

TOGGLE: Once you know, then what?

DOOFUS: Enough, Draggle. He's getting angry.

TOGGLE: You came here on purpose to make me angry. Am I right?

DRAGGLE: I just want to know the price of your gun.

TOGGLE: Expensive! You hear? It costs a lot! What else do you want?

DRAGGLE: If it's truly expensive better you should sell it.

TOGGLE: What?

DRAGGLE: Yes, sell it to get rid of our problems. The problems of poverty and ignorance in this country.

(DRAGGLE *and* DOOFUS *quickly exit.*)

5.

Total silence. TOGGLE *stands guard. Offstage, the sounds of the clacking wooden mask and jingling bells are heard from afar. Then, there's the sound of a loud typewriter.* TOGGLE *listens carefully. He readies his gun.*

Silence returns.

Time passes.

The sounds return. TOGGLE *jumps down from his post. He looks infuriated, bothered by the sounds.*

The sound of the typewriter gets louder and faster.

TOGGLE: It's that reporter again! It must be! This is too much! This could cause Stickler to relapse. Unacceptable!

(TOGGLE *becomes more agitated.*)

All Stickler needs to do is give the order to take out that reporter. I could definitely obliterate her. She's just a troublemaker![4]

(*Silence returns.*

Time passes.

All of a sudden, DRAGGLE*'s and* DOOFUS'*s wooden mask and ankle bells sound close by.* TOGGLE *leaps in the direction of the sounds but they suddenly go silent. Then, from some other place, the sound of typewriter begins again.* TOGGLE *gets angry. He cocks his rifle. He moves toward the source of the typewriter sound and yells.*)

TOGGLE: It can't go on like this!

(*The sound of the typewriter suddenly stops.* TOGGLE *becomes more introspective.*)

Draggle and Doofus probably made a statement to that reporter who is now typing up an article. The news will then be broadcast in all the newspapers. They really have no respect! Conspiring against Stickler! Against me! How dare that reporter! I'll wipe her out now I know how she feels! Why should newspapers only be filled with criticism, criticism, criticism! Can't they report anything positive? She's truly evil! Her work causes never-ending pain. Criticize this! Criticize that! Like the greatest person ever! Like a know-it-all! Like she knows more than Intel! Damn it! But where does she get her stories from? How come someone close to Stickler like me, doesn't know?

Perhaps Intel is her source? Ack! How could Intel betray Stickler? Nah! It doesn't make sense! Intel is pro-Stickler! No way would Intel betray Stickler! Perhaps there is foreign intel openly hostile to Stickler! Yup, the reporter herself is foreign intel! Definitely a foreign operative! That must be it! Damnation! But why hasn't Intel reported to Stickler that she's a foreign agent? If it's true, Intel would've reported it! But it's possible Intel doesn't know yet! Clever those foreigners. They use our people as their stooges so it becomes hard to identify them. But I can't be duped.

Just look at their newspapers. They criticize their own countries. They defame their own people. Doesn't she always badmouth Stickler? Why expose our country's squalor and ignorance in the newspaper? That's just stirring the pot! As for ignorance, just how much ignorance is there here? And poverty? Are our people eating stones? Of course, there's ugliness, but just keep it a bit hidden. That's what's called being a developing nation. Stop criticizing every little thing! Criticizing Mr. Stickler? What's wrong with Mr. Stickler? Mr. Stickler is second to none in our country! He's a demi-god! What possible shortcoming could he have? Bah! It's her job to slander other people! Mr. Stickler is the single greatest Stickler in the world! Who doesn't admire him? She's the only one arrogant enough to criticize Stickler. No one else! That's because the others are honest! Because the others aren't spiteful and malicious! This one reporter is disrespectful!

I'm in awe of Stickler. The others are just like me. When Stickler stands at the podium and delivers a speech, who can match him? He fires up our passion for life and dedication! "We must continue the fight!" Stickler says. "We must continue to develop!" Stickler says. Aren't those inspiring words? And the name Stickler is revered in other countries. He's admired abroad, except by his enemies, of course. That's normal, they're enemies! And that reporter? She should also be considered an enemy!

"We must first pass through hell if we are to get to heaven!" That's what Stickler says! And Stickler is always right, never wrong! He's a god! "This park being built will be nourishment! The park will also be an investment! The skyscrapers will be ingenious!" That's what Stickler says! And Stickler is always right! It's normal there are still people like Draggle and Doofus. That's fate. Should we fight fate?

Of course we must fight for the best fate, and only Stickler is up for that fight. We can only progress under Stickler's leadership. Poverty and ignorance will disappear from our country. That's not just a promise, but it's in Mr. Stickler's speeches and his message is always great because the point is inspirational. So we must trust it. We must be optimistic at all times. Don't be so pessimistic like that reporter!

Or maybe the reporter doesn't understand what Mr. Stickler's speeches are about?

No way! Even I understand them! Draggle and Doofus are exceptions. I get why they may not understand, but the reporter? Reporters are supposed to be smart, right?

Phooey! She couldn't be stupid! But maybe she's cut from the same cloth as Doofus! How could someone stupid become a reporter? Aha! That's the root of the matter! That reporter is stupid! No wonder the reporter is like Doofus and Draggle! Didn't they also criticize me? That's why he wanted me to sell my rifle. Outrageous! Insane! The reporter must be a lunatic! Disgraceful! How can a nut job become a reporter? No wonder newspaper content is so ridiculous! She's a beast! Barbarian!

(TOGGLE *paces back and forth babbling in annoyance. Meanwhile, the typewriter sound continues. It becomes louder and louder. All of his griping is directed at the sound of the typewriter. He prepares by cocking his gun while continuing to gripe. He even challenges* REPORTER *to a duel. He rants and raves. Suddenly* TOGGLE *opens fire in the direction of the typewriter sound. The gunshot causes* STICKLER *to abruptly wake up.*)

STICKLER: Toggle!

(TOGGLE *startles. The sound of the typewriter disappears.* TOGGLE *faces* STICKLER.)

STICKLER: What are you doing?

TOGGLE: Me, sir?

STICKLER: Yes, you. Who else?

TOGGLE: I'm guarding!

STICKLER: Guarding or dreaming?

TOGGLE: Right, sir!

STICKLER: Right?

TOGGLE: I mean you are always right, sir!

STICKLER: You're nauseating!

TOGGLE: Right, sir!

STICKLER: Right right right! Stop using that word! I don't want to hear you answer like that again! Do you understand?

TOGGLE: Understood, sir.

STICKLER: And now back to your guard post! Get up there!

(TOGGLE *climbs on the wagon.*)

STICKLER: That is where you belong! Not below! Not pacing back and forth!

TOGGLE: I wasn't pacing back and forth, sir. I was guarding, sir!

STICKLER: Guarding guarding guarding! You think I didn't see what you were doing? Was that guarding?

TOGGLE: Yes, sir. That is called guarding.

STICKLER: Do you or I have the right to name names here?

TOGGLE: Mr. Stickler.

STICKLER: Now get down!

TOGGLE: Don't make me get down, sir. I will be more disciplined from now on.

STICKLER: Good! So you will follow my orders? So you will get down now? Get down, I say!

TOGGLE: Yes, sir!

(TOGGLE *gets down from the wagon.*)

STICKLER: Now do what you were doing while I was asleep. Do it! From start to finish. In order, step by step.

(TOGGLE *starts to climb back up on the wagon.*)

STICKLER: You wretch! Up again! Get down I say!

TOGGLE: But you ordered me to do what I did from the start and I started up here!

STICKLER: You're hopeless! All right, climb up!

(TOGGLE *climbs on the wagon. He guards. He acts as if he hears something. He climbs down from the wagon and hides behind it.*)

STICKLER: What's that?

TOGGLE: Hiding, sir.

STICKLER: Guarding or hiding?

TOGGLE: But I've already cocked my gun. The sound came from that.

STICKLER: I don't care! The point is you must be at your post, on the top! Climb up again!

TOGGLE: But, sir…

STICKLER: Since when have you been permitted to use the word "but"? Follow my orders! I say "climb up," you must climb up! I say "guard," you must guard! Do you understand?

TOGGLE: Understood, sir!

STICKLER: If you understand, climb up then! You're hopeless!

(TOGGLE *climbs on the wagon.* TOGGLE *guards vigilantly. Suddenly there is the sound of the typewriter in the distance. The sound gets closer. It makes* STICKLER *jump.*)

STICKLER: Tog! Toggle! Do you hear that?

TOGGLE: That's what was bothering me earlier. It's that reporter!

STICKLER: Was she here?

TOGGLE: She wouldn't dare. Do you want me wipe her out?

STICKLER: Who ordered you to wipe her out?

TOGGLE: I mean if Mr. Stickler orders me to, I will.

STICKLER: Enough! Don't talk so much! Call Intel!

TOGGLE: But what about guarding?

STICKLER: I said call Intel!

TOGGLE: The order to guard has been cancelled?

STICKLER: You're hopeless! You really can't use your head, can you! Get down and call Intel!

(*Just as* TOGGLE *crosses downstage toward the audience to call* INTEL, INTEL *enters. He rides in a toy car. Its wheels are noisy. The sound startles* TOGGLE *and* STICKLER.)

TOGGLE: You've arrived before I had a chance to call you?

STICKLER: You surprised me!

(INTEL *chortles.*)

There's nothing to laugh about! You think the sound of that typewriter is fun?

(*The three of them listen to the sound of the typewriter.*)

So what now?

TOGGLE: Do you have documents to prove she's a foreign agent?

INTEL: Nope.

TOGGLE: Really?

INTEL: What else do you want? That's the truth.

TOGGLE: Just eliminate her, sir.

STICKLER: Are you giving me orders?

TOGGLE: I mean, I suggest, if I may—

STICKLER: No, you may not!

(INTEL *giggles with glee seeing* TOGGLE *being scolded by* STICKLER. TOGGLE *gets mad at* INTEL *for laughing at him.* TOGGLE *lunges at* INTEL. TOGGLE *and* INTEL *wrestle.* STICKLER *blows up at the sight.*)

STICKLER: Hey, hey, hey! What's all this? Hey!! You!! Stop this nonsense!

(*They stop fighting. The pack of candy has fallen out of* INTEL*'s pocket onto the ground.* TOGGLE *sees the candy.*)

TOGGLE: There! The thief is revealed! You, right?

(TOGGLE *moves to pounce on* INTEL *again.* INTEL *dodges him and picks up the candy.* TOGGLE *chases* INTEL. *They scramble.* STICKLER *becomes furious.*)

STICKLER: Toggle!

(TOGGLE *stops chasing* INTEL.)

TOGGLE: But Intel stole my candy. You gave it to me as a reward!

STICKLER: Intel! Come here! Give back the candy!

(INTEL *throws the pack of candy at* TOGGLE*'s feet.* TOGGLE *picks it up.*)

STICKLER: Now no more commotion. The situation is already plenty serious. That deranged reporter needs to be taken care of.

(*The three of them confer in whispers using the wagon as a conference table. Their whispered debate is quite passionate. Suddenly,* STICKLER *pounds loudly on the wagon. The others falls silent.* STICKLER *continues to whisper while* TOGGLE *and* INTEL *just listen and nod.*

Time passes.

Meanwhile, the typing sound stops. The discussion ends. INTEL *exits riding in his toy car.*)

STICKLER: Toggle? Before tackling this major project, I must rest. No disturbances like before. You must guard my safety. Everything and everyone depends on me, on my safety. Now go up to your guard post! Hurry up!

(TOGGLE *climbs on the wagon.*)

STICKLER: Don't make the same mistake again. Your job is to guard and nothing else. Your only duty is to follow my commands and directions. Do what I tell you. Your initiative is not needed. I have taken the initiative. All initiative begins with me, from here on, from this brain of mine. If necessary, I might issue an order, "Hit that wall, Toggle!" You must hit it! Do you understand what I mean?

TOGGLE: Understood, sir.

STICKLER: It means you must be willing to sacrifice to the last drop of blood for me. Do you understand?

TOGGLE: Understood, sir!

STICKLER: We're fighting, we're developing. Do you understand?

TOGGLE: I understand completely.

STICKLER: Good! Now what's your job?

TOGGLE: To guard, sir!

STICKLER: Where do you guard?

TOGGLE: Up here!

STICKLER: Whose safety are you guarding?

TOGGLE: Mr. Stickler's safety.

STICKLER: Who am I?

TOGGLE: The one with the power.

STICKLER: Good! We're on par with the mighty rhino! You deserve your traditional reward from me but you still have a lot of candy, right?

(TOGGLE *inspects his candy.*)

TOGGLE: What! Gone again! That little devil again!

STICKLER: Forget it! No more squabbles over candy!

TOGGLE: But what about my reward, sir?

STICKLER: You're incorrigible!

(STICKLER *takes out a pack of candy from his pocket.*)

STICKLER: You can't even guard your candy!

TOGGLE: Because of that little devil!

STICKLER: Here then!

(TOGGLE *happily accepts the candy.*)

STICKLER: Candy is only given to elephants and you are indeed a determined elephant. You are more formidable than our founding fathers and fearless military troops. You are a more splendid volcano than Mount Merapi. You're as mighty as Krakatau! My enemies will be crushed when you defeat them!

TOGGLE: It's all thanks to Mr. Stickler's speeches and the pre-sucked candy.

STICKLER: Luckily you understand these things! Now go guard!

TOGGLE: Ready, sir!

STICKLER: Don't give yourself orders.

TOGGLE: I won't leave my post even if Krakatau erupts again!

STICKLER: Good!

(STICKLER *returns to where he had been sleeping.* TOGGLE *stands guard and sucks his candy.* STICKLER *falls asleep and snores. Nothing moves. Total silence.*

Time passes.

Blackout.)

Act II
Suppression

1.

Quiet. Stage is dark. Spotlight up on TOGGLE*'s face while the rest of his body remains in darkness. He's on guard. Simultaneously, lights up slowly behind the screen so that it looks like a shadow puppet screen. Gradually, the sound of the typewriter is heard from far away, but gets closer little by little until it's loud enough that it's coming from behind the screen.*

TOGGLE: There it is again! It must be that lunatic reporter! Crazy!

(DRAGGLE *and* DOOFUS *enter behind the screen so that their shadows are cast upon the screen but the performers are not visible.* DRAGGLE *and* DOOFUS *perform a kind of dance. He moves the wooden mask so that it clacks. She moves the oil lamp around so that everything dances dynamically. They cry out every once in a while. Suffering souls crying out against oppression.*)

DRAGGLE: We don't want to be trampled on!

DOOFUS: We don't want to be raped!

DRAGGLE: Our destitution is not because of fate!

DOOFUS: Our ignorance is not because of fate!

DRAGGLE and DOOFUS: We have the right to live decently as human beings!

TOGGLE: Ack! What if this gets out! On the front page no less! What if foreigners read it? That's stirring the pot! That damn lunatic reporter! Crazy!

(DRAGGLE *and* DOOFUS *become more spirited. They pound the floor with anger. Their anger escalates until they are out of control. Their anger overcomes them and, in the end, they wail in agony. Eventually they run out of energy. The sound of the typewriter grows louder.* REPORTER *speaks from behind the screen. The sound of the typewriter subsides.*)

REPORTER: After the era of our independence, after the era that brought us together, after we've persisted as a big family, after opportunities became more widely available, there are still those obsessed with rank, obsessed with adulation, obsessed with power. There are even those who are greedy and insatiable and deceitful and cruel.

DRAGGLE and DOOFUS: They are cruel! Evil!

TOGGLE: Damn reporter! Her work is inciting the wretched and foolish!

REPORTER: He, who loves the crowds of huddled masses; but only for the applause that follows the grandiose promises he spits out.... He, who loves the throng of multitudes; but only those who agree with him. And the passions of those everyday people light up like a million candles on a wide and desolate field, ablaze and burning. When their imaginary enemies are destroyed by his fantasies, he serves up mounds of make-believe victories on that desolate field where a million candles burn. The packed multitudes ravenously suck it up, greedily suck it up, blindly. Myopic and mindless. Submissive and ridiculous.

TOGGLE: So rude! This is offensive! Offensive!

REPORTER: They, who come for an opportunity—for the chance to applaud and beat their chests—arrive ready to escape their daily misery, willing to take part in the victory of empty promises. Empty promises! Nonsense spewed from his mouth that reeks of gunpowder smoke.

TOGGLE: It's obvious this reporter is the enemy! She's definitely the enemy! A foreign accomplice!

REPORTER: He, who has dubious work potential—

TOGGLE: Scumbag!

REPORTER: He, who is obviously lying and rotten to the core—

TOGGLE: This reporter is such a bitch!

REPORTER: He, who believes the world can be built with canned speeches.... He, who believes the world can be built on debt.... He, who believes the world belongs to him and his inner circle.... He, who believes the world can be bought with votes and gunpower...

TOGGLE: What! She means me! Wow! How dare she! Go at it one-on-one with me? Yikes! Yikes!

(DRAGGLE *and* DOOFUS *fiercely cry out again. They convulse with anger. The wooden mask clacks aggressively. Then, suddenly* DRAGGLE *and* DOOFUS *are silent, but they remain on standby.*)

DRAGGLE and DOOFUS: He, who forgets that if he wants to advance the world, he must exist as part of it.

REPORTER: Not floating between heaven and earth...

DRAGGLE and DOOFUS: He must be grounded by a clean and honest personality.

REPORTER: Not a greedy and deceitful heart...

DRAGGLE and DOOFUS: He must be mindful of the common interest—not self-enrichment, not his wife's enrichment, not his siblings' enrichment.

REPORTER: Not just for the benefit of his own family and closest friends whose job it is to enthusiastically lick his ass.

DRAGGLE: This squalor insults our human dignity!

DOOFUS: This ignorance insults our human dignity!

(*They growl again. They move about fiercely.*)

REPORTER: He's evil!

DRAGGLE and DOOFUS: He's evil!

REPORTER: He, who wants it to be easiest for him to get delicious food for his own stomach and those closest to him…

DRAGGLE: He, who wants it to be easiest for him to obtain luxurious clothes to mask his filthy core and the mange that covers his body and the minds and bodies of those closest to him…

DOOFUS: He, who wants it to be easiest for him to satisfy his own lust and the lust of those closest to him…

TOGGLE: This has crossed the line! It's all slander! Lies! Lies! So cruel!

(*Meanwhile,* DRAGGLE *and* DOOFUS *continue to move about fiercely. They growl loudly.* REPORTER *also growls loudly. The sound of the typewriter gets louder. The movements, the sounds, and the voices escalate and build to a climax.* TOGGLE *becomes increasingly agitated, but it only shows in his face. He also looks furious. When everything climaxes,* TOGGLE *abruptly shoots his gun upwards. All at once, everything goes silent. Immediate blackout. Darkness everywhere. Oppressive silence.*)

2.

STICKLER *and* TOGGLE *hide. The stage is empty. Lights up on the top of the raffia ropes. Everything else remains in darkness. There is now a mound of soil onstage.* INTEL *enters. He uses a flashlight to light his way.*

INTEL: Shhh…!!!

STICKLER: Shhh…!!!

TOGGLE: Shhh…!!!

(*They meet. They whisper.* STICKLER *gives orders. They hide. They peer into the darkness. It is very quiet.*

Time passes.

Spotlight up on the mound of earth. It is very quiet. Another spotlight up on another area. As the second spotlight appears, the spotlight on the mound of earth goes out. In that way, the illuminated area of the stage shifts from one place to another. The shifting spotlights reveal STICKLER, TOGGLE, *and* INTEL *lurking in their hiding places. The three of them remain vigilant.* TOGGLE *is ready with a noose made of rope.* INTEL *is ready with his pistol.*

Time passes.

REPORTER *enters. She carries a wooden mask on her shoulders. One hand holds onto the mask, the other holds an oil lamp. They belong to* DRAGGLE *and* DOOFUS. REPORTER *is in mourning. She walks toward the mound of earth. She stops in front of it. Dispiritedly, she places the oil lamp on the ground near the mound and lowers the wooden mask. Then she sits cross-legged in front of the mound. She puts the wooden mask and the oil lamp on top of the mound. Spotlight out. The only light on stage is from the oil lamp on top of the mound and the light on the tops of the raffia ropes.* REPORTER *sits in contemplation. The mood is somber.*)

REPORTER: God, I feel so ashamed today. Even on this rich earth of ours, in this land of intelligent people, there are so many Draggles impoverished, so many Doofuses fooled. I am so ashamed.

(*Beat.*)

I'm not criticizing you for all of this.

(*Beat.*)

I'm not blaming all of this on divine fate.

(*Beat.*)

God, all this is our responsibility alone: the presence of Draggles and Doofuses in this country, in the post-independence era, is our fault alone. Doofus, Draggle, forgive me, I haven't done much for you guys, but my conviction has never wavered knowing that your existence, along with all the other Draggles and along with all the other Doofuses, is a tangible sign of a plague that gnaws away at this country, a plague that continues to grow and spread.

(*Beat.*)

I swear before you, in the presence of the Doofuses and the Draggles and God Almighty, I will never stand idly by. There is work to be done. I won't blink even for a second. I will continue to face the plague that lies ahead; I will continue to hunt down the evil that haunts us. It doesn't matter who or where the culprits are, it doesn't matter what rank they hold or how powerful they are, I will continue to act as much as I can, as much as my limited abilities allow.

(*Beat.*)

Forgive my human limitations.

(*Beat.*)

Yet I am convinced that life can be given meaning. Life cannot be wasted—this one life.

(*Beat.*)

God, I deeply understand, I clearly hear your voice, pure and inspiring—your voice, continuing to enrich my sense of honesty. I thank you.

(*Beat.*)

God, I feel so ashamed today. Accept these departed souls, Draggle and Doofus, by your side. Amen.

(*Very quiet. Yet, in the silence,* STICKLER, TOGGLE, *and* INTEL *prepare to ambush* REPORTER. *Then, after a time, they trap her with the noose. Bedlam ensues! Whistles are heard everywhere. After a while,* REPORTER *stops moving.* TOGGLE *tightens the rope.* STICKLER *and* INTEL *just watch, while keeping guard.*

Lights up on stage so that REPORTER *and* STICKLER *are clearly visible.* STICKLER *crosses over to* REPORTER.)

REPORTER: It's you!

(STICKLER *sniggers cynically.*)

REPORTER: What's that for?

STICKLER: You've forgotten the Dutch saying, "Silence is golden"!

REPORTER: This kind of suppression is just like the Dutch colonizers!

STICKLER: Shut up! I set the standards around here! Furthermore, everyone knows I'm not a colonialist! I am a native! Alright, if you don't like the Dutch saying, how about: "Your mouth is your tiger"? Now do you understand?

REPORTER: But what did I do wrong?

STICKLER: Definitely something!

REPORTER: You have to prove I'm guilty under the law, in a court of law!

STICKLER: Who says I won't stick to the law? Who says I won't take you to court? But first you must be arrested.

(REPORTER *does not answer.*)

STICKLER: There! You see? This action is accordance with regulations.

TOGGLE: Protected by the law.

REPORTER: As long as you remember there's a time limit for detaining a person.

TOGGLE: You don't have to teach us about that stuff!

REPORTER: And don't forget, I have the right to defend myself and, if necessary, to bring charges against you in a court of law.

STICKLER: (*Bemused*) Court of law?! (*Laughs scornfully*) Of course, of course, of course! But the important thing is that from now on, you have to.... Shhh…!!!

TOGGLE: Shhh…!!!

INTEL: Shhh…!!! (*To* STICKLER) Bye-bye, boss.

(INTEL *exits quickly.* STICKLER *takes out a notebook from his pocket. He writes something in it.*)

STICKLER: I'm doing this specifically to satisfy you. I really don't need to write down something like this, but since you like court procedures, fine! Listen to this carefully, Tog!

TOGGLE: Yes, sir.

STICKLER: Read this! Speak up!

(STICKLER *hands* TOGGLE *the notebook.*)

TOGGLE: "Arrest Warrant. Period. I, Stickler with the power, am obliged to order the arrest of the person listed below colon. Name Reporter; occupation reporter; address not important; age not important; education not important; newspaper title you know it. Grounds for arrest colon forthcoming period signed Stickler."

STICKLER: Satisfied?

REPORTER: How could I be satisfied? At least you should have the rough details about my offense. Which news story, on what page, what date, and so on, necessitated my arrest and investigation.

STICKLER: What day do you want?

REPORTER: What?

STICKLER: Well? Today? Details exist! Yesterday? Details exit! A week ago? Details exist! A month ago? Details exist! In fact, there will be details tomorrow as long as your newspaper isn't shut down today.

TOGGLE: Clear where the problem lies?

STICKLER: Want to ask on which pages? Just count all the pages in your newspaper! The answer is: on every page of your newspaper!

TOGGLE: Clear where the problem lies?

STICKLER: That's everything I'll be using as evidence later.

REPORTER: Evidence of what?

STICKLER: The warrant Toggle read wasn't clear?

TOGGLE: Was my voice not loud enough? Do I need to shout when I read it?

STICKLER: Deal with her, Tog!

(STICKLER *walks away from them.*)

TOGGLE: Do I need to read it again? Or do you want to read yourself? Here! Read it!

REPORTER: But here it says, "Grounds for Arrest colon forthcoming"!

STICKLER: Of course they're forthcoming!

TOGGLE: That's how it is! He's right!

REPORTER: But why?

TOGGLE: Oh boy! She's a chatty one, sir.

STICKLER: (*To* TOGGLE) Come here!

(TOGGLE *crosses to* STICKLER. STICKLER *whispers something to* TOGGLE.)

STICKLER: Can you explain it?

TOGGLE: No prob!

STICKLER: No mistakes this time!

TOGGLE: If I do good, there's a prize, right?

STICKLER: Yes, okay!

(TOGGLE *confronts* REPORTER *again.*)

TOGGLE: Of course it's forthcoming! Why? Because everything is being arranged by a committee. The committee's job is to gather the data. The data will be processed. During the processing, everything will be categorized: which ones are classified as major wrongs, which ones are classified as minor ones, between the most major and the most minor. Of course there will be some in-between. In addition, there needs to be an introduction, and if there's an introduction, there must be a conclusion. That's what's called a perfect format, but perfection alone is not enough. There must also be… must also be…

(*To* STICKLER) How must it be, sir?

STICKLER: Give me a break!

(STICKLER *whispers something into* TOGGLE'*s ear.*)

TOGGLE: (*To* REPORTER) But perfection alone is not enough. First, strength must be studied. That means strength must be tested first. Someone has to attack, then block, attack, block, wrestle, slam, kick, punt, punch, pin, and so on, and so on, and so on. If you pass this test, only then can you be judged to be on par with my strength. But, believe you me, you won't be able to beat me. I am not just Mount Merapi, says Mr. Stickler, but also the great volcano Krakatau!

STICKLER: Toggle!

TOGGLE: Yes, sir!

STICKLER: Where are you going with this?

TOGGLE: I'm lecturing her so she knows my strength, so she won't dare to criticize you again.(*To* REPORTER) Because if you criticize Mr. Stickler, that means you gotta face me! Get it?

STICKLER: Enough! Shut up! Geez, you're a crafty one, Tog!

REPORTER: That's messed up!

TOGGLE: What? Who's messed up?

REPORTER: You!

STICKLER: Tog! Toggle! Get over here.

(TOGGLE *quickly goes to* STICKLER. *They whisper.*)

REPORTER: So, this is going to take a while?

STICKLER: Depends!

REPORTER: Depends on what?

STICKLER: Depends... depends on time!

(STICKLER *laughs.* TOGGLE *joins in.*)

STICKLER: If time says, "Hurry!" it will be quick. If time says "Slow down, sir," What happens, Tog?

TOGGLE: It will be slow!

(STICKLER *and* TOGGLE *burst out laughing.*)

REPORTER: Not funny at all.

TOGGLE: Of course not! Nothing is funny to you.

(STICKLER *chuckles.* TOGGLE *also chuckles.*)

REPORTER: So, actually, in other words, you aren't ready, yet you shamelessly make this arrest!

(STICKLER *moves closer to* REPORTER *again.*)

STICKLER: This is what you don't know, young lady! Your experience is undeniably different than mine. People with my experience, counting those from centuries ago and until whenever in the future, know when it's time to make an arrest. We have a special feeling about this.

REPORTER: So it's based on a feeling?

STICKLER: I understand if that surprises you. We're admittedly different, but it doesn't mean that reporters don't have feeling. You can be sure, a good reporter must have some kind of feeling and the feeling that reporters have is self-restraint. That means knowing the limits: for example, when to withhold certain news from dissemination because it would be bad for them if published.

REPORTER: Not bad for me but bad for you.

TOGGLE: Don't interrupt when Mr. Stickler is speaking! Mind your manners!

STICKLER: Take a look for yourself. Even Toggle knows more on the subject of feeling.

REPORTER: Because he's a tool of your power.

TOGGLE: Of course I'm Mr. Stickler's tool! What's wrong with that? My position is as his legal tool, in accordance with the law!

STICKLER: Keep lecturing her, Tog!

TOGGLE: Because Mr. Stickler is everything here, reporters must also be a tool of his power.

STICKLER: (*Claps*) Nicely done, Tog!

REPORTER: To hell with your indoctrination!

TOGGLE: What? Why so rude?

STICKLER: Don't attack her yet, Tog.

TOGGLE: How hard is it to report good news—news that gives everyone pleasure and especially pleases Mr. Stickler? What's so difficult?

REPORTER: It's difficult because reality isn't like that.

TOGGLE: Says who?

REPORTER: Reality is based on real facts. I can't be forced to lie. These actions of yours, Stickler, these actions of yours trample any sense of human decency!

STICKLER: (*Laughs*) You're awfully grandiose, young lady.

REPORTER: I can't compromise. I will still report crime facts as crime facts. It doesn't matter where they took place or who committed them. The people's misery remains agonizing. To hell with your theory of feeling!

(TOGGLE *grabs* REPORTER *furiously.*)

TOGGLE: So disrespectful!

STICKLER: Tog!

TOGGLE: This mouth is begging to be whacked with my shoe!

STICKLER: Not yet, Tog!

(TOGGLE *grudgingly releases his grip.*)

Your mouth is your tiger, young lady.

TOGGLE: If necessary your mouth's gonna be acquainted with the steel toe of my boot. Get it?!

(TOGGLE *drags* REPORTER *over by the hanging raffia ropes. There, he ties* REPORTER *even tighter until she can't move at all.*)

REPORTER: When will I be tried?

STICKLER: Shhh…!!!

REPORTER: Take me to court now! We'll prove to the country who's the evil one and guilty of wrongdoing!

TOGGLE: Shhh…!!!

(*A sound is heard from offstage. It gets closer. It makes* TOGGLE *and* STICKLER *tense.* TOGGL*E safeguards* STICKLER.)

REPORTER: Aren't you going to try me? Am I going to be held without a trial? This is injustice!

(STICKLER *becomes angry with* REPORTER. *He rushes over to her with a large handkerchief taken from the wagon. He uses the handkerchief to gag* REPORTER*'s mouth. Just before she's gagged,* REPORTER *snaps at* STICKLER.)

I can smell your brain rot! You are truly black-hearted!

(*Now* REPORTER *can no longer speak or move.* STICKLER *hides.* TOGGLE *stands guard by the wagon. His gun is at the ready. The sound is now very close by. It comes from the squeaky wheels of* INTEL*'s toy car.* INTEL *is very animated. He goes directly over to* TOGGLE.)

TOGGLE: Oh, it's you!

INTEL: Shhh…!!! Where's Stickler?

TOGGLE: What do you want?

(STICKLER *comes out of hiding on his own.* INTEL *rushes over to* STICKLER *as soon as he sees him.* INTEL *produces a file from under his shirt and immediately hands it over to*

STICKLER. *Then he whispers something in* STICKLER*'s ear.* STICKLER *is unnerved and angry.* INTEL *quickly exits in his noisy toy car. Everything happens so quickly that* TOGGLE *is immobilized.*)

STICKLER: Toggle!

TOGGLE: Yes, sir!

STICKLER: Bring the reporter here!

TOGGLE: Right, sir!

(TOGGLE *does as instructed.*)

STICKLER: The gag is too messy. We need to shut her mouth completely.

TOGGLE: Just use Band-Aids, sir.

STICKLER: Band-Aids, masking tape, electrical tape… whatever!

TOGGLE: But the best would be Band-Aids, sir. Masking tape isn't strong enough. People will think she's has an extension cord in her mouth if we use electrical tape.

STICKLER: Are Band-Aids really appropriate?

TOGGLE: She's sick, isn't she? So Band-Aids would be best!

STICKLER: I order you to first remove her current gag, then get the most suitable supplies and, lastly, gag her mouth tightly. Can you do that?

TOGGLE: No problem!

(TOGGLE *fetches the supplies.*)

REPORTER: How do you have the right to do all this? What's the meaning of our legal institutions? What's the meaning of our monuments to independence that were built with our blood and lives? You've become despotic!

STICKLER: The country's in danger! Shut up!

REPORTER: Who's in danger? The country or you personally?

STICKLER: Can't you see that my safety is the safety of the country?

REPORTER: It's precisely because you managed to save yourself and your position as Stickler that the country is now threatened. You're driving the inhabitants of this country to the brink of disaster. The people are losing their ability to set limits on your extravagance and whims. You have become despotic and a plague that will rule every legitimate institution. You and your people are leeches who will continue to suck the blood of our people.

(TOGGLE *can't ignore what she's saying. He ferociously strikes* REPORTER.)

STICKLER: Muzzle her!

(TOGGLE *is ready with the Band-Aids. He roughly closes up* REPORTER'*S mouth with Band-Aids. Because she's tied up,* REPORTER *can't do anything but surrender.*)

STICKLER: We'll just jail her first. Put her court appearance on hold so she can't take advantage of the court venue. She's too clever with her agile tongue; she'll probably use the court setting to incite again.

TOGGLE: What about the committee drawing up the charges?

STICKLER: What committee?

TOGGLE: The one you mentioned.

STICKLER: Oh... that?

(STICKLER *laughs.* TOGGLE *laughs too.* INTEL *enters abruptly, in a great hurry.*)

INTEL: Shhh...!!!

(STICKLER *and* TOGGLE *are startled. They immediately stop laughing.* INTEL *goes directly to* STICKLER. *He whispers something.* INTEL *finishes delivering his whispered message. He begins to exit.*)

Hurry! It's time!

(INTEL *exits.* STICKLER *crosses over to* TOGGLE. *He whispers something in* TOGGLE'*s ear.* REPORTER *is dragged to the raffia ropes and hidden in them.* STICKLER *cleans up the wagon.* TOGGLE *helps* STICKLER. *They busy themselves tidying up everything onstage. They bury the wooden mask brought by* REPORTER *in the mound of soil. They extinguish the oil lamp. The whole stage is cleaned up. Slowly, the lights dim until it becomes extremely dark. They continue their activity for a moment.*

Time passes.

Silence.

Blackout.)

ACT III
Prohibition

Stage is dark. A flute is playing. Muted chanting. Enter the TORCH BEARERS *upstage left and upstage right. They carry lit torches and move about in front of the backdrop until all gather behind the shadow screen. The muted chanting becomes clearer. The shadow screen is being readied for a shadow puppet performance with the torchlight behind it.*

Time passes.

The stage is still empty as before.

Time passes.

DALANG *appears among* TORCH BEARERS. *The only thing visible is* DALANG'*s shadow cast on the screen.* INTEL *sneaks onstage into the darkness. He carries a flashlight with which he examines the stage. He's most interested in the area of the screen but he doesn't aim his flashlight at it.*

Time passes.

INTEL *returns to the place where he had just entered onstage.* TOGGLE *enters from the same place. They whisper for a moment. Then* TOGGLE *exits again.* INTEL *crosses the stage to the other side. He stays there.*

Time passes.

TOGGLE *and* STICKLER *enter from the same place as earlier. From across the stage,* INTEL *turns on his flashlight.* TOGGLE, *who also has a flashlight, does the same as* INTEL.

INTEL: Shhh…!!!

TOGGLE: Shhh…!!!

(TOGGLE *escorts* STICKLER *across the stage.* INTEL *also begins to cross the stage from the other side. They meet in front of the shadow screen, but they are still quite far from it.*)

INTEL: (*Whispers*) The dalang is meditating.

STICKLER: It's really him?

INTEL: There's no mistake

STICKLER: What's the title of the play?

INTEL: "Lambs of the Revolution."

TOGGLE: Oh! I was told it was "Big Brother."

INTEL: Same thing! [5]

TOGGLE: They're different!

INTEL: The content is the same!

STICKLER: So maybe the title is different for this performance?

INTEL: Maybe. I don't know how many times the title has changed, but the story's always the same. What's clear though is that it's never been given the title "Stickler."

TOGGLE: Stickler?

STICKLER: Shhh…!!!

(DALANG *lifts his hands toward the sky.*)

DALANG: Good evening! Good evening, gatekeeper of the world of the departed, I come only as a spirit. My body is just a shadow, arriving to fetch the departed souls of Draggle and Doofus. Draggle…? Doofus…?

TORCH BEARERS: Draggle…? Doofus…? We are all Draggles. We are all Doofuses. We miss you.

(DALANG *waves his hands. It is very quiet for a moment.*

Time passes.

Two shadows of bodies appear on the screen. They are the spirits of the deceased DRAGGLE *and* DOOFUS.)

DALANG: Thank you, gatekeeper of the world of the departed. Tonight, Draggle and Doofus will take part in our performance.

(*The muted chanting begins again. The tempo rises and falls. In keeping with the tempo of the chanting,* DRAGGLE *and* DOOFUS *begin to dance, but their rhythmical movements aren't smooth. They stumble as if their bodies are broken and on the verge of falling.*)

TOGGLE: What should be done, sir?

STICKLER: Best I take immediate action! You must be ready the moment I need you.

TOGGLE: Right, sir!

STICKLER: (*To* INTEL) You go now and return right away. Bring the files with evidence of this dalang's activities. I need them.

(INTEL *quickly exits.*)

TOGGLE: Shall we start, sir?

STICKLER: Yes!

TOGGLE: Now?

STICKLER: Now!

(*Suddenly, whistles are heard everywhere. The torches behind the curtains move nervously. As a result,* DALANG*'s shadow appears to move nervously although* DALANG *doesn't actually move. The same for the shadows of* DRAGGLE *and* DOOFUS. STICKLER *stands facing the shadow screen. The whistles are joined by other sounds creating pandemonium. The shadows of* DRAGGLE *and* DOOFUS *disappear from the screen.*)

DALANG: (*Surprised and disappointed*) Draggle...! Doofus...! Don't go yet!

DRAGGLE and DOOFUS: (*From afar*) I'm allergic to Stickler. He is pestilence and plague. The spirit world must not be infected.

TORCH BEARERS: Draggle…! Doofus…!

DRAGGLE and DOOFUS: We no longer need to be brave. If you truly want to change your destiny, be brave. Be brave, be brave.

(*Their voices get farther away until they disappear completely. Sounds of people wailing, people cursing, people screaming. Complete bedlam. The* TORCH BEARERS *move nervously.* STICKLER *gives a signal to* TOGGLE. TOGGLE *swiftly fires into the air. The mood abruptly turns chilly, silent, and still.* DALANG *and* STICKLER *face each other. They are only separated by the screen.* DALANG *is still in the form of a shadow on the screen.*)

STICKLER: Who are you?

DALANG: I'm a dalang.

STICKLER: I know that but what's your name?

TORCH BEARERS: His name is Bambang the Concerned.

STICKLER: What?

DALANG: I knew you wouldn't like my name.

STICKLER: So you deliberately chose a name that would displease me?

DALANG: I didn't choose it.

TORCH BEARERS: We gave him a name. Tonight, his name is Bambang the Concerned.

STICKLER: You all have no right to use that name! That name is evil! That name wreaks havoc! Do you mean to cause trouble here?

(*Silence. No one answers.*)

I am the only one who has the right to give you a name, Puppeteer!

(DALANG *doesn't reply.*)

TOGGLE: (*Loudly*) Puppeteer!!!

(DALANG *still doesn't reply.*)

Maybe he's deaf!

STICKLER: Maybe he wants to be deaf?

TOGGLE: Shall I make him deaf, sir?

STICKLER: It's not time for that yet, Tog!

DALANG: My name is Bambang the Concerned. There's no way for you to change it.

TOGGLE: Defying Stickler, are you? That means you are dealing with me!

DALANG: You're the one who asked. My name is Bambang the Concerned.

STICKLER: Not allowed!

TOGGLE: That name is forbidden! It's not appropriate for the spirit of the times.

STICKLER: Look! Even Toggle understands this simple matter!

DALANG: That depends! The spirit of the times, in your opinion? Or in ours?

STICKLER: Ours, you say? Who do you mean by ours?

TOGGLE: Seems there's some sort of conspiracy here!

TORCH BEARERS: We are made up of millions of Draggles and Doofuses. We are one country, one nation, one language with you!

STICKLER: Puppeteer! Listen carefully. Starting tonight your name is Bambang the Truth King. You can't be called a true dalang yet. You're newly a puppeteer-in-training. You have a great gift, but your mind and soul have yet to be infused by the words of my speeches, have yet to be saturated by my thoughts and essential nature. You and all the others must become my tools. I am Stickler, the one with the power.

TOGGLE: I am also Stickler's tool, legally and protected by law.

STICKLER: As a puppeteer-in-training, you need to undergo an upgrade. Once that's done, then you'll be a real dalang. Understand?

DALANG: That's totally outrageous! You bury the facts after our hard-won freedom to reveal them. Now is the time for the freedom to create works of art. What's guiding you as you develop this country if you're not brave enough to witness the truth, if you're not brave enough to listen to the voices of the living?

STICKLER: I know what I'm doing!

TOGGLE: Stickler knows everything!

DALANG: You guys only know what makes yourselves happy!

STICKLER: You only want what justifies yourself! You only want to exaggerate your role and the role of your art.

TOGGLE: Like that lunatic reporter!

DALANG: Your words are nonsense, devoid of meaning except as a ploy to cover up your mangy soul!

TOGGLE: Your language! Mind your manners!

DALANG: Embezzlement will flourish without transparent supervision directly by society. Illegal fees will rule like infernal bloodsuckers. Kickbacks will give birth to high-level sprawling malignancies. Corruption will become a way of life that renders this country no different from the colonial era.

TOGGLE: Bastard! How dare you!

DALANG: The people know who's responsible for the misfortunes undermining our country and from where they come!

(INTEL *enters hastily. He gives the file he carries to* STICKLER. STICKLER *immediately goes behind the screen, so that he becomes a shadow, like* DALANG. TOGGLE *does the same.* INTEL *hastily exits.*)

DALANG: Is that the file on the history of my artistic activities? You don't need to show it to me!

TOGGLE: Wow! You're giving him orders now?!

DALANG: You don't need to collect data about me and my art. I can explain it to you directly. That's usual for me as an artist; honesty is my flesh and blood.

STICKLER: So it's true then, you've actually performed the story of Stickler?

DALANG: It's true. The Legend of Stickler is a treasure of our culture

TOGGLE: Stickler? Stickler is a legendary character?

DALANG: You truly have never been educated about your native culture, have you?

TOGGLE: So there is a legend about Stickler? That's amazing!

DALANG: I am afraid your Mr. Stickler doesn't agree with you.

TOGGLE: Huh? What should be done, sir?

STICKLER: What I've been asking you for a while, Toggle! Shut your mouth! What do you know about the legend! You want to know? It's forbidden to perform that legend. Not only during my lifetime, but it's been codified into law. You get it?

TOGGLE: Got it, sir!

DALANG: But I don't perform that legend.

STICKLER: Just now you claimed to be the most honest person. Now it's back to word gymnastics! Drag him outta here, Tog!

DALANG: (*Panics*) I need to explain. Admittedly, the Legend of Stickler was my jumping off point, but I've merged it with present day reality.

STICKLER: Merged or not, the result is the same. I've studied this file. The content of the story you perform offends me, insults me, rebukes me.

DALANG: I'm sorry if that's the case.

STICKLER: Your apology is too late!

DALANG: What I mean when I apologize doesn't mean I take back what I've performed or want to deny it. I'm just being polite.

STICKLER: So you oppose me?

DALANG: Oh wow!

(TOGGLE *roughly drags* DALANG *out from behind the screen.* STICKLER *follows. The three of them are now downstage of the screen. Lights up on the area so their faces are clearly seen. Meanwhile, the* TORCH BEARERS, *who had been illuminating the shadow screen, scatter and exit. Sounds of whistles and rowdiness overwhelm the space.*

Time passes.)

STICKLER: At your advanced age, old man, it's unseemly for you to act like that, while the young accept it because they appreciate the importance of our singular strength to develop our country.

DALANG: But what's wrong with the story I perform?

STICKLER: Your story has the potential to disturb the peace in the workplace. It has the potential to interfere with our collective welfare.

DALANG: But what can I do if revealing the truth shows too much wrongdoing and that we're truly in an age of darkness? Must I become a liar? If what I see hurts us all, must I transform it into something pleasant?

STICKLER: That's enough! Without realizing it, you've gotten yourself trapped in a pessimistic pattern of art-making. Have you ever thought about killing yourself?

DALANG: On the contrary! It's because I want to live a long life that I've discovered a powerful reason to keep on living. I emphasize that reason in my work. I will continue to create stories. I draw from the wealth of our native cultures and merge them with the reality of our lives today. The pain of our nation's people deserves a place of honor. That place is in my art.

STICKLER: Enough! I don't need to be schooled by you. Toggle!

TOGGLE: Yes, sir!

STICKLER: Restrain this dissident!

DALANG: Hey!

(DALANG *is tied up.*)

STICKLER: He'll have to get special upgrading while he's in detention.

DALANG: (*Furious*) I don't need your upgrading! Just take me to court if you can actually prove my guilt!

STICKLER: You think I'm stupid? A court of law for you? You just want a forum. In such a forum, you could sell your sauce and incite the people with your fairy tales! Ho ho! I'm not that stupid! No! I've decided you will get an upgrading. You need a prototype for your art. Model yourself after artists who've received my blessing. They depict my thoughts and feelings in their work. They're all good tools. Use them as examples!

DALANG: I'm too old to backpedal. Too old to start over again as a dissembler. My measure of freedom isn't whether or not I'm in jail, but whether I am a liar or a truth-teller. Your tools do indeed remain out of prison and dine with you, enjoying the results of scheming with you, but actually you've imprisoned all of them. But not me!

STICKLER: Toggle! Shut his mouth!

(TOGGLE *gags* DALANG'*s mouth with Band-Aids, then binds his whole body including his hands.*)

So that he knows what is actually a prison and what is freedom!

(*Blackout. Silence.*)

Act IV
Stickler's Version of Freedom

Stage is dark. A flurry of activity. Whistles from all directions. Also other sounds.

Time passes.

Suddenly, a gunshot. Spotlight up onstage. TORCH BEARERS *move behind the screen.* STICKLER *sits on a beautiful and valuable rug. In front of him, there is an extravagant and sumptuous display of food. He eagerly eats the food.* TOGGLE *stands tall with his weapon across his chest. He munches on candy. In his hands, he holds two ropes that bind the hands of* REPORTER *and* DALANG. *Their bodies are tied up and their mouths are shut tightly with Band-Aids. They look exhausted. Elsewhere,* INTEL *busily cleans his little pistol. The corpses of* DRAGGLE *and* DOOFUS *are laid out downstage close to the audience. Together, they form a kind of family portrait.*

Sudden blackout.

TOGGLE: Who says we aren't yet liberated?

STICKLER: Who says we aren't yet prosperous?

INTEL: Who says we aren't yet secure?

(*Lights up. A family portrait. Blackout. They laugh happily.*)

STICKLER: Laughter is healthy!

(*Lights up. A family portrait. Blackout. They laugh happily.*)

TOGGLE: This is Stickler's version of freedom!

(*Lights up. A family portrait.*

Total silence.

Time passes.)

THE END

Alternate Endings

1. Dajal kills Stickler, Toggle, and Intel.
2. Dialogue between Dajal, Reporter, and Dalang.

3a. Reporter and Dalang are shot dead; the sun is shot dead; Person is overcome by fear.

3b. Interview with audience. What do they want? Discussion with audience.

Mask 1

Production Notes

Mask 1 was originally titled *A-him-pom-pong*. It was devised at the University of California, Davis when I was a guest lecturer/artist-in-residence there in 1974. The work was conceived during the "Workshop Toward a Performance," a special course I taught for theater majors.

The workshop was an attempt to produce a performance that doesn't start as a scripted drama, or even life experiences or stories. It was derived from an exploration of body movement in space and time, freely, without being tied to the burden of a realistic flow. At first, it was performed by individuals, then continued in pairs, and finally developed into a group piece. Each bit generated was codified and called a "segment": my imagined correlation with the segmented body of an insect.

The segments were then re-mixed, combined with one another, or remained on their own. The finished segments were then re-internalized by the performers. At this stage, vocalizations were added which then developed into words.

The words were derived from existing poems that had been divided into fragments. At the time, I included not only fragments of my poems, but also poems by the Indonesian poet Chairil Anwar (1922–1949).

Then we added costumes, makeup, props, as well as the set and lighting, all the visuals that make up the performance. We also added the mask. After the addition of the vocals, rhythmic and lyrical sounds naturally followed and so music was added.

Because expression and recognition are important in the creative process, it was inevitable that life itself would become a part of the work. Besides me, those who participated in devising *A-him-pom-pong* included John Vickery, Jean Bucknel, Maureen White, Tony Bruskas, and others.

That is how *A-him-pom-pong* was born. That is the embryo that led to the birth of *Mask 1* (*Topeng 1*). *Mask 1* is no longer the same as *A-him-pom-pong,* just as a cultured adult is no longer the same as its embryo.

In *Mask 1*, Chairil Anwar's poems were cut and a number of new segments added apart from my poetry. Each theatrical performance brought new and changing elements, including the mask, the music, the stage setting, the lighting, etc.

I gave the title *Mask 1* because it is the first of a series that includes #2, #3, #4, #5, and God willing, the next numbers will be born. All of my works of this type have been collected under a single title: *The Rite of Masks* (*Ritus Topeng*).

The first production of *Mask 1* was at Taman Ismail Marzuki in Jakarta in 1980 in the Arena Theater. Those who participated in the production were members of Teater Saja, including: Ik (Ikranagara), Mal (Jamal Kheler), Maxi (Maxi Manongko), Pra (Mamok Pratomo), Ran (Iran AR), Tik (Atiek Cancer), and Win (Wienda Daniel).

Teater Saja has also performed *Mask 1* in Kuala Lumpur, Malaysia, in 1986, while an English version was staged in Taipei, Taiwan, in 1984, and Singapore in 1986. In 1990, students in the Drama Department of Drama at Ohio State University, Columbus, Ohio, performed the play in English under my direction.[6]

Ikranagara (1987)

Characters

MAXI A big, strong man. He wears a long-sleeved tight fitting t-shirt and tight fitting pants like those worn by ballet dancers, but made from thicker material. He wears a cape made from hanging plastic cords that swing freely. Bottle caps and small emblems are attached to the cords. His head is wrapped in plastic and tied up with plastic string. Two plastic cords are stretched tightly from one ear to the other: one across his bridge of his nose and the other under his chin. A number of small ankle bells are wrapped around his right ankle. He wears shoes.

MINIONS Maxi's minions, including MAL, RAN, TIK, PRA, and WIN, are all dressed like Maxi, except they wear vests rather than capes.

IK A faceless creature with a fetid and frayed body. His face is a giant bird mask, with a moss green beak, pink gums and tongue, and pearly white fangs. His eyes protrude. Take a look at Balinese Garuda masks for inspiration, or make your own design.

PAR An old man. His face and body look ancient. Even his clothes are old and shabby.

OFF STAGE VOICES

♦

Setting

Along the upstage edge of the performance space, a thick wall of raffia ropes hangs from above. Five long pipes hang in this raffia wall. There is a platform just downstage of the raffia wall. Several platforms of increasingly smaller size are stacked with the highest point upstage center, forming a tower of platforms. There is a large metal throne on the topmost platform with a place to hang Maxi's cape next to it. The performers can climb up and down the platforms like stairs. There is an open flat playing area in front of the platform tower with a large tree stump downstage left and a pile of stones stage right. Round segments of bamboo, each containing an unlit candle, are scattered along the downstage edge of the performance space from stage left to stage right.

Segment 1

Dark. Desolate. Silent. After a while, breathing is heard, voiced as a long, single tone "Aaaaa...." Red lights dimly illuminate downstage left revealing WIN*'s entire corpse lying face up on a stretcher.* MAL, RAN, TIK, *and PRA carry* WIN *on their shoulders. They are lined up behind* MAXI, *who carries a very large, round, shiny emblem in both hands raised above his head. They stand erect stage left in a solemn ceremonial procession line facing stage right. The breathing is vocalized by the* MINIONS.

Meanwhile, IK sits cross-legged on a large tree stump downstage left with the procession behind him. IK sits as still as a statue, his faceless body facing downstage. His bird face mask is on the ground in front of him.

PAR, *old and stooped over, stands downstage right. He holds a small gong in his left hand and its mallet in his right hand.*

Unlit candles in bamboo holders are scattered across the downstage edge of the playing space.

The breathing grows clearer and louder until it fills the space.

Time passes.

MAXI: (*Loudly*) Ssssaaaahhhh...!

(*The breathing stops! Silence!*

PAR *slowly and solemnly strikes the gong. Not only does the gong sway from side to side, but so does PAR's body. Then, while continuing to play the gong one strike at a time, PAR heads upstage center to the highest platform on the tower. When he arrives at the top, he pauses a moment, while still striking the gong. Then he descends to the back of the stage, walks through the raffia wall, and exits.*

PAR *is no longer onstage, but the sound of the gong continues as it travels into the distance until it fades away.*)

Segment 2

MAXI: Ssssaaaaahhhhh...!

(*MAXI crosses to center stage. Each step starts with the cry, "Sah…!" He climbs to the highest platform where PAR had been. However, he doesn't follow PAR, but turns around to face downstage and boldly stands holding the large round emblem high above his head.*

Spotlight up on the emblem. On the dimly lit stage, the illuminated emblem is like a full moon in a sky of raffia streamers. Silence returns.

Time passes.

MAXI stamps the floor with his right foot.)

MAXI: SSSssssaaaahhhh...!

(*This cues his* MINIONS *to march forward carrying the corpse.*)

MINIONS: (*With each step*) Huuuh… hah…! Huuuh…hah…! Huuuh… hah…! (*Repeats.*)

IK: Bird feathers bathed in blood on the martyr's breast. Bird feathers bathed in blood on the martyr's breast. Bird feathers bathed in blood on the martyr's breast. (*Repeats*)

(*The* MINIONS *carry* WIN*'s body to the area below the metal throne, downstage of the platform tower.*)

MAXI: Ssssaaaahhhh...!

(MAXI *cries out just as his* MINIONS *arrive in front of the metal throne and stop walking. IK stops chanting when* MAXI *cries out. Silence!*

MAXI *steps down a platform level at a time in front of the throne. He cries "Sah…! " with each step.*

MAXI *arrives at his destination. His* MINIONS *place the stretcher on the ground at* MAXI*'s feet. They then back away from the body, stooped over with their arms dangling at their sides, and sit facing* MAXI *with heads bowed. The mood remains solemn.*)

MAXI: I'm not ready to face death after death. I've never prepared myself. As if we would never die.

(MAXI *turns in slow motion to face the metal throne. He climbs up the platforms one by one, still crying "Sah…!" with each step. He doesn't sit right away. First, he hangs the large emblem on the back of the throne. Then takes off his cape and hangs it up. After that, he sits on the throne and listens to indistinct voices as they grow louder and clearer.*)

VOICES: Good night. Good night. Good night. Sleep well. Sweet dreams…

(MAXI *falls into a deep sleep. Lights fade out on the throne. Silence!*

Time passes.

Green spotlight up on IK.)

IK: Bird feathers scatter in a squall/
Bird feathers scatter on the edge of the forest/
Bird feathers bathed in blood on the martyr's breast/
Song bird feathers exist behind silence/
Spirit bird feathers vibrate within us/ (*Repeats.*)

(The small gong is struck. Lights up upstage behind the raffia wall. PAR *is revealed holding and striking the gong. The* MINIONS, *including WIN's corpse, awaken and move to the rhythm of the gong. They stand up, moving like fish in the depths as if searching for something. They don't move upstage toward the sound of the gong; instead they cross to the pile of stones placed stage right. They each pick up two stones, then hit them together making a musical sound. A music composition is created with the stones accompanied by the small gong and IK's repetitive chanting. As they continue, the green light on IK dims, but doesn't go out. Green light comes up gradually on the* MINIONS. *The light grows brighter and brighter.*

The MINIONS *dance enthusiastically to the rhythm of the music they are making. WIN performs a solo for the others who continue to create music and dance around the space. From far off, animal noises are heard during breaks in the music. Then, wolves howl.*

Time passes.

Suddenly, a siren goes off, drowning out all the other sounds. MAXI *is jolted awake. Spotlight up on* MAXI *and the throne. Green spotlight out on* IK. *Lights out also on* PAR *so he's no longer seen behind the raffia wall. Light on the* MINIONS *stays up, but is no longer green.* MAXI *stands up straight with bulging eyes! The* MINIONS *drop the stones from their hands and panic!)*

MAXI: (*Loudly rebukes*) Ssssaaaahhhh...! Himpong-himpong! Himpong-himpong!

(*The* MINIONS, *including* WIN, *quickly get in line and stand at attention, ready for orders.*)

Segment 3

MAXI: Join me! Come on! Himpong-himpong! Himpong-himpong!

MINIONS: Himpong-himpong!

MAXI: Himm! Himm-himm!

MINIONS: Himm! Himm-himm! Himm! Himm-himm! Himm! Himm-himm! Himm! Himm-himm! (*Repeats*)

(MAL, RAN, TIKTIK, PRA, *and* WIN *walk in place in time with their rhythmic vocalizing. Their bodies move from left to right and their shoulders go up and down without moving their hands. Their movements become faster as their vocalizing gets louder, the pitch rises, and the tempo quickens. From where he stands, MAXI enjoys the vocalizing by performing some dance moves.*

Time passes.)

MAXI: (*Forcefully*) Teeeeeeee…!

(*That is the signal for the* MINIONS *to stop.* WIN, TIK PRA, RAN, *and* MAL *return to their positions to wait for orders.*

Silence!)

MAXI: (*Not robotically*) As if we would never die, I never prepared myself to face my own death.

MINIONS: (*Robotically*) As if we would never die, I never prepared myself to face my own death.

MAXI: Sssssaaaahhhh...! Join me! Come on! Switch it up! Himm…!

WIN: (*Bowing forward*) Himm!

MAXI: Pong…!

TIK and PRA: (*Bowing forward*) Pong…!

WIN: Himm…!

(WIN *flings body, hands, and head upward.*)

TIK and PRA: Pong…!

(TIK *and* PRA *fling their bodies, hands, and heads upward.*)

WIN: (*Bows forward*) Himm…!

TIK and PRA: (*Bowing forward*) Pong…!

(*As if performing an established dance,* WIN, *followed by* TIK *and* PRA, *repeat their words with alternating forward and upward movements. They make their way past the centerstage platform tower toward the upstage left platform adjacent to the raffia wall. That becomes their spot.*

WIN, TIK, *and* PRA *each grab one of the five long pipes hanging in the raffia wall. While continuing to repeat "Himm" and "Pong," they move the pipes more vigorously in the rhythm of people doing various kinds of routine work.*

Time passes.)

MAXI: Teeeeeeee…!

(*That is the signal for* WIN, TIK, *and* PRA *to stop their activities. It is also the signal for* RAN *and* MAL *to begin to chant "himpong-himpong" and to walk in step past the platform tower to the backstage platform adjacent to the raffia wall.* RAN *and* MAL *don't move toward the plastic pipes in the same way as* WIN, TIK, *and* PRA *had. Instead, their movements give the impression they are hitting each other and dodging the other's blows, like a power-struggle dance.*

All five MINIONS *line up in a row on the upstage platform where they move the plastic pipes as if working. They become increasingly energetic and chant "himpong-himpong" in unison. Atmospheric sounds from different work locations, including a factory, an office, and others, ending with the stock market, play in the background.*

The sounds create environmental music. Meanwhile, MAXI *moves in a kind of dance that depicts giving orders, indicating approval or expressing disapproval, all various actions a boss normally carries out.* WIN, TIK, PRA, RAN, *and* MAL *end up moving robotically, like a dance of stilted mechanical creatures. The various atmospheric background sounds fade out and are replaced by a siren that begins softly at first, but grows louder and louder!*)

MAXI: Teeeeeeee…!

(*That's the signal for his* MINIONS *to end their activities and for the siren to stop. Silence!*)

Segment 4

MAXI: (*Not robotically*) I'm amazed by this life!

MINIONS: (*Robotically*) I'm amazed by this life!

MAXI: Life and passion are readily available.

MINIONS: Life and passion are readily available.

MAXI: Rapture!

WIN: (*Not robotically*) I want! I want I want I want I want!!

MAL: Coffee with sugar!

TIK: Sweet tea with milk!

RAN: Fried eggs!

PRA: Fried rice!

WIN: Bread and jam!

PRA: Leather shoes!

MAL: Wool pants!

RAN: A leather belt!

TIK: A leather bag!

WIN: Lipstick!

TIK: A pencil mini skirt!

WIN: A watch!

TIK: An umbrella!

RAN: A car!

MAL: A typewriter!

PRA: A computer!

(And so on! They name things they like for everyday use, for work, or other needs. After that, they begin to name objects they offer for sale. They act as merchants noisily selling their wares.)

WIN: New books! Colored pencils! Magazines! Magazines! Magazines!

MAL: Tennis balls! Running shoes!

TIK: Children's bikes! Children's bikes! Children's bikes!

RAN: Radios! CD players! TVs! TVs! TVs!

PRA: Trending suit jackets! Long-sleeved shirts!

TIK: Limited stock! Limited stock! Buy now!

RAN: Airplanes! Helicopters! Helicopters!

PRA: Machine guns! Cannons!

MAL: Guided missiles! Bullets!

RAN: Bombs!

WIN: Bombs!

PRA: Bombs!

TIK: Limited supplies. Limited supplies! Buy now!

MAL: Nuclear reactors! Nuclear reactors!

RAN: Nuclear bombs! Nuclear bombs!

TIK: Limited supplies! Limited supplies! Buy now!

PRA: Nuclear war! nuclear war!

MAL: Germ warfare! Germ warfare!

PRA: Limited supplies! Limited supplies! Buy now!

(*And so on! Then each speaks as if on the phone, using the plastic pipe in their hands.*)

WIN: Hello!

MAL: Hello!

PRA: Hello hello!!

RAN: Hello hello hello !!!

TIK: Helll… oooo….!

MINIONS: Hello hello hello!

(*They try to communicate, but get stuck and can only repeat "hello!" over and over. They grow more and more frustrated, then angry until they go berserk because their hellos go unanswered.*

Time passes.

MAXI *falls back into a deep sleep. Meanwhile,* TIK *steps down from the upstage platform to the open space downstage, while the others continue their efforts to communicate.* TIK *finds a bicycle bell on the ground, picks it up, and closely studies it as if it were something unusual.* TIK *rings the bicycle bell a few times. The others fall silent and turn their attention to* TIK *who repeatedly rings the bell.* WIN, PRA, RAN, *and* MAL *leave the upstage platform and crawl over to* TIK. *They marvel at the bell* TIK *keeps ringing.* TIK *delights in the sound of the bell.*)

TIK: (*Chortles with glee*) On sale! On sale! Cheap price! Cheap price!

(*The others join with* TIK*'s delight and gleeful laughter as* TIK *rings the bicycle bell.* TIK *convulses with laughter and falls backward, but is caught by the* MINIONS.)

(*Emphatically*) I never thought about it. Never once! What if all of this vanishes in the future! (*Laughs*)

MINIONS: (*Laughing*) Never!

(*The* MINIONS *laugh gleefully and repeat "never" over and over.*

Time passes.

They are overcome by laughter. They continue to repeat "never" but their voices grow weaker and weaker. They tire. As they tire, they begin to question.)

WIN: Never?

RAN: Never?

PRA: Never?

MAL: Never?

TIK: Never?

(*They are no longer tired. They keep asking. They think hard. The mood turns serious. They gradually become sad as they repeat "never?" over and over. By continuing the repetition, the* MINIONS *grow bitter, which makes them angry.*)

WIN: What if all of this goes extinct?

MAL: If all of it disappears?

TIK: Have we thought about it?

PRA: We have thought about it!

RAN: We have!

WIN: We have!

MINIONS: We have! We have! We have!

(*Meanwhile,* MAXI *has woken up. He observes his* MINIONS *from the metal throne and is not pleased. He stands up!*)

MAXI: Sssssaaaahhhh….!

(*His* MINIONS *are startled, then frightened. They freeze in place.*

MAXI *descends from his throne. He takes a section of plastic pipe from under the throne. It's as long as an overseer's whip or one used by a circus animal trainer! Upon reaching centerstage,* MAXI *swings the plastic pipe around and loudly strikes the ground with it. His* MINIONS *quickly return to the upstage platform where they had been working. Each grabs a plastic pipe and stands at the ready to receive* MAXI*'s orders.*)

MAXI: Follow me! Come on! Switch it up! Himpong-himpong! Don't think about that! Do not!!!

MINIONS: (*Robotically*) Do not! Do not think about that!

MAXI: Do not!

MINIONS: Do not!

MAXI: Do ooo ooo!

MINIONS: Do ooo ooo!

MAXI: Nnn… o… ttt!

MINIONS: Nn… o… ttt!

MAXI: Do… not!

MINIONS: Do… not!

MAXI: Do… not!

MINIONS: Do… not!

MAXI: Don't!

MINIONS: Don't!

MAXI: Do not think about that!

MINIONS: Don't think about that!

MAXI: Do ooo ooo!

MINIONS: Do ooo ooo!

MAXI: Do ooo ooo!

MINIONS: Do ooo ooo!

MAXI: Do… do!

MINIONS: Do… do!

MAXI: Do do doodoodoodoo do do!

MINIONS: Do do doodoodoodoo do do!

(*And so on.* MAXI *rhythmically sings "do do" inspiring him to dance downstage with the long plastic pipe in front of the metal throne. His* MINIONS *also sing along, but robotically.*

Time passes.)

MAXI: Teeeeeeee…!!!

(*His* MINIONS *stop all their activity.*)

MAXI: (*Not robotically*) I am amazed by this life.

MINIONS: (*Robotically*) I am amazed by this life.

MAXI: How beautiful burly bodies are.

MINIONS: How beautiful burly bodies are.

MAXI: Bodies dripping wet with sweat.

MINIONS: Bodies dripping wet with sweat.

MAXI: Bright eyes.

MINIONS: Bright eyes.

MAXI: Snorting.

MINIONS: Snorting.

MAXI: And throbbing!

MINIONS: And throbbing!

MAXI: Throbbing!

MINIONS: Throbbing!

MAXI: Throbbing!

MINIONS: Throbbing!

MAXI: Life and passion are readily available.

MINIONS: Life and passion are readily available.

MAXI: Rapture!

MINIONS: Rapture!

MAXI: I want!

MINIONS: I want!

MAXI: Definitely!

MINIONS: Definitely!

MAXI: Definitely!

MINIONS: Definitely!

MAXI: Life provides the sun!

MINIONS: Life provides the sun!

MAXI: Life provides the beach!

MINIONS: Life provides the beach!

MAXI: Life provides lust!

MINIONS: Life provides lust!

MAXI: Sex!

MINIONS: Sex!

MAXI: Let me drown in life!

MINIONS: Let me drown in life!

Max: Let me drink up this life until I've had enough!

MINIONS: Let me drink up this life until I've had enough!

Max: Eeenufff...!!!

MINIONS: Eeenufff...!!!

MAXI: Without rest!

MINIONS: Without rest!

MAXI: Like on the disco floor!

MINIONS: Like on the disco floor!

MAXI: Music!

MINIONS: Music!

(*Boisterous music fills the stage!* MAXI *dances. His* MINIONS *also dance, a dance of mechanical creatures.*

Time passes.

MAXI *eventually ascends the throne and goes back to sleep. His* MINIONS *are also tired and fall fast asleep on different levels of the platform tower.*)

SEGMENT 5

The entire stage is bathed in a dim green light creating a gloomy, ghostly atmosphere. Silence. Two flickering candle lights appear from behind the raffia wall where PAR *has been hiding.* PAR, *holding a candle in each hand, enters from behind the upstage raffia wall. He carefully climbs up and over the platform tower to the open playing area downstage. One by one, he lights the many candles in bamboo holders scattered across the downstage edge of the performance space. While lighting the candles,* PAR *utters an incantation that vacillates between audible and inaudible.*

Time passes.

PAR *crosses to where* IK *sits on the tree stump.*

PAR: Bird feathers are friends with whomever
Has been made useless /
Bird feathers' ragged friends
Are made destitute /
Bird feathers' idiot friends
Are made to look foolish /
Bird feathers' closest friends
Go blind /
Bird feathers are friends with whomever
Has been made useless /
Bird feathers do have friends
So they say /
Bird feathers stand bravely
On the altar of independence.

(IK *pats* PAR *on the shoulder.*)

IK: Speak up! Stand tall!

(PAR *exits to his hiding place behind the upstage raffia wall.*)

SEGMENT 6

Spotlight up on PAR.

PAR: (*Summons loudly*) Bird feathers…! Bird feathers…! Bird feathers…! Bird feathers…! (*Repeats*)

(*Time passes.*

WIN *wakes up.* WIN *hears* PAR*'s voice calling, but can't tell where it's coming from.*)

WIN: Your voice. I hear your voice from inside a cave. Which cave is your cave among the millions of caves within the self? Which cave?

PAR: Bird feathers…! Come, come…! Into the cave of bird feathers…! Come…!

(*Meanwhile, the other* MINIONS *also wake up. They observe* WIN *while also looking for the source of* PAR*'s voice. The* MINIONS *restrain* WIN *as* WIN *begins to climb down the platform tower.* IK *remains silent.*)

WIN: Where are we? What is our place here? What?

TIK: We've never thought about that!

PRA: Never!

RAN: Do do do!

MAL: Himpong-himpong!

WIN: We've thought about it!

PRA: Never!

WIN: We once questioned it! Once! Once! Once!

PRA: Never never never!

RAN: Himpong himpong himpong himpong himpong!

MAL: Doodoo do doodoodoodoo do!

TIK: Himpong himpong himpong himpong himpong!

WIN: Once once once! We once questioned it!

(*The argument gets heated, then becomes a struggle between* WIN *on one side against all the others.* WIN *is captured and stretched out like a cowhide drying in the hot sun as it's tanned into leather.*

IK *speaks again. His loud voice startles the* MINIONS. *They freeze like statues while* WIN *is still stretched out like a cowhide.*)

IK: Spirit bird feathers vibrate within us. Song bird feathers exist behind silence. Hear it…! Listen…!

(*The* MINIONS *hear IK's voice clearly and the hostility between them disappears. They look for the source of the voice from where they stand on the platform tower.*)

WIN: What is our place here?

TIK: What?

PRA: This is our place.

WIN: What is our place here?

TIK: What?

PRA: The back of a porcupine!

RAN: A giant porcupine!

MAL: The back of a giant porcupine!

WIN, TIK: Heed the spiny steel needles, spiny steel needles, spiny, spiny…!

MAL, RAN, PRA: Heed the spiny steel needles…!

(*They are in extreme anguish. WIN crawls to the ground from the platform tower, still holding the plastic pipe. The others follow* WIN, *but they no longer hold plastic pipes. They crawl behind* WIN *on the ground.*)

WIN: (*Crawling*) Where is my moon?

TIK: (*Standing with difficulty*) The moon is alone. Its face slashed. Slashed…

MAL, RAN, PRA: Slashed…

TIK: Blood drips non-stop… incessantly…

MAL, RAN, PRA: Pus festers. Festers…

TIK: The moon is alone… fenced in by iron bars… iron bars…

RAN, MAL, PRA: Iron bars…

(*At the same time,* WIN *continues crawling to where* IK *sits in meditation.* WIN *sits solemnly facing* IK, *still holding the plastic pipe. The upstage raffia wall sways whenever WIN pulls on the pipe because it's attached to and hangs as part of the wall.*

TIK, MAL, RAN, *and* PRA *crawl over to the lit candles in the bamboo holders. They lie prone on the ground with each of their faces directly over one of the candles so their faces are clearly illuminated.*

Nothing moves for a while, except for the raffia wall that sways due to the pipe in WIN's *hands.*

Time passes.)

SEGMENT 7

WIN *lets go of the plastic pipe. At the same moment,* PAR *strikes the small gong from behind the raffia wall.*

MAL, RAN, PRA, *and* TIK *each pick up a candle and stand up slowly and carefully. As they stand up, their attention remains fixed on the candlelight, held close to and illuminating their faces.* MAL, RAN, PRA, *and* TIK *step carefully, slightly bent over, toward* IK. *Once they reach* IK, *they also sit facing* IK, *solemnly like* WIN. *The sound of* PAR*'s small gong continues in the background.*

WIN *stands up after picking up the giant bird mask and walks slowly behind* IK *so that* WIN*'s feet touch* IK*'s back. The gong grows louder.* PAR *begins to intone again, starting faintly and gradually becoming louder. His incantations are followed by a wolf howl and other animal sounds.* WIN *moves the giant bird mask until it's exactly in front of* IK*'s faceless head so that from the front it looks like it's attached to him as his face. At that moment,* MAL, RAN, PRA, *and* TIK *raise their respective candles near the mask, illuminating it. They don't stand, but remain kneeling.*

IK *begins to recite his poetry again. And while he is chanting the poetry,* WIN *slowly moves the giant bird mask up until it is over the top of his head.*

IK: Spirit bird feathers vibrate
        within us /
    Song bird feathers exist
        behind silence /
    Bird feathers slip between fingers
        become quills /
    Bird feathers stand bravely
        on the altar of independence /
    Bird feathers soar on high
        become battle flags.

(Meanwhile, IK *stretches his hands out and up, signaling for* WIN *to give him the giant bird mask.* WIN *understands the gesture and lowers the giant bird mask from over his head. At last, the giant bird mask is in* IK*'s grasp. Gripping the mask with both hands,* IK *positions the giant bird mask directly in front of his head as* WIN *had done earlier.*

PAR *enters through the raffia curtain while striking his small gong. He's visibly animated! Other increasingly exuberant sounds fill the space, not only animal sounds, but also musical instruments. The mood becomes genuinely lively.*

IK *dances in place. At the same time,* MAL, RAN, PRA, *and* TIK *put their candle holders on the ground and join with* IK*'s dance moves.*

IK *gets down from his place on the tree stump. Where* IK *had been sitting,* WIN *now sits meditation in exactly the same position as* IK *earlier.* WIN *also recites the "Bird feathers" poem, just like* IK *had.*

MAL, RAN, PRA, *and* TIK *form a line facing* IK, *who stands motionless and at the ready to be attacked. The line attacks* IK. IK *stands his ground! They try hard to knock him down but they bounce off and end up sprawled on the ground.*

IK *dances while moving the giant bird mask in his hands.* MAL, RAN, PRA, *and* TIK *stand up and form a line, creating a tail behind* IK. *They dance along with* IK. MAL *bends over and holds* IK*'s waist,* RAN *bends over and holds onto* MAL*'s hips,* PRA *bends over and holds onto* RAN*'s hips, and lastly* TIK *bends over and holds onto* PRA*'s hips. The combination of* IK *and* MAL, RAN, PRA, *and* TIK *circle throughout the space, moving like a many-legged long-bodied creature with* IK*'s body acting as the creature's neck.* PAR *doesn't want to be left out of the dance, so an interaction develops between* PAR, *who plays the* *small gong, and the movements of the many legged creature.* WIN *doesn't just recite the poetry, but sings it. They have a good time. Festive!*

Time passes.)

SEGMENT 8

MAXI *wakes up from his sleep.* MAXI *hears the revelers! He looks about and listens for the source of all the noise.* MAXI *sees the festivity! He is not happy!*

MAXI: (*Vehemently*) Teeeeeeee…!

(*The dancing and singing abruptly stop!*)

MAXI: Himpong-himpong! Himpong-himpong! Himpong-himpong!

(MAXI *descends from the metal throne.* MAXI *and the creature face each other.*)

MAXI: Himpong-himpong! Himpong-himpong!

Segment 9

A fierce battle of strength takes place between MAXI *and the creature formed by* IK, MAL, RAN, PRA, *and* TIK.

The music grows rowdy. PAR clearly roots for the creature formed by IK, MAL, RAN, PRA, *and* TIK.

Ultimately, a battle breaks out between MAXI *and* IK *only, while* MAL, RAN, PRA, *and* TIK *only occasionally help to block* MAXI. IK *defeats* MAXI, *who lies on the ground.* IK*'s group celebrates their victory with dance and music.* IK *stands on the metal throne, dancing.*

Time passes.

PAR: (*Points at* MAXI) Get rid of it!

(MAL, RAN, PRA, *and* TIK *cross over to* MAXI. *They carry* MAXI *as if carrying a corpse.*

But suddenly MAXI *stirs and comes back to life. A fight breaks out between* MAXI *and* MAL, RAN, PRA *and* TIK. MAXI *wins the fight.*)

MAXI: I am A-him-pong-pong...!

(MAL, RAN, PRA, *and* TIK *seek protection from* IK *near the throne.* IK *is ready to fight again with* MAXI. *Bedlam!*

Time passes.

The battle of strength between MAXI *and* IK *ends with* IK*'s defeat.* IK *lies dead on the ground. The ruckus ends.*)

Segment 10

MAXI *ascends the metal throne. He puts his cape back on.* MAXI *stands magnificently in front of the throne while holding the large round emblem up high with both hands.*

MAXI: Sssssaaaaahhhhh...!

(MAL, RAN, PRA, *and* TIK *solemnly carry* IK*'s corpse accompanied by funereal music. There are also rhythmic and solemn incantations.* IK *is carried around the playing space before finally arriving behind* WIN. IK *is placed standing erect behind where* WIN *sits. Next,* WIN *lets out a loud mournful scream as she rolls down onto the ground. Dead.* IK *sits again on the tree stump, cross-legged as before. A giant bird mask is placed in front where he sits, also as before.* MAL, RAN, PRA, *and* TIK *carry* WIN*'s corpse. After circling the playing space, they arrive back at the trees stump where* IK *sits. They stand exactly as they had in the beginning.*

Time passes.

The funereal music and chanting continues while MAXI *walks step by step toward the corpse bearers. The battles are over.* MAXI, WIN, MAL, RAN, PRA *and* TIK *stand close together as they had in the opening tableau. Silence.*

Time passes.)

Segment 11

PAR *steps slowly and unsteadily, striking the small gong one beat at a time as he makes his way downstage. Once there, one by one he puts out the candles in the bamboo holders with the gong mallet. Once all the candles are out,* PAR *returns to where he had been standing at the beginning. Even the lighting returns to how it was at the beginning.*

Time passes.

Eventually the MINIONS *begin again with "Aaaaa..." also exactly as in the beginning.*

Then everything continues as it had previously...

THE END

Era of the Bat

Production Notes

Zaman Kalong (*Era of the Bat*) was first performed at Teater Tertutup in Jakarta's Taman Ismail Marzuki January 7–10, 1980. It was part of a two-play program called *Topeng Pajegan Ikranagara* that also included the play *Ritus Topeng* (Mask Rites). Ikranagara wrote, directed, and performed both plays.

In the original performance, four musicians, each playing several instruments, provided the musical accompaniment and background sounds:

1. I Gusti Kompiang Raka– *Gendang 3, Kecek, Cengceng*
2. I Wayan Sadra– *Gendang 2, Semara Pegulingan, Gender Wayang, Suling 2*
3. Winaya–*Rebab, Suling 1, Gender Wayang*
4. Roda–*Gendang 1, Gentora, Cengceng*

Musical Instruments

For readers unfamiliar with Indonesian musical instruments, a glossary containing brief descriptions of the musical instruments used in the original performance is provided below. Note that the metallophones, cymbals, and bells continue to reverberate unless dampened.

cengceng	A set of small cymbals on a wooden block struck with small cymbals held in each hand
gendang	A double-sided cylindrical membrane drum, played with the hands to keep the beat
gender wayang	Metallophone with brass keys suspended over bamboo resonators, played with mallets and used for *wayang kulit* (shadow puppet) performances

gentora	An upright post surrounded by rings with hanging bells
kecek	Similar to *cengceng,* a set of brass plates on the back of a carved wooden turtle struck with small hand-held cymbals
rebab	A two-stringed instrument played with a bow
semara pegulingan	The oldest form of Balinese gamelan associated with the courts, made up of several metallophones, gongs, drums, cymbals etc.
suling	Bamboo flute

Translator's Note

Era of the Bat is a type of *topeng*, one of Bali's masked dance-drama genres performed during ritual ceremonies and as secular entertainment. In this play, Ikranagara experiments with the solo performer *topeng* form called *topeng pajegan*. All the roles are enacted by a single performer who dons a different mask for each character while wearing the same basic costume throughout the performance. The gamelan (referring to both the ensemble of instruments and the musicians) and the performer work off each other as accompaniment and/or to set the tone and pace of the scenes. Traditionally, the performer changes masks in full view of the audience and often jokes with members of the gamelan and speaks directly to the audience.

Ikranagara wrote and performed his *topeng pajegan* plays, *Zaman Kalong* and *Ritus Topeng*, in 1980 during the New Order regime, the years when autocratic President Soeharto was in power from 1967 to 1998. During the New Order, freedom of speech was severely curtailed. Government censors would clamp down on any kind of protest or critique that they believed could lead to social unrest. It was illegal to criticize government policies, the ruling party, or Soeharto. Playwrights, who wanted to make political statements and social critiques through their performances, had to find ways to do this covertly in order to avoid being censored, shut down, or jailed. One way a number of playwrights did this, including Ikranagara, was to borrow from the structure and aesthetics of traditional performance genres. For the most part, traditional performances weren't considered dangerous to the government's campaign to maintain peace and order.

In 1980, government censors monitoring *Era of the Bat*, after having seen the opening scenes with traditional Balinese masks and music, might have left early satisfied that it was a traditional performance that presented no danger. If they stayed long enough, they would have heard the audience cheering at the political cues. Throughout the play, the characters representing the activist and the poor complain about the banyan tree, which was the symbol of Soeharto's Golongan Karya (Golkar) political party during the New Order.

Focusing on the banyan tree provided Ikranagara a foil to create meaning on more than one level. The banyan tree is an apt metaphor, not only because it was the symbol for Soeharto's Golkar party, but because of the characteristics of the tree itself that tends to encase its surroundings in its tendrils. Banyan trees start out living on other plants. As they grow, they produce aerial roots that hang down and germinate wherever they touch the ground. These thick roots make the tree appear to have several trunks. It can get to about a hundred feet wide and some have been known to spread over several acres.

The banyan tree and the bats associated with it (symbols of Golkar, Soeharto's family, and his cronies) appear later in the play, after the government censors had left—it was hoped—satisfied that the play posed no threat. The banyan tree and the bats suggest, through veiled references, the political issues of the day, such as shoddy government housing for the poor, concessions to Soeharto's family for profits from agricultural products, censorship of printed news by literally redacting criticism with black ink, a staged attack by the government with an ammonia bomb at a dissident artist's poetry reading,[7] the frequency of army spies on campus, and growing unemployment.

The bats referred to in the title of the play, *kalong*, are flying foxes, the largest type of bat indigenous to Indonesia and other Southeast Asian islands. They are primarily nocturnal, fruit-eating, and can have wingspans up to 5 feet across. Highly social, they congregate in large numbers to noisily forage for fruit and to roost in open trees where they hang upside down and wrap themselves in their large wings. Unlike some of the references to blindness of bats in the play, flying foxes have very good eyesight and don't use echolocation.

Readers might also like to know something about Balinese traditional naming conventions, to better understand the relationship between the characters in the play.

A Balinese Hindu person's name is conventionally comprised of several parts that indicate, in order, the person's gender, caste (if applicable), birth order, and a given name that is often related to something surrounding the circumstances of the child's birth or character. For example, "I" (pronounced ee, a long "e") indicates the person is male, whereas "Ni" (which sounds like "knee") indicates the person is female. If the person has a caste, it would follow I or Ni. The next name indicates birth order. "Wayan" ("why- yahn"), for instance, indicates that he or she is either the first-born or fifth-born child. (There are four birth-order names that begin with Wayan and then repeat beginning with the fifth and ninth child, and so forth). Lastly, there is the given name, such as Chongek ("chong-eck") which literally means a weeping inner ear infection, but is often used to refer to people who are either deaf or who refuse to listen. Wira-Wiri (we're-uh we're-ee) is not a Balinese name but an Indonesian phrase which means to pace back and forth.

Cobina Gillitt

Characters

(All characters are performed by a solo actor)

I WAYAN, an activist

I CHONGEK, a homeless man

WARA-WIRI, a richly dressed official

Setting

An empty stage.

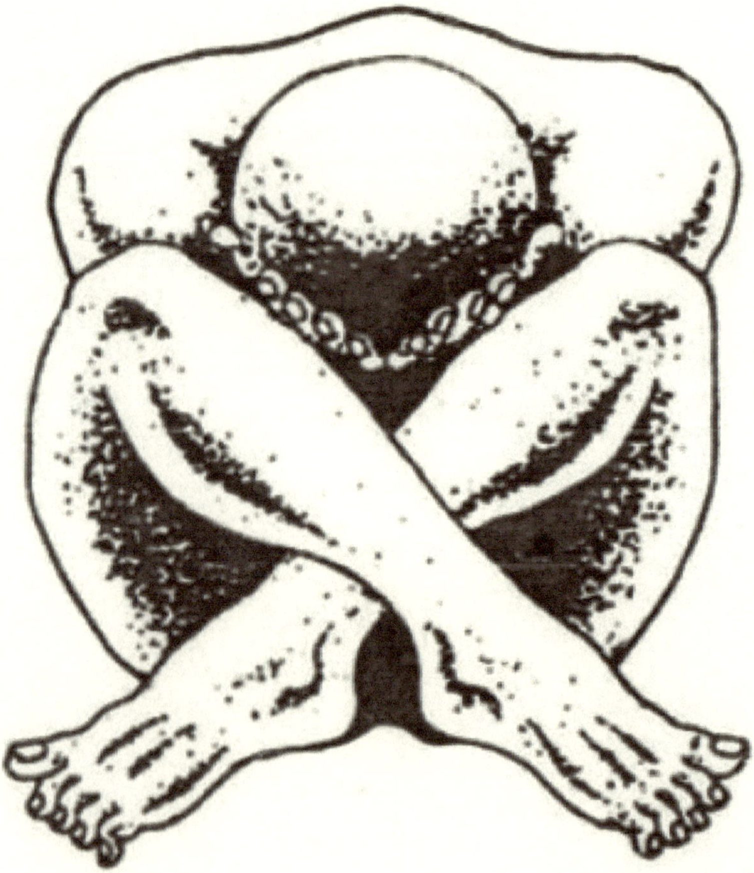

Prologue

Musical notation cues in the dialogue: @ = a single loud strike of one or several instruments; # = a single "dug" sound without any reverberation.

Stage Atmosphere and Sounds	Stage Cues and Dialogue
Gentora: subtle, faint jingling for a minute or so	*The stage is dark. The* ACTOR *sits cross-legged in the middle of the empty space. All is quiet for a moment.*
Rebab: vague fluttering waves, sad—whining, becoming louder and louder—for about two minutes	*Almost at the same time as the first sounds of the rebab are heard, the lights come up slowly, focusing on the* ACTOR.
All musical instruments: playing noisily together, culminating with the *rebab* and *gentora*	*Full lights up on the* ACTOR. *He doesn't wear a costume or a mask, but is* I WAYAN *somewhere beyond the bounds of reality. He sits so that he looks like a ball, or like a curled up pangolin, or perhaps like an embryo about to be born. Or maybe it's more suitable to compare his position to that of the naked men in the Balinese statues commonly called "I Mokoh" (Fatso), or "I Kemud" (The Shy One).* *He's dejected. Hopeless. He's disconnected from reality. In retreat. However, he's actually in the process of wanting to return to reality. The impulse grows stronger within him.* *This conflict has become his inner music. The feeling eventually grows critical, reaching its climax so that he can't help but come to a decision in order to stop the commotion within himself.*

Suling 1: sad, mysterious, hopeless	Fine… fine… fine… alright. I'm back. Back to reality. It's just that I don't know how to react to this new reality.?[8] But… new reality? What's new? The only thing that's new is the people. New people. New people in power in my region. But, the new in the new leader…. What's new about this honorable Mr. Wira-Wiri?
Gendang 1, *Kecek*	I suspect that reality will always remain the same as yesterday, as today, and as tomorrow, unchanged! @
	(*He freezes and is tense for a moment, then relaxes.*)
Gendang 1: "Dug" sound, irregular and infrequent	Yikes! # It appears I've lost faith # in hope.
	(# *He feels as if he's retreating again. The music of disappointment again fills his inner core.*)
Rebab	In that case, I'm # still far, way out there! # I haven't completely returned here yet. I'm not yet completely # back to reality.
Semara Pegulingan	Ah… hope! Once # hope has betrayed us, it's hard for us to trust again. # There's a feeling of reluctance! Why, why, why, why… # why! Obviously it's difficult to give hope a second chance!
	(*But there is another music in his core, an uplifting music, creating a conflict within. Finally, he arrives at a decision. He is able to put an end to the conflicting music inside.*)
Gendang 2: nervous, accompanying the dialogue	But whatever I feel inside, whatever, whoever, however, wherever, whenever, whatever the risk, whoever, whatever, whatever, whatever,

what matters is what is now! Now! Now I have decided to return to reality.

Add Gendang 2

Add Gentora

(*#... The* ACTOR *puts on his basic costume and the* I WAYAN *mask. Now, he is ready.*)

I, I Wayan, will return to play my role here. I will take part! I cannot do otherwise!

All instruments: follow the movements of the actor

(*With a loud cry, he jumps up. He moves with certainty, full of energy. His dance is in sync with the music that lives in his core now: he has regained his zest for life. He is spirited. His keen eyes focus on the reality that he now enters. He is fully in it now. He moves from one place to another until he arrives at the roots of a giant banyan tree and is startled when he stubs his foot. He jerks it back, ready to roughly and explosively trample on the roots. For a moment he is frozen and silent. But he pounds his feet and cries in outrage.*)

Rebab: louder and more expressive

That giant banyan tree root again! It's everywhere, with no regard to place, heedless to time, arbitrary, just popping up and down into the ground, indiscriminately as it sees fit!
Argh… argh… argh!

(*He squats, overcome by the feeling of hopelessness again. The music of his disappointment lasts for a time. Ultimately, he arrives at a feeling of anger that hurls from his chest.*)

Aaaaahhhhh!!!

Rebab, Gentora, Semara Pegulingan: teasing, illustrative

(*He stops squatting. His eyes burn with ferocity.*)

Endlessly complaining won't solve the problem. I must stop complaining; there's no place for whining now. Now it's time to snarl and roar!

All instruments: accompany the movements and gestures of the actor	(*He moves about energetically.*) I need to get a passionate group lined up as quickly as I can to storm and snarl. (*He stops moving. He stands at attention.*) Now! This is the only way to welcome the honorable Wira-Wiri, by snarling! Our collective fury! Our patience has run out, sir!
Stop...	That giant tree must be cut down, sir! It must!
Start again	Our first task is to cut down that giant tree! You are the new leader here. There's no policy as important as cutting down that giant tree! That tree is a source of anxiety for our people.
Stop at different times	We have demanded this for this for a long time. But the leader before you only gave us hope. Broken promises! We were deceived! All the while, the giant tree just kept getting bigger and bigger. It's growing more openly now, its roots running wild everywhere it wants! Those that live within its branches and roots, those infernal bats, are multiplying and terrorizing us at will, shitting anywhere they want.
Quiet, then silent	Over time, our region has become nothing more than a huge toilet! A toilet with a tree growing in it! A single organism! That giant tree! Damned roots! Our home has become an open sewer for those diabolical bats to shit in. Damn bats! (*He groans loudly and protractedly.*) Ugh! Ugh ugh ugh ugh ugh!

Musicians join in the laughter	(*He laughs at himself recognizing his unhinged state.*)
	I'm rambling.
	(*He laughs amusedly to himself.*)
	It seems my emotions have taken over.
	(*He laughs to his heart's content.*)
	What's important is that I'm finally here. I'm back in reality, completely! I also know how I should react to this new not-new reality. To the honorable Mr. Wira-Wiri!
All instruments: noisy for a moment but stopping when the ACTOR moves	Yeeesss…!
Semara Pegulingan	I need to organize my crowd of snarlers as quickly as I can. We need to seize the moment. This unsettling Era of the Bat must end immediately. The source of the people's discontent must be brought to an end immediately.
All instruments: rowdy, noisy	Okayyyyy…!
Cengceng: noisy	(*With that, he leaps energetically, ready to fight guided by the music thundering in his chest.*
All sounds end	*Lights out. Streaks of flashlight beams crisscross each other in the bustling darkness, while the music becomes louder. The flashlights go out as the cengceng reverberations die out.*)

Episode 1

Lights up. The ACTOR *dons the mask of* I CHONGEK *who wears a shabby hat that's a little bit torn. At first we don't see his face.*

Suling, *Semara Pegulingan*, *Gendang 3*: cheerful, light-hearted accompaniment

Ong namo namo/ Amun mati abo ke sema/ Amun idup anggon naymo.[9] Ho ho ho ho…!

(I CHONGEK *is now fully visible. He has a comical appearance, from head to toe.*)

Ong namo namo!

Comical music when the ACTOR calls for it, builds up, stops a moment, starts again

If dead, to the grave/ If alive, be family. Ho ho ho ho. I Wayan is not dead. I Wayan is alive. Ho ho ho ho… I'm glad, I'm glad! At any rate, my fate is back to… not so bad!

Stop

Ho ho ho ho! I'm glad, I'm glad.

Oh boy, when I Wayan isn't here, wherever it is he goes, my head spins! All I know is Wayan disappears. Just disappears! Where to? Who knows! Anyway, it's hard to understand. And when he returns, ack, I really don't get it. He just reappears out of the blue. Where from? Who knows?

All instruments: comical accompaniment

It's even hard for smart people to understand. Never mind! It's none of my business!
"I Chongek?" I hear a voice calling me, like this. "Chongek! I Chongek!" Calling my name! I immediately turn around! To see him!

Stop

Whoa...! Ho ho ho ho ho!

Begin again but softer

I'm glad! I'm glad! There's no mistake! He's the one calling me! Wayan! Out of the blue! Like usual! Where from? I don't care! The important thing is Wayan is back! I'm glad, I'm glad, I'm glad! Whereas before my head was spinning! But, even if my head is spinning at full speed or half speed or one third speed, as long as Wayan is here, everything is okay. Wayan is the sure cure for my spinning head.

So, like I said. As soon as we ran into each other, I immediately said, "Brother Wayan! My head's spinning out of control, man!"

He knew what I meant. He knows my coded language. How could he not? I just have one code, what else? I just say, "Spinning out of control."

Stop

He immediately reaches into his pocket. Cash! Money! Ho ho ho ho!

Begin again

"Chongek, Chongek! When will you get a steady income?" he asks as he gives me cash.

I'm happy to accept the cash and I say, "I'll have a steady income once I have a steady job." What else can I say? And I then I usually say, "It's a loan, right, brother Wayan, right?"

Louder, then suddenly stop

At any rate, as long as Wayan is here, that means my life is… not so bad!

Suling 1, *Semara Pegulingan*, *Gendang 3*: comical accompaniment

Ong namo-namo/ Amun mati mbo ke semo/ Ong namo-namo.

If dead, to the grave/ If alive, borrow money!

Stop...

Ho ho ho ho! I'm glad, I'm glad! I'm rich!

All instruments: accompany a little bit

(I CHONGEK *dances about foolishly and happily.*)

The matter of repaying… that comes later. Ha! That's the art of being in debt! Ha... art! What kind of art is that?

Stop	Ho ho ho… art! Chongek's art! Ho ho ho ho…!
<u>All instruments</u>: rowdy–boisterous #, noisy for a while–then stop suddenly	The thing is, if you're in debt, there's one thing you must keep in mind about the art of it. That's the art of pretending to forget! Pretend to never to be in debt! That's the art of it! This is my method, and it's not just any random method. It's been proven to work.
Quiet	Go ahead and try to add it up. How much do I owe Wayan? A lot! Too much to count! But, not once has he asked for any of it back! The thing is… I pretend to forget! Just think, if I remembered and didn't pretend to forget, I would probably say, "Brother Wayan, I owe you money, man, right?" And Wayan would definitely say, "Yes, that's right. Pay it back now!" Gak…! My head would spin at least half speed if not more! At any rate, I never remind Wayan that I've borrowed money from him. It's not that I forget, but I practice the art of pretending to forget. This practice is contagious, so that Wayan also forgets. Or, at least maybe he pretends to forget, too, like me. He's infected by my art! And because of that… I'm alright!
<u>*Suling 1*</u>, <u>*Semara Pegulingan*</u>, <u>*Gendang 2*</u>: comical accompaniment.	If I'm spinning out of control and meet Wayan, I don't need to worry. I just say "Spinning out of control". Apparently my code works, because he always immediately reaches into his pocket, and gives me some money!
	Not too shabby! Ho ho ho ho! I'm glad, I'm glad.
	Ong namo namo/ Amun mati abo ke semo/ Ong namo namo.
Each instrument stops one by one	If dead/ to the grave. If alive/ hopefully he'll remain forgetful!

Ho ho ho ho…! So I'm forever alright!

Ooooo… Wayan asked me for help. Asked for help!

"Chongek? Please round up all the unemployed. As many as possible!" Wow… easy-peasy! Rounding up the unemployed around here, that's no sweat! No problem!

Quiet Easy things suit me. Difficult, complicated things, those are for smart guys, not me.
To my right? Out of work! To my left? Jobless! Behind me? Looking for work! Over here? Fired! Over there? Between jobs. Over here? Laid off! Over there? On unemployment. Way over there? Let go. More! More! More! Unemployed, unemployed, unemployed, unemployed, unemployed, unemployed, unemployed, unemployed, unemployed, unemployed, unemployed! Everywhere… Unemployed! All unemployed! Only unemployed! So many! Easy! No problem!

And… here?

(*He points to himself.*)

Unemployed! Ho ho ho ho…! Hah! It's no secret!

Quiet Anyway… it's simple! Finding unemployed people is easy work! The best kind of job for me. No need to worry. I can find however many you need. I'm the one and only agent! Plenty of stock! Don't worry! You want them sent by sea or air? Express? C.O.D? Done! Whatever you want! Ho ho ho ho…!

Wow! Wayan says he wants a lot of them. And express!

Don't worry! There's plenty of stock!

To pass the time, I casually asked him, "What is it for, Brother Wayan?"

Boy! His answer was strange. I totally don't get it. Because Wayan said, "To snarl!" That's what he said. What does that mean? Who cares? I don't want to worry about it! Wayan can take care of the hard part, the easy part is for me. Keeping things real!

But that's not all of it. The rest of his answer was even more confusing. He said, "Snarling is the proper way to welcome our new leader, the honorable Mr. Wira-Wiri."

Semara Pegulingan: quick and rather loud

Snarling…? Welcome…? Honorable…? Wha'? I'm confused!

It doesn't matter, ack! But… snarling? Like … a tiger?

Does Wayan want to greet the honorable Mr. Wira-Wiri with a circus performance? That's probably it! At least something circus-like! With something tiger-like! Tigers created by the unemployed! Wow, that could be fun! What a surprise! Might as well!

Semara Pegulingan, *Suling 1*, *Gendang 3*, *Gentora*: calm accompaniment

(I CHONGEK *sneaks offstage until he's no longer visible.*)

Ong namo-namo/ Amun mati abo ke semo/ Amun idup anggon nayamo/ Ong namo-namo.

If dead, to the grave/ If alive, have a circus!

<u>Gender Wayang</u>, <u>Suling 1</u> <u>Gendang 2</u>, <u>Cengceng</u>: one instrument occasionally hangs while accompanying the movements of the TIGER's shadow

(*The* ACTOR *reappears as* I CHONGEK *wearing a* TIGER *mask. He snarls like a tiger. Sporadically, all that is visible is the* TIGER*'s shadow created by* I CHONGEK *in the* TIGER *mask when it is cast upon a shadow puppet screen. The* TIGER *demonstrates its circus skills, like jumping through hoops, etc.*)

Episode 2

<u>Gendang 1</u>, <u>2</u>, <u>3</u> *Lights up.* ACTOR *puts on the* WIRA-WIRI *mask.*

WIRA-WIRI, *a regional government employee, wears a grand garment over the basic costume. The polished gold decorations on his garment give an appearance of authority. He stands with his back to the audience.*

Sounds of marching in unison. Clamorous voices. He stands calmly facing it all.

In the midst of the clamor, we hear demands that the giant banyan tree be cut down, as well as curses directed at its roots and the bats that live in its branches.

The clamor peaks. Suddenly, WIRA-WIRI *turns around. Silence abruptly cuts off everything, and the voices disappear.*

<u>Gender Wayang</u>, <u>Gendang 2</u> (*He walks with full authority. Step by step. Each step makes an echoing thud. He stops. He stands majestically.*)

"The honorable Mr. Wira-Wiri!" they said. But it's clear the emphasis on the word "honorable" was not said out of respect but intended the opposite. I'm offended because he deliberately wants to insult me and my authority as the new leader in this region. I am offended because I understand where he's going with his contempt.

Without a doubt, he's the driving force. The rally wasn't something spontaneous; it was preplanned and thought out beforehand. I Wayan is the mastermind behind all of it!

I already have quite a bit of data on him. He always shows up whenever there's a demonstration. Who else should appear if not him, because he's the mastermind!

Demand this, demand that, demand, demand! That's all they can do. You may, go ahead, go ahead, go ahead and make demands. But how? This is not the proper procedure! This is not only a violation of the procedure that should be followed, it's a direct slap to my face, the face of this region's authority, the face of the highest authority in this region. This is nothing less than a political act! There's political ambition behind all of this! There's ambition for power behind all of this! They must all be political derelicts being driven forward by intellectual derelicts. That's why their demands are nothing more than the voices of mere homeless bums! Not supported by mature reasoning!

Gender, Gendang 1 (*He walks about, contemplating the problems he faces.*)

Bums! He's smart though. He mobilizes the homeless. There must be a pretty good assortment of bums. Clearly there are political bums and intellectual bums. There must also be economic bums, artist bums, student bums, and bum bums! He definitely has a strategy: if we arrest them, we lose. Getting arrested would be a blessing for them. At least they would get free food and drink in jail. No wonder none of my assistants suggested they be arrested.

If we let them go free, they'll definitely be more daring tomorrow. What they just did can't be called brave but it was audaciously disrespectful.

Tomorrow, the next time, and if beyond that, then what? How will they treat me? If the first step was that easy, what about the second, third, fourth…? Damn! @

All instruments — (WIRA-WIRI *is shocked by the tremor in his heart.*)

Semara Pegulingan, Gender — Wayan has suddenly become a menace!

Is that right? Does he have ambitions to overthrow me, so that he himself can be in power? Could be! Why not? Anything is possible in politics. Anything can happen and can happen without warning!

Just look at my own experience. Who would have thought that I'd be named the leader here? The regional leader before me was removed all of a sudden. I don't know why, and I don't want to know, and I don't need to look into it. That's my superior's business. The important thing for me is to always consult with my superiors because they approved me for this position. See? Everything happened so fast. Everything was unexpected. Just like that! But I've always known that one day I would succeed. Success is achieving a position of authority over a region. If not this one, then another. If not now, then next year, or the next. The point is, I was certain. Because I chose the right path. Because I can read situations thanks to my flawless instinct. I was determined to rule. Of course, I had to enter into the existing orbits of power if I wanted to succeed! And the proof? I did it!

But this Wayan? He wants power, but the path he's chosen is outside the power orbit! How

	could he succeed? He's incapable of reading the situation! He's a deadbeat barking up the wrong tree! So! Naturally he's destined to incompetence!
	Just wait for game on to see if I need to grandstand! Don't think that my power isn't supported by the powers that be, the legitimate power, the true authorities!
<u>*Gendang 3*</u>	(WIRA-WIRI *strides forward with heart-felt conviction, but then falters as doubt enters his heart.*)
Getting louder	I have data about all his activities so far. But now there's proof that he can bring about an unexpected turn of events! There wasn't a single advance report that he was going to carry out all of that. Clearly, this shows that there is a weak point in my power network.
Getting louder, then later ending with an echo	Oh oh oh oh… this could jeopardize my standing. Yes yes yes yes… I have to deal with Wayan carefully. I can't consider my opponents trivial. This is the key I must hold fast. All opponents are serious. So I have to take him seriously.
Dialogue begins when the echo ends	I must watch out for Wayan. I must!
<u>All metallophones</u>: as loudly as possible–play without dampening for about two minutes–then stop with the sound of the <u>*kecek*</u> ringing	(WIRA-WIRI *is nervous.*) Provocateur! (WIRA-WIRI *treads carefully and suspiciously.*) Provocateur!

Episode 3

Semara Pegulingan, Gendang 3, Cengceng: accompanies the movement, one instrument hangs at a time

The ACTOR *wears the* I CHONGEK *mask.* I CHONGEK*'s mouth and nose are covered by a rag tied around the back of his head. In his free hand he holds several posters with protest slogans and demands as intended by* I WAYAN. *He seems like he has been working hard. He hangs the posters in several places. Then he removes the rag from his face. He rests.*

Humph…! I'm pooped. But it's enjoyable! It's fun!

Loads of them! Multitudes marching! Crowds filling the streets! Along the whole street! It was great!

Quiet

Useless ol' me managed to get as many unemployed people as possible!

What did I say? Rounding up unemployed people is simple! Easy! The proof? Masses of them! Masses! Masses!

Gendang 1

I'm glad, I'm glad! Ho ho ho ho! #

But Wayan was the greatest. He's truly a leader. Commanding! # He's a first-rate protector.

But I was also amazed. Washed-up? They were all # trained by me to snarl. A mass snarl! That's what he said. You know? Only snarling as one, no speaking allowed, not any sound at all! #

He managed to convince us. He said, "We are actually tigers, my fellow unemployed! But don't forget. # We are tigers on the prowl. So

	even our footsteps must make no sound. No raised voices at all. # Not a sound! # Like tigers on the prowl!" he said.
Gender Wayang	No one could disagree. No one? # Because he's right. He's the one who knows what this is about. We all completely trust Wayan. All of us? # How else could it be? He has proven to us, this whole time, that he is our number one protector! The unemployed trust him, not because he asked for it, # not because he demands it! How could he force us? He's an ordinary person. He doesn't have any weapons. What power does he have? The point is # the unemployed trust him based on experience and actual evidence. The unemployed don't doubt Wayan, he's their first-class protector.#
Quiet...	Ho ho ho ho…! I'm glad! Why not? Wayan trusts me. I didn't ask him to either. He trusts me because I can prove what I can do. Useless ol' me… to him… must have become a top-rate safeguard!
Suling 1, *Semara Pegulingan*, *Gendang 3*: Accompanying, amusing	Ho ho ho ho!
	Ong namo-namo/ Aman mati abo ke semo…. Amun idup anggon nyamo/ Ong namo-namo.
	If alive/ become a leader! Ho ho ho ho!
	Crowds of them! Crowds!
	But… quiet!
Rebab	Sssh…!
Stop...	(*Quiet for a moment.*)
Start again...	Ho ho ho ho…!

Stop...	(*Quiet for a moment.*)
Start again	Even after arriving at the honorable Mr. Wira-Wiri's office, the quiet got quieter because the sound of footsteps stopped. Exactly like the quiet when a tiger is close to its prey, a tiger ready to jump, snarling as it pounces on its prey! Dead silent! Shhh!
Stop...	(*Quiet for a moment.*)
Suling 2: starts again	Ho ho ho ho…! Amazing! Another shocker. Different from the others! Wayan is great! So smart! Even more so when Wayan read the demands to the honorable Mr. Wira-Wiri. Extraordinary! He's truly incredible! @
All metallophones, *Rebab*, *Gendang 1*, *Gendang 2*	(*Suddenly he makes a startled jump.*) # Those bats! # Them too # gathering into a crowd! But they were noisy! # They were yelling! # They were making trouble! # Emerging suddenly! # Flocks of them from # their nests! From that giant # banyan tree. Troublemakers! #
Gentora	But we all remained silent, persisting, and Wayan just went on reading the demands. It was only when the bats were not only yelling, but also shitting on us, that the chaos and confusion began. Thugs! Rotten! Those rotten shits! But that's not all! The giant banyan roots suddenly rose up from the earth where Wayan was

standing! Wayan almost fell as he was pushed by the roots tearing the earth apart! But Wayan was alert. The people around here are used to being suddenly jostled by the roots of the banyan tree. We've all learned not to be surprised.

But apparently the chaos caused by the bats, along with giant banyan tree roots, was comical. In fact, some people laughed instead of getting angry. To be honest, because some people laughed, I went from being angry to laughing too! Laughter is better than anger! It fits my character. Whatever the situation, laughing is always fun!

Suling 1, Semara Pegulingan, Gendang 3

Ho ho ho ho! Ong namo namo/ Amun mati abo ke semo/ Amun idup anggan nyamo/ Ong namo-namo!

If dead, to the grave/ If alive, keep on laughing!

Ho ho ho ho! Maybe if that giant banyan tree is cut down, the tree is destroyed, perhaps if it's gone, vanished, perhaps that will mean one less thing to laugh at!

It's a good policy to cut down the giant banyan tree. Like Wayan says, it means work for the unemployed. The work of cutting down the giant tree. For the unemployed. That means money goes to the unemployed. Doesn't money make us happy? Happiness means laughing. Money also makes me laugh.

Quiet

But, who can't help but laugh, because it happens so often. The giant banyan tree roots just appear in the living room! The roots of the giant banyan tree appear just like that in the middle of the living room. They damage the living room floor! And the social atmosphere enjoyed by the host and guests is destroyed because of the sudden visit by the tree roots!

Ho ho ho ho! But that's nothing! What about when they show up in the bathtub? Wow!

Ho ho ho ho! The tub leaks, the water runs out, and those who want to bathe have to give up their plans and go to the river!

Ho ho ho ho! The latest news about the giant banyan tree roots is about what's happened on the outskirts of town over there. Isn't that the area where the cheap housing was just built?

Cheap housing? What's cheap? Here's proof. For example, I myself live from hand to mouth spending little on food.

But that's no problem!

And the cheap housing that was just built is still unoccupied. Suddenly the walls and the foundations cracked, some have collapsed and this is all because of the surfacing of the giant tree roots there! Of course, some people have been really disappointed by that event. But what can you do?

To me, it was totally hilarious! Ho ho ho ho!

But the bats don't want to lose! They sweep up all the fruit! Bananas, guava, fruit, fruit, any and all fruit! Those bats are pretty strange too. I mean, they aren't ordinary bats. They make off with all the coconuts too! And all the coffee berries! Sometimes, the rice in the fields! Finally, to the surprise of the people here, these bats are fond of cloves! And tobacco!

Ho ho ho ho! The latest word is those bats are wild about visiting art events and the offices of news and magazine editors! Don't be surprised if you pick up a magazine or newspaper, and find parts of it can't be read. Why? There are parts that are all black! Ordinary black would be okay, but this black has a smell, the smell of rotten bat shit! The art event news was interesting.

Quiet There had been a poetry reading. All of a sudden, the audience panicked. There was a bomb! Ammonia gas! Next thing I know… it wasn't true! What do you think? It was just bat piss!

Ho ho ho ho!

As for the university campus, it has come to the point where the giant banyan tree roots and bats regularly cause disturbances. It's easy to find roots bursting out of the ground all over the campus. It's easy to find piles of bat shit everywhere. Maybe the bats are trying to nourish the campus because bat shit is fertilizer? Special fertilizer!

Ho ho ho ho! When the People's Representative Council meets, the giant tree roots aren't invited, but they usually come anyway in the middle of the session, emerging from under the assembly room floor to join the meeting!

Ho ho ho ho! Wayan says the activities of the bats and giant tree roots have risen to the level of terrorism.

Quiet I believe everything he says. I've memorized it! I know it by heart!

	But, personally, I don't actually agree with Wayan. For me, it's all a source of laughter.
Suling 1, Semara Pegulingan, Gendang 3	Ho ho ho ho! Ong namo-namo/ Amun mati abo ke semo/ Amun idup anggon nyamo/ Ong namo-namo!
Suling 1, Gentora	(I CHONGEK *dances happily for a while and then tires. He is sleepy. He prepares himself for sleep. Eventually he falls sound asleep. All of a sudden he wakes up and is immediately angry.*) Damn it! Waking up someone who's asleep! Disturbing me! Is there no other place to emerge? Damned roots! Hey!
All instruments	(*He quickly takes his posters, then flies into a rage at the roots that disturbed his sleep.*) Take that! And that! (*But* I CHONGEK *is outdone by the roots.*)
Quiet	What...? Still shooting up? I've gotten angry and yet you're still growing? You're stubborn, eh? Stubborn roots!
Rebab, Gender Wayang: dim, vague accompaniment	Ho ho ho ho! How come I'm angry? Isn't getting angry bad for you? Besides, this is funny! I fell asleep and then these giant banyan tree roots came up from below, and I woke up, angry. That's funny! Ho ho ho ho! Ong namo-namo... (*He walks away.*)

Episode 4

<u>*Semara Pegulingan*</u>: as illustration

The ACTOR *switches to the* I WAYAN *mask.* I WAYAN *appears swiftly. He seems to be busy.*

<u>*Gender*</u>, <u>*Gendang 3*</u>: only accompanies when the actor moves

It appears that this honorable Mr. Wira-Wiri is difficult to engage in dialogue.

I'd better not be wrongly accused. I'll probably be accused of being power hungry. I might be seen as hostile. Don't think I'm jealous of his position. Ah ah ah...! This could get complicated!

Those in power are preoccupied with their power. Everything else comes second. Their priority is only to make sure their positions are secure. That's why they're so cruel. Hot-headed. They only want to brag about their power all the time! To show off!

Evidently, the honorable Mr. Wira-Wiri is that kind of official. Ah ah ah ah… ah!

But what really made a mess of everything were those damned bats! Those evil giant tree roots! They're all evil! Messing everything up!

Whereas I had arranged everything to be as orderly as possible, even as quiet as possible!

Damn those bats!

(*He takes control of his anger.*)

But... that could be good too. It should be considered direct evidence seen by the honorable Mr. Wira-Wiri that the bats and the giant roots are the source of the disorder around here! But... is he able to judge the situation? He should be able to! But... if he's already like those bats? What then? What if he's blind to the situation, blind because he only thinks about his position and power, what then? Ah ah ah ah... ah!

(*Suddenly he laughs bitterly.*)

It would be funny if they accuse me of being ambitious, of being power hungry.

Someone like me? Dreaming of a position? Of power?

Someone like me? Dreaming of a position? Of power?

(I WAYAN *amuses himself thinking about it.*)

But here's the problem. How to convince the authorities that I absolutely have no such ambition.

Definitely not easy! Most likely, I'll be under surveillance from now on.

What can I do...? This new leader doesn't seem to care about our demands for the unemployed. He's stonewalling... stonewalling!

(*He lets go of his feelings of annoyance.*)

Would it be wrong if we were to find out in the end that our regional leader is the one who's indirectly nurturing the giant tree and the bats that live in it?

Would we be wrong if we were to conclude that the source of public unrest is none other than the regional leader himself?

I might be arrested if I said any of this. Maybe it would be better if I were. In court, at least I could defend myself, even though I know I would lose.

	Would that bring everything to an end? How else? In the Era of the Bat, uh, justice is Bat Justice.
	But the worst would be if I were just held indefinitely without trial, and if they were satisfied with torturing me, imprisoning me, then just letting me go, as long as I sign a statement that I had never been imprisoned! This is really the Era of the Bat!
	But when they say they need procedures based on sound reasoning, could they accept procedures proposed by anyone other than themselves? This is the problem! If procedures only come from the ruling party, or are in line with the ruling party, then those aren't procedures, man, but indoctrination!
Stop	But what can I say? It's the Era of the Bat!
Quiet a moment	(*He is silent for a moment, thinking it over.*)
Start again	I've made a decision and have even taken the preliminary steps. I will not back down. I must achieve my objective. This path I have chosen and am on is the righteous and correct one.
Louder and faster	All sane people will agree with me. What we need now are projects that can employ as much of the workforce as possible in order to reduce unemployment. Destroying that giant banyan tree is a good project for my purpose.
Stop	I cannot back down!
All instruments: strongly and very loudly	(*He swiftly walks away.*)

Episode 5

Semara Pegulingan, Gender, Cengceng, Gendang 3: accompany movements and dialogue

The ACTOR *switches to the* WIRA-WIRI *mask and dons his official attire. He appears happy and dashing in his splendor. Each step he takes still makes an echoing thud, and this time is accompanied by stately music.*

Now! This is good fortune! Instructions from above have arrived at last. And from my point of view, the most important thing is instructions from above. I must carry them out quickly and well. Voices from above are the most important. Voices from below, from the community, don't decide the manner or strength of my position as the leader in this region. It's voices from above, instructions from my superiors, that make the determinations.

At any rate, I won't act like the former leader. The leader before me was hesitant. He was uncertain whether he should listen to the voices from below or the voices from above. And so, because he didn't follow instructions from above, of course his superiors weren't happy, of course his superiors removed him from the position of regional leader before his term was over! His own fault.

But I never hesitate to carry out instructions from above.

And the instructions that have come from above in connection with this giant tree will be carried out without hesitation! I just have to create a working plan and implement it, which I will do as quickly as possible.

Now! It would be nonsensical for the voices from below to continue to protest! Instead, Wayan's group should express their support and show their joy because it has been decided that the giant tree will be cut down. Yes! No mistake! I will cut down the giant tree in accordance with the instructions from above, which, as it happens, will also make the community happy! Truly good fortune!

Gender, Semara Pegulingan: louder, faster — If good luck continues to come my way well, well! I'll really enjoy working here. It's pleasurable! And I definitely won't be dismissed before my term ends. In fact, it's very possible my term will be extended.

At any rate, my future looks bright, thanks to my ability to read the situation!

Dance music — (WIRA-WIRI *happily walks away. He's accompanied by an inner music full of a passion for life.*)

Episode 6

<u>Suling 2</u>, <u>Gender</u> *The* ACTOR *puts on the* I CHONGEK *mask.* I CHONGEK *is busy looking for* I WAYAN. *He calls his name anxiously.*

Wayan! Where did he go? He's just gone! Just disappeared! But where to? Smart people are hard to understand! But the problem is my head's spinning out of control. I need to meet with Wayan.

(I CHONGEK *searches. But is unsuccessful.*)

Boy, this sucks! Where should I find a replacement? Among my fellow unemployed? How could they help cure my spinning head? They themselves are suffering from spinning heads! Man!

When was the last time we met...? Oh right! When that giant saw arrived! That machine is really something! It's enormous! Everything about it is completely modern. Suddenly, it feels like everything is progressing fast. Modern! Thanks to modern machines!

Ho ho ho ho! It's too bad Wayan won't get to see those machines at work. I heard the giant banyan tree will be cut down tomorrow. Or next week? The trouble is that they have to import machine operators from another country first. They're waiting for them to arrive.

Those machines are so cool!

But where has Wayan gone, huh? He looked gloomy the last time we met. No mistake. I remember that he was sad, disappointed, because he hadn't been able to find a steady job for me. I felt bad for him. He really meant to help me.

Only, he never asked if I really wanted a steady job or not. Well, honestly, if I could answer honestly, I would say, "I really want to make money. But a steady job? Isn't it possible to get a steady income without a steady job, but work uh... part-time?"

But I wouldn't dare say that to Wayan. At most, if he offered me a steady job, I'd give it to someone else who's unemployed. And if that happened, Wayan would probably misunderstand my motive. He'd say I have a big heart!

Gendang 3, Gentora Ho ho ho ho! Ong namo-namo/ Amun mati abo ke semo/ Amun idun anggon nyamo/ Ong namo-namo!

If dead, to the grave/ If alive, be good!

Ho ho ho ho!

Ah... apparently it's not time yet for me to get a remedy for my spinning head. That's okay! Who cares? I don't want to think about difficult stuff, heavy stuff, because what's most important to me is how to be happy. Whether in a sad or bad place, I will still laugh. That's my nature. What can I do!

Episode 7

The ACTOR *puts on the* I WAYAN *mask.* I WAYAN *looks despondent. He feels hopeless. He feels lonely. But he is also angry because he feels oppressed and defeated.*

Rebab, Gender, Gendang 1 — Yes... indeed... the giant tree is going to be cut down. Fitting. # In agreement with the demands of the public. This should be good news. Should be! And it's not impossible that some members of the community are happy. Of course, especially the honorable Mr. Wira-Wiri # because it was a directive from above, and by implementing it, Mr. Wira-Wiri's name will likely be promoted among the upper echelons. #

But I cannot be happy. How could I be happy? That giant banyan tree will be cut down, but the project doesn't involve the unemployed! That's what makes me unhappy, what has created this feeling of disappointment, the reason for this hole in my soul. #

Really depressing!

They don't think about the fate of the unemployed. We could ease the unemployment problem with this project. The number of unemployed is enormous; how come they can't they see that? Baffling! #

Maybe it's because the directive came from above; how could they know what really goes on down here from all the way up there? But, Wira-Wiri should have reported what's actually happening around here.

Right! Why would he report it? You can bet

he reports that things just are fine here, as long as the boss happy, everything's okay!

For sure, the directive from above to cut down the tree is not from anyone who knows that the giant tree has been terrorizing the people # in this area. No way!

But you can bet they want to make as much profit as they can from this venture.

Expressive Man... oh man, oh man. It just goes on, non-stop!

<u>*Gentora*</u> No question that the giant tree # has become a source of public anguish. Those bats entrenched in the tree are also a source of public anguish.

But isn't just the state of being unemployed, # anxiety-inducing? It's precisely this type of anxiety, mixed with the emotions and power of the masses, precisely this kind of anxiety that can lead to agitation, # agitating agitation, hidden threats, malignant melanomas under the skin, embers smoldering in the ashes, buried dynamite...# ticking time bombs!

Insane! Just to cut down a tree, they bring in modern machines! Even though there's a deluge of unemployed workers! Just to cut down a tree, they buy machines from abroad. Even though the unemployment rate is increasing!

Insane! This is what's called procedure based on sound reasoning?

Insane! Reasoning by people blind like bats! Reasoning by people whose feet are above, their heads below, seeing everything upside down, like bats!

What can I say? Hope has slipped through our fingers.

Epilogue

Gendang 3: begins disorderly and rowdy but suddenly stops

The ACTOR *as* I WAYAN *sits so that he looks like a ball, or like a curled up pangolin, or perhaps like an embryo about to be born. Or maybe it's more suitable to compare his position to that of the naked men in the Balinese statues commonly called "I Mokoh" (Fatso), or "I Kemud" (The Shy One). He's dejected. Hopeless. He's disconnected from reality. In retreat.*

When the actor is already sitting, steady and calmly…

Suling 2: plays a sad Balinese song for about two minutes, then…

Gentora: vague, tinkling, together as the lights slowly dim to black

THE END

Knock Knock Knock

A Psychological Drama in Three Parts

◆

Production Notes

Knock, Knock Knock (*Tok Tok Tok*) was first performed by Teater Saja August 26–September 1, 1982 at Taman Ismail Marzuki, Jakarta, with the title *Terdakwa* (The Accused). It was performed again in 1986 as *Tok Tok Tok.* It was also adapted by student theater groups and performed on campuses.

Characters

ATMA, a judge

KAROMAN, a poet

NARRATOR, appears in three forms:
Karoman as a teenager; an old maid; an old man

VILLAGERS:
TUK SYAM, a fisherman
MATASIK, a fisherman
SIDDIK, a fisherman
MA OLONG, a mother
MORNI, a wife
A CORPSE

MOMOK OBLONGACHAK, an enormous ghostly monster/machine

Setting

The stage is the space "inside the head" of a judge named Atma. A shadow puppet screen is stretched from stage right on an angle toward upstage where it meets a gray wall. This meeting point functions as an entrance from behind the shadow screen.

Several drama blocks create levels and are utilized as set pieces, such as a table, chair, steps, floor, etc. The table will need to break apart and have empty space inside. Downstage left of the table, there is a pile of over-sized books, mixed with boxes, bundles, old typewriters and so on, under which is hidden a pile of bloody stones and a pair of black military boots.

Part One

Atma Daydreams

1.

ATMA *sits pensively in a chair, smoking a cigarette. On the table, there is a large ashtray filled with cigarette butts and ashes, a water bottle, a pill bottle of sedatives, and a judge's gavel. Amber spotlight up* ATMA, *casting a much larger than life shadow of his head and upper body onto the shadow puppet screen.*

Time passes.

Blue light up behind the shadow screen casting KAROMAN*'s shadow to his left onto the screen exactly inside the shadow of* ATMA*'s head.* KAROMAN *cannot be seen directly because he's standing behind the shadow screen.*

ATMA: Karoman?

KAROMAN: Yes, Atma.

ATMA: Why have you appeared, Karoman?

KAROMAN: Because you were thinking about me.

ATMA: Why was I thinking about you?

KAROMAN: You were thinking about me because–

ATMA: (*Interrupts*) Don't answer!

(*Beat.*)

I should be asked that question. Don't answer! If you ask, I'll answer.

(*Beat.*)

Ask, Karoman.

(*Beat.*)

Come on, Karoman, ask, so I can think of the answer.

KAROMAN: What for?

ATMA: So we can have an inner dialog in this space, in my daydream. Come on, Karoman.

(*Beat.*)

Karoman? Are you still there?

KAROMAN: You know very well I can't leave as long as you want me here.

ATMA: I don't want you to go.

KAROMAN: I'm here because you willed it.

ATMA: And I want you to ask me.

KAROMAN: (*Half-heartedly*) Why were you thinking about me?

ATMA: (*Offended*) You didn't mean that, Karoman! Ask me seriously. Be serious, Karoman!

KAROMAN: (*Irritated*) Why were you thinking about me?

ATMA: Well... no need to be annoyed, buddy.

KAROMAN: It's always this way! You want to control everything!

ATMA: I can't help it. You know me. I want everything to be in order, according to the rules.

KAROMAN: That's why you finally became a judge and I didn't. We are different—

ATMA: (*Interrupts*) Never mind! Also, don't bring up human rights just because you're an artist, a poet. It's simple. You're in my head space. Yes! My head, Karoman. So, it's only natural for me to want to organize everything in my head, so that its contents don't get mixed up, all discombobulated, so they're easy to understand—

KAROMAN: (*Interrupts*) And easy for you to control?

ATMA: What's wrong with me controlling everything in my own

head? Enough already, Karoman, let's not argue any longer. Come on!

(*Time passes.*)

KAROMAN: You said I appeared because you were thinking about me.

ATMA: Hold on! I have another idea! Let's just forget about all those questions and answers. Okay?

(KAROMAN *exits quickly. The blue light behind the shadow screen fades to black, and lights up onstage in the area in front of the shadow screen.* KAROMAN *appears in the light in front of the shadow screen, in the same space as* ATMA. ATMA *welcomes* KAROMAN *warmly.*)

ATMA: There! That's better.

KAROMAN: (*Looking about*) Atma? When are we now?

ATMA: Now is sixteen years ago, when we were teenagers, when we were still in high school. Still virgins! (*Laughs*)

KAROMAN: Oh... I get it. Yes, nostalgia. You like nostalgia, because nostalgia—

ATMA: Stop! There's no need to come up with a reason based on rational analysis.

KAROMAN: But it's true, right? You're just recalling pleasant things from the past, for the purpose of—

ATMA: That's enough. There's no need for a reason; no need for a purpose. The nostalgia is happening right now!

KAROMAN: But why?

ATMA: Fine, if you insist.

KAROMAN: Answer!

ATMA: Because… of your presence. Yes! Just because of that. You were my friend when we were teenagers. We studied law together after high school. After that, we went our separate ways because we had different professional callings. When two old friends meet again, it's only natural that nostalgia for the past comes up. It just comes up, and… that's it! (*Laughs*) Now is the past—

KAROMAN: Alright, alright, I give up for now. Of course. Nostalgia. When it's in the past, even a lousy experience can make us feel nostalgic. The bad will fade away; it can even make the bad experience seem like a good memory. Like caterpillars. Disgusting creepy crawly creatures. But after spending some time in a cocoon, the creepy crawly creature transforms into a beautiful butterfly, fluttering and caressing flower blossoms...

ATMA: (*Clapping*) You're a whiz at wielding words. Your elegant sentences touch my soul.

KAROMAN: I know how mushy you are! (*Laughs*)

ATMA: What's with you? I don't understand you artists. I commend you on your way with words. I appreciate your work with a lay person's understanding of the arts and then... you mock me as mushy.

(KAROMAN *laughs again*)

ATMA: You are peculiar, Karoman. But never mind! You and I share a lot of memories.

(*They look happy. Spontaneously, they sing a children's song while playing a crisscross clapping game.*)

ATMA: A pinch of chili on my cherry

KAROMAN: The pretty girl we shall marry

ATMA: Hey hey hey!

KAROMAN: Hey hey hey!
(*They laugh with glee.*)

ATMA: If you go by boat

KAROMAN: Make sure it will float

ATMA: If you go by air

KAROMAN: Money will be spare

ATMA: Money!

KAROMAN: Money!

ATMA: Money!

KAROMAN: Money!

ATMA and KAROMAN: Money money money… hey!

(*Time passes.*)

2.

ATMA *and* KAROMAN *are jubilant.*

ATMA: Nostalgia…!

KAROMAN: Nostalgia…!
(*They laugh out loud.*)

ATMA: Karoman?
(KAROMAN *listens.*)
Do you still remember this nostalgic event?

KAROMAN: Show me!
(ATMA *stands solemnly, then claps his hand three times, like a*

magician.)

ATMA: Abracadabra!

(ATMA *snaps his fingers. Lights up behind the shadow screen so it looks like a giant TV screen. At first the TV screen is blank. The* NARRATOR *appears on the screen, wearing short pants and a short-sleeved shirt, so he looks like a high school student. He's playing the role of teenage Karoman.*)

NARRATOR: Hot hot hottttt! Ow ow ow! Spicy, hot, ow!

(ATMA *laughs out loud.* KAROMAN *grins.*)

I just peed... oh... oh... hot, hot... uh. I just ate, just drank, ate, ate, drank, drank, so hungry, ate, hot sauce, chili pepper, chili pepper... oh... spicy spicy spicy! Too much chili, too much drink, drink... spicy, spicy... so need to pee, run to pee behind the bushes... forgot hands are covered with chili sauce... chili, chili... ow wow wow... chili on little willy... little willy feels really hot! Hot hot hottttt!

(*The* NARRATOR *disappears from the screen while continuing to howl.* ATMA *bursts out laughing.* KAROMAN *joins in laughing, but not as hard as* ATMA.)

ATMA: You still remember that?

(KAROMAN *just grins.*)

That happened to you, Karoman, when we went on a picnic in the mountains and I became a laughing stock in front of our classmates who were there.

(ATMA *and* KAROMAN *laugh with amusement.*

Time passes.)

Here's another one, Karoman. But still from your past.

(ATMA *laughs. Again he claps his hands three time like a*

magician. The NARRATOR *reappears on the TV screen, still as teenage* KAROMAN.)

NARRATOR: I'm sooooo embarrassed embarrassed embarrassed! I feel so self-conscious! Too shy in public, too shy to hang out with the girls, I'm totally helpless in front of girls, even though we go to the same school, and especially if they aren't in my class. But what happened this morning was too much. It killed me, I want to die, I'm dead! I'm soooooo embarrassed embarrassed embarrassed embarrassed!

(ATMA *laughs, amused.* KAROMAN *just grins.*)

ATMA: Do you remember, Karoman?

NARRATOR: As usual every morning, the polished cement hallway between classrooms has just been mopped. It's wet and slick, and of course… slippery! I have to use that hallway to get to my class. Unfortunately, there are already packs of girls on both sides of the hallway, laughing it up. Are they talking about me? Are they laughing at me? You see, there's a girl there who's rumored to have a crush on me.

ATMA: But, am I right? You have a crush on her?

NARRATOR: I hesitate because I'm afraid to pass the group of girls. But, I have to get to my class! How can I? I'm totally stuck. But then I begin to worry about something else. I'm afraid the girls will know I'm too shy to pass them. Oh boy! Disaster! So, with determination and a fighting spirit, I carry on, walking really fast. But, as a result... I slip… and fall in front of the girls, who scream with laughter! They laugh at me! Oh boy... I'm soooo embarrassed, embarrassed embarrassed embarrassed!

(*The* NARRATOR *disappears from the TV screen.*)

ATMA: (*Laughing out loud*) You played hooky that day, Karoman!

The history teacher asked us where you'd been, Karoman... why had you been absent? (*Laughs*) We naturally told the history teacher about the "historic event" that had taken place downstairs! (*Laughs.*)

(*The* NARRATOR *appears again on the TV screen, still acting as young* KAROMAN.)

NARRATOR: You told her?

ATMA: She burst out laughing.

NARRATOR: That pretty history teacher?

ATMA: Yes! Who else, if not her?

NARRATOR: Oh boy, I'm soooo embarrassed, embarrassed embarrassed embarrassed!

(*The* NARRATOR *disappears from the screen.* ATMA *and* KAROMAN *laugh amusedly again.*)

KAROMAN: That girl with a crush on me sent a letter because of that "historic event" on the wet floor.

(ATMA *laughs, but quickly stops himself.*)

After that we exchanged letters!

ATMA: (*Surprised*) What?! You wrote letters to each other?

KAROMAN: The first letter wasn't just any letter. It was typed, not written by hand. You want to know what it said?

ATMA: She expressed sympathy and compassion about your historic event. She said that she didn't laugh like the others, rather she got angry with her friends who laughed. Why should they laugh at you when it was an accident?

KAROMAN: Wait! How do you know what was in the letter?

(ATMA *laughs.*)

I kept that secret and never told anyone!

(ATMA *laughs.*)

How could you guess so exactly? I bet—

ATMA: It's not a guess! Because the one who wrote the first letter and typed it was… me!

(ATMA *laughs.*)

KAROMAN: Dang!

ATMA: But then you answered the letter?

KAROMAN: Yes. Of course I replied! It was a golden opportunity!

ATMA: And she wrote back?

KAROMAN: Yes! She answered! Surreal!

ATMA: Huh… so it was a golden opportunity for her too?

(KAROMAN *extends his hand to* ATMA. ATMA *takes it and they shake hands.*)

KAROMAN: Thank you!

(*They laugh happily, They sing a goofy song.*

Time passes.)

3.

ATMA *claps his hands three times like a magician.*

KAROMAN: Hold on! You've gone already. Now it's my turn.

(ATMA *agrees.* KAROMAN *claps his hands three times like a magician.*)

Abracadabra!

(*After these words,* KAROMAN *snaps his fingers. The* NARRATOR *reappears onstage in front of the screen, but this time as an old maid.* ATMA *is taken aback and displeased.*)

ATMA: When are we now, Karoman?

KAROMAN: Now is not sixteen years ago.

ATMA: Then when?

KAROMAN: Last year!

ATMA: No! I disagree. Let's not get too close to the present. We're going back to sixteen years ago, when we were teenagers in high school, that's all!

KAROMAN: You'll like this, don't worry. Do you remember her? She was the host at last year's law school reunion. Remember?

ATMA: I know, I remember. Enough, the point is I disagree. Let's return to our nostalgic teenage years.

KAROMAN: Atma! It's my turn, Atma. (*To the* NARRATOR) Go ahead, ma'am.

ATMA: I need a sedative. Excuse me! (*Swallows a pill.*)

NARRATOR: Husbands and wives, widowers and widows, bachelors and old maids, like me. Am I right? Am I right? We've got all kinds at this reunion. Or are there some I haven't yet mentioned? Maybe mistresses? Or sugar daddies? Or unmarried couples living together? At any rate, to all those present, we're clearly no longer teenagers. Some of you even have sons or daughters-in-law. Or are potential daughters-in-law, like me. I haven't been taken yet, although my price has gone down, like the price of oil on the world market. A real bargain! But pay in U.S. dollars! You know … but I digress. My apologies!

So, we've all become real "people." Am I right? Am I right? All set in our stations in life. The difference is that some of us have been slow to get rich, while others were quick, depending on their station and if they were able to get on the express train or not. But there are also those of us who are freeloaders, whose salaries don't last until the end of the month. Always in debt! In debt to foreign countries! You know it!

Okay, the next item on the agenda is voluntary contributions, unrestricted and mandatory, in the form of an activity that's become expensive these days. Because, unlike the falling price of oil, the price of poetry reading has soared in the free market, up to millions! It seems that poetry reading is now an important non-oil-and-gas commodity. Am I right? Am I right?

Please go ahead, esteemed poet. Don't ask for an honorarium though, alright, sir?

(*The* NARRATOR *giggles as she exits.*)

KAROMAN: It's hard to be a poet. Poor? Mocked. Rich? Mocked even more. Protesting? Praised. Arrested? No one helps. Alright! One poem.

(*Beat.*)

KAROMAN: When I worry about
my child's future
        becoming an adult,
The Jogading River
        from olden days
        visits my recollections.
The Jogading River
        for ages has not visited

the town of my birth.
Until now
it has not left its banks
where I first encountered
horse tracks in the black sand.

(*Beat.*)

Like my life path
flowing relentlessly toward the harbor
and before merging with the ocean
consorts with a girl at the waterfall.
Fishermen come, fishermen go
with salt and coconut husks in their boats,
to an inlet with shrimp and sardinella
like crocodiles in the mangroves.

(*Beat.*)

But is the child as worried as I
Watching your child separate and take its own path
Creating swamps and mangroves along the way.

(*Beat.*)

What is the child's fate in the dry season?

(*Beat.*)

Even now, I don't know if the child succeeds in reaching the ocean.

(*Beat.*)

Woe is me.
Jogading from olden days can only deliver silence.
It is the same with the future from which I've yet to hear a peep.

(KAROMAN *lowers his head as a sign that he is finished and to show respect to the audience. Thunderous applause.* ATMA *also claps.*)

ATMA: Thank you, Karoman!

(ATMA *shakes* KAROMAN*'s hand warmly.*)

You know very well I liked the vibe at our reunion, you know very well I like your poetry, especially that one about the river, the river that flowed through our hometown. Think of it! The river! Yes, the river has paid you a visit. Truly, with your poem, our friends and I shared your inner experience… the river arrives… to visit! Thank you, Karoman!

(ATMA *shakes* KAROMAN*'s hand again, then hugs him warmly.*)

Only poets have the God-given gift to experience such a whimsical, unique, and enjoyable thing. Thank you, Karoman, thank you!

KAROMAN: You exaggerate.

ATMA: No, Karoman. At least, speaking for myself. But people say that poets and artists are quirky by nature. I agree with that, I can accept that in its most positive sense. It means that an artist's eccentricities help other people experience the sensuous pleasures of the work. So it's more than appropriate for me to thank you, Karoman. Thank you!

(KAROMAN *blushes.*)

ATMA: Take that poem for example. Enjoyable! Really, Karoman, I'm not just being polite to an old friend. Come on, what about your other weirder, scrumptious poems, I want to get drunk on your poetry, Karoman.

(KAROMAN *begins to look annoyed.*)

KAROMAN: (*Irritated*) Atma! Don't use me as a lock and key to shut the door to your present, closing the door on a visitor who's been waiting for an opportunity to appear here in your head space! Get in here!

ATMA: But you are my special guest… you bring pleasure… bring a river... a girl bathing in a waterfall… high school nostalgia…

KAROMAN: But there are also threats hiding in the mangroves! The crocodile in the mangroves! The dry season! A bygone era that can't express anything but silence. An uncertain future!

ATMA: Enough, Karoman! I beg you, don't go yet. You and our sweet nostalgia…

KAROMAN: Let your real guest come in, Atma!

ATMA: No! No, Karoman, no…!

(KAROMAN *claps his hands three times. The* NARRATOR *reappears, this time as an old man, with a with a long beard and mustache. He carries a folded white cloth that he gives to* KAROMAN. *Exits.*)

KAROMAN: Look at this!

(KAROMAN *spreads out the white cloth. On it is an image of a human figure. It's drawn on the cloth in blood red as an outline of a body, with no facial features or other details. It's reminiscent of chalk outlines drawn by the police to mark the ground where a victim's body has fallen.*)

Your guest left this with me. Now it's no longer a year ago, Atma!

ATMA: Give me that drawing!

KAROMAN: (*Contemptuously*) Ordering, scolding!

ATMA: Karoman, this is none of your business. This is my business, the business of a judge, not an artist!

KAROMAN: Why? What's wrong with me being an artist?

ATMA: The point is that you have no reason to meddle in this business!

KAROMAN: Isn't it enough that I'm human, that I'm a citizen of this country?

ATMA: Artists are truly bizarre!

KAROMAN: Your thanks to me has only just crossed your lips and suddenly you're back to disparaging artists for their eccentricities!

ATMA: Forget it, Karoman, don't let us fight.

KAROMAN: (*More cynically*) Don't don't don't! How many kinds of "don't" have you strewn about?

ATMA: Karoman?

KAROMAN "Don't!" you say. Don't do this, don't do that… don't don't! over and over. Can't you use any other words than "don't," Mr. Judge?

ATMA: Is there anything else that you, as an artist, can do besides criticize every situation?

KAROMAN: Do you realize what you just said?

(*Beat.*)

You said "don't" again, but in the form of a question that smacks of ridicule. Or was it a threat, Atma?

ATMA: Karoman…

KAROMAN: You must know, Atma, those categories of yours, whether the term is criticism, or protest, or something even stronger, and the like, none of them is important to me. It's just a matter of mere naming. Hmm, although, it's not out of the question that there's more than just simplifying the matter.

There may be certain hidden intentions behind the creation of these categories or this brand… that brand! Perhaps there's… a sledge hammer behind it all, Atma?

ATMA: Enough already! Soon you'll be nothing more than a sleazy, biased lawyer with bad judgement. Give me that drawing, Karoman!

(*But* ATMA *isn't able to grab the white cloth with the drawing on it before* KAROMAN *throws it away so that it lands in a pile downstage.*

Beat.

ATMA *starts toward the pile of white cloth, but stops with the sudden sound of people howling and moaning in agony.*

Time passes.

After the heart-rending cries disappear, ATMA *starts again toward the white cloth, but this time he stops when* MA OLONG *and* MORNI *enter downstage. They trudge with the heavy steps of those who suffer from the burdens they bear. The first of the two women carries a bamboo pole with a lighted lantern on one end. Their lamentations fill* ATMA*'s head space.*

Time passes.

MA OLONG *and* MORNI *pick up the white cloth and, full of sorrow, carry it on their shoulders as if it were a corpse. They cross along the downstage edge of the performance space and exit. Silence.*

Time passes.)

Part Two
Atma Contemplates

1.

ATMA *is weary. It's evident as he makes his way back to the table. He takes a pill from the small bottle on the table and swallows it along with a glass of water.*

KAROMAN: I feel sorry for you, Atma. A sedative isn't going to help, especially with the strength needed to drive away the current contents of your head space, let alone to force your nostalgic memories in to replace them.

ATMA: When are we now?

KAROMAN: What's certain is that now is now, not the past, not a year ago, and not sixteen years ago. No nostalgia, but the reality you're arousing as you contemplate.

ATMA: Reality. Now.

KAROMAN: Let your real guest enter, Atma.

(*Quiet.*

Time passes.

ATMA *returns to the same position as he was in at the play's opening. An amber spotlight casts a large shadow of* ATMA*'s head and upper body onto the shadow screen.*

ATMA *claps his hands three times. Blue light up behind the shadow screen, casting shadows of three men,* SIDDIK, MATASIK *and* TUK SYAM, *who are members of the* VILLAGERS.

KAROMAN *is upset and skeptical. He disapproves.*)

KAROMAN: Wait, why are they here, Atma?

ATMA: They are my guests, Karoman. Don't meddle by managing the contents of my contemplation. This is the reality I'm wrestling with now. You can't classify this as me interfering with the past. Enough already! Let them enter my contemplation, Karoman.

KAROMAN: (*Strained*) Do as you like!

(*The shadows of* SIDDIK, MATASIK *and* TUK SYAM *disappear from the shadow screen. Lights up downstage of the shadow screen where the* VILLAGERS *reappear in the same space as* KAROMAN *and* ATMA. *The spotlight on* ATMA *and the blue light behind the screen fade out.*

The VILLAGERS *look miserable. Their clothes are in shreds, with traces of blood and dirt.* MATASIK*'s head is wrapped in bloody bandages. His face is wounded and bandaged as well.* SIDDIK*'s condition is not much different; he looks like someone who has just been discharged from the hospital after having been treated for a serious accident. Meanwhile* TUK SYAM *is even worse off, with one leg in a cast and using a cane.*)

ATMA: Familiar faces to you, Karoman.

KAROMAN: Yes. Faces awaiting your verdict.

ATMA: I know, but be quiet, Karoman.

KAROMAN: Death sentence, Atma?

ATMA: Quiet!

KAROMAN: Firing squad, Atma?

ATMA: Shut up! Shut up, I said! This is none of your business! This a judge's business! Legal business! Court business!

(KAROMAN *is quiet.*)

There is something called crime, there are those who are the victims of criminals, there are those who commit the crimes, there are those who must be punished, all in accordance with existing laws that are in accordance with our universal sense of justice!

(KAROMAN *remains silent.*)

I am only a judge, a servant of the law. Justice must be served. Those found guilty must be punished! Is that wrong? If wrong, then blame the world's justice institutions, don't put me on the defensive just because I'm a judge whose decisions offend our humanity, which is as tender and delicate as the wings of a butterfly.

(KAROMAN *remains silent.*)

Now, interrogate them about what they've done, Karoman, until you're satisfied! Let there be no suspicion in your heart about whether I am being fair or not!

(KAROMAN *remains silent.*)

Put yourself in the judge's shoes! Gauge their actions against the legal norms you once knew! I'm sure you understand because we studied law together, Karoman! Cross-examine them!

KAROMAN: I already know everything.

ATMA: But I don't know what you know about it.

KAROMAN: As a matter of fact, I know that they total not just three, but forty men.

ATMA: Excellent! You're correct. But I want you to ask them, for example, whether it's true they are forty in total, and if not, how many?

KAROMAN: (*Irritated*) Fine!

(KAROMAN *stands facing the three* VILLAGERS.)

KAROMAN: So, there are only three of you?

MATASIK: No. There are forty of us in all.

KAROMAN: (*To* ATMA) You heard it yourself.

ATMA: Yes! But I want you to drill down for details.

KAROMAN: In other words, you have doubts about me, whether what I know about them is correct, and whether what I know matches what you know about them. Right?

ATMA: Right!

KAROMAN: In that case, why don't you cross-examine yourself? Your Honor?

ATMA: Cross-examine myself?

KAROMAN: That's not what I meant!

ATMA: Then you'd accuse me of being self-serving!

KAROMAN: But you're more skilled and experienced at prosecuting a case!

ATMA: (*Laughs delightedly*) So you can appreciate my position as a judicial officer.

KAROMAN: (*Trapped*) Damn! (*Laughs*) How could I not?

(ATMA *and* KAROMAN *laugh. It seems the two are friends again, the tension between them gone.*)

It's the artist's destiny to forever appear suspicious to government officials!

ATMA: But it's also the unfortunate destiny of government officials to be the target of criticism and protests by artists!

KAROMAN: Of course it is! If power is not open to correction, criticism, and protest, it will become absolute and controlled by the corrupt!

ATMA: Enough! We can discuss politics another time!

KAROMAN: (*Laughs sarcastically*) It turns out you aren't that different from those officials who fear the people's demands for government that's unblemished, open, fair, and corruption-free in all sectors!

ATMA: (*Irritated*) Do you want me to investigate the case of these forty villagers or not?

KAROMAN: You're the one who's willed it all. I'm only a guest here. Arrange everything to suit your desires, Your Honor!

(*Time passes.*)

2.

ATMA *knocks the gavel on the table, as if court is in session.*

ATMA: I'm not going to ask a lot of questions. I invite you to tell me everything, in detail. Please, go ahead!

VILLAGERS: We plead guilty, Your Honor.

ATMA: Not that! Whether you are guilty or not will be decided at trial. But here and now, I'm asking you for an honest explanation of the appalling events that occurred in your fishing village, as completely as possible, just as it was, the facts. Proceed!

(MATASIK, TUK SYAM *and* SIDDIK *look at each other, each indicating another one go first.*

Time passes.

ATMA *knocks the gavel on the table again, so all attention turns to him.*)

Anyone can go first.

MATASIK: Tuk Syam should go first.

TUK SYAM: Siddik would be more appropriate because it started with him, right?

SIDDIK: But… in my opinion, Matasik is even more appropriate, because Matasik clearly knows who our Village Head is. Besides, he genuinely understands the circumstances and the general situation in our village.

ATMA: Alright, alright, alright! It's best to start from the beginning so it's in chronological order, one by one until everything is clear down to the details.

TUK SYAM: Then Siddik is the one who should go first, followed by Matasik, and finally, I'll go last.

SIDDIK: Thank you for giving me this opportunity. Permit me, Your Honor.

ATMA: Proceed!

SIDDIK: May God protect me from the demons who tempt humans, so that my words are pure, free from all lies and deceit. Amen!

ALL: Amen!

SIDDIK: It was when I went to the office of the Village Head, which is at his home. The purpose of my visit was only to request permission to have my wedding in another village, my fiancée's village. That's our custom. But apparently our Village Head, Mr. Tabrani, was deliberately making it difficult for the official permit to be issued.

(*Beat.*)

I know what the problem was.

(*Beat.*)

Your Honor, if I may, I'd like to tell you about an issue that involved my parents, my own dad. My dad had asked the Village Head for an official certificate so that he could get credit to buy fishing gear and Petromax lamps from the fishing cooperative managed by the Village Head himself. But my dad didn't get it, because he couldn't deliver what the Village Head asked for in return. At the time, Mr. Tabrani asked for cement.

KAROMAN: Cement for what?

SIDDIK: Well… for construction. Officially.

ATMA: A kind of development fund, right?

SIDDIK: (*Confused*) Uh, how to say this? Um… yeah, Your Honor.

ATMA: That's great! Well, fishing villages need development. Do you watch TV? This is indeed the era of development, development in all fields and in all corners of the region, including your fishing village. Physical development as well as spiritual. Villagers must also contribute to the development and improvement of your villages. Wouldn't it be nice if your village could progress? Right? That's great!

MATASIK: But… excuse me for interrupting, Your Honor. The cement was not for improving the village, not for the benefit of the people.

ATMA: Then? What for?

MATASIK: (*To* SIDDIK) Be honest.

SIDDIK: As I recall, Your Honor, the cement Mr. Tabrani asked for was to build… his bathroom.

KAROMAN: (*Laughs out loud*) Build his bathroom? Building bathrooms for officials by exhorting money from the people's pockets! (*Laughs.*) Development, development…. You're not wrong, but too many are partial to corruption! Sweet! (*Laughs and claps his hands.*)

ATMA: But it must be proven before it can be taken as fact!

KAROMAN: The proof is these people!

SIDDIK: You can ask the whole village if there's anyone who hadn't been charged fees beyond the official ones. Everyone has, and most of them more than once.

MATASIK: I was, many times, Your Honor.

KAROMAN: It's common practice everywhere.

MATASIK: As wretched as I am, I used to be a kerosene and cigarette agent in our fishing village. As wretched as I am, I used to have a small shop, a private business, Your Honor. But since the village cooperative was taken over by Mr. Tabrani, that is, our village fishing cooperative, my share of kerosene decreased, also cigarettes, soap, and finally my small shop was forced out of business. Actually, if you think about it, the capital to form the cooperative came from the fishermen, but only Mr. Tabrani and his family enjoyed the benefits. In the end, it was a cooperative in name only. In practice, it was nothing more than Mr. Tabrani's personal business, which was only for his family's benefit and profit.

ATMA: Hold on a moment! Isn't everything you're telling me just a search for an excuse?

MATASIK: (*Surprised*) A… a… search? For a what?

ATMA: To excuse your inability to become a successful entrepreneur, for example?

TUK SYAM: My apologies, Your Honor! I have to speak up here because Matasik's assessment of his own abilities is inaccurate. With regard to his ability as an entrepreneur, the fact is his shop was thriving and always crowded. When he said it was a small shop, he was just being humble. Actually, his shop was quite large, in fact much bigger than the cooperative that Mr. Tabrani was managing. Matasik's idea to open a shop was his own, using his own initiative, without vying for facilities or backing. Matasik is known to be honest and trusting of others, so our fishing community entrusted the cooperative to him. He never mixed the cooperative business with his own shop. He's topnotch!

MATASIK: Thank you, Tuk Syam.

TUK SYAM: I speak the truth. So, when Mr. Tabrani became Village Head, he transferred the management of the cooperative to the Village Head. This was at the insistence of Mr. Tabrani himself, and he gave all kinds of reasons. We villagers don't know the details of the regulations for cooperatives, but according to Mr. Tabrani, cooperatives must be "officially" managed in order to get formal approval for bank credit and available services. "Officially" meant in official hands, meaning in the hands of the Village Head, Mr. Tabrani.

(*Beat.*)

That's what happened in our village. I don't know about any issues in other villages.

KAROMAN: Impressive, that Tabrani. Not only was he in control of government affairs, but he also monopolized all trade and economic activities in the village.

ATMA: Enough! Enough has been said to end here. Even if all of this is true, it doesn't justify taking the law into your own hands! So, none of this is relevant!

MATASIK: Forgive me, Your Honor. I don't mean to imply that I'm planning on filing a lawsuit against Mr. Tabrani. I don't intend to demand compensation for the closure of my shop, or for the loss of my position as head of the fisherman cooperative.

KAROMAN: Of course, that's not what you meant by explaining all that. All of it is relevant!

ATMA: Karoman! I hope you don't mean to justify the vigilante actions of these forty men from the fishing village!

KAROMAN: It's not so simple that the problem ends here. There are circumstances, indeed, many situations that cause a person to act, sometimes as part a group.

ATMA: Under the rule of law, all actions and behavior of our citizens must be measured and judged by the prevailing norms of law and justice!

(*Time passes.*)

3.

ATMA knocks his gavel on the table three times. All attention turns to him.

ATMA: We've already wasted enough time with irrelevant stuff. (*Knocks the gavel.*) Therefore, I must warn you all that from now on we will limit ourselves to what's relevant.

TUK SYAM: Alright, Your Honor. Please allow me to disclose the most important thing concerning human dignity in our village, as a male human, as a man.

ATMA: I'm afraid this will just be a waste of time!

KAROMAN: Objection! I don't agree with this kind of censorship. We agreed to seek the truth here. What is relevant or irrelevant cannot be determined from your point of view alone. Because everything you think is irrelevant, I believe is actually relevant. And who knows, the important things that Tuk Syam will disclose may in fact be relevant.

ATMA: But I'm the judge here, Karoman, I consider the law and justice here.

KAROMAN: All you're doing is convincing me that judges are nothing more than robots or computers, programmed by someone or other with official facts, two plus two always equals four. Uninspired! A rejection of human beings as unique and complicated creatures!

ATMA: We do have different opinions, Karoman! But it's very wrong of you to think that I'm equating or degrading the role of judges to robots and computers. Wrong! So wrong! And you, Karoman, with such an opinion, you have insulted the court. Contempt of court!

KAROMAN: (*Laughs mockingly*) Contempt of court? It's you who are in contempt of court. You've arbitrarily censored these villagers. It's clear you want absolute control to win. Perhaps you're planning on banning any difference of opinion.

ATMA: Look! You've insulted me again!

KAROMAN: You're the one who's insulting!

(ATMA *and* KAROMAN *throw accusations at each other! Chaos! The villagers join in adding to the chaos. A loud gong is struck, followed by Balinese gamelan music that accompanies topeng, a traditional masked dance-drama.* ATMA *quickly swallows another sedative followed by a sip of water.*

The NARRATOR *appears again, still in the form of an old man with a mustache and long beard.*)

NARRATOR: What's going on here, son? What is this? Why has the space in your head been transformed into a chaotic courtroom? Here, we seek the truth. Uphold the truth and drive out dishonesty, but with patience. That's how it should be, in accordance with God's commandments! Okay? Jeez!

(*The* NARRATOR *exits.*

Time passes.

ATMA *knocks the gavel on the table three times.*)

ATMA: Alright! Continue with what you were saying, Tuk Syam.

TUK SYAM: Forgive me, Your Honor, I can't leave out something important that you need to consider because it affects us men who live and were raised in this special environment, our fishing village.

ATMA: (*Irritated*) Just go ahead, no need to preface everything. (*Grumbles*) Like a goddamn dissertation!

(*Beat.*)

TUK SYAM: Mr. Tabrani was a master. Powerful hands. Powerful boxer. Awesome at martial arts.

(*Beat.*)

Most people in our fishing village have been on the receiving end of those hands, his punches, his slaps, his kicks, and even his spit. That, Your Honor, is in addition to his harsh, crude, insulting words when he was angry if people didn't do what he wanted. So, Your Honor, if you want to talk about taking the law into your own hands, Mr. Tabrani is a prime example, and he did it for years without anyone able to stop him. He wasn't just the law, he was the executioner!

(TUK SYAM *nears* ATMA.)

Your Honor, I've never seen you use a gun to enforce your directives.

ATMA: Of course not! I'm a judge!

TUK SYAM: But Mr. Tabrani, our Village Head, besides being the judge and executioner, enforced his commands with a gun.

KAROMAN: A gun?

TUK SYAM: Yes, a gun!

KAROMAN: That's nuts!

MATASIK: Mr. Tabrani also had a cowboy hat.

SIDDIK: And boots!

MATASIK: And a horse!

KAROMAN: (*Shaking his head*) Tsk, tsk, tsk, tsk.

ATMA: All this must be proven before we accept it as fact!

TUK SYAM: Siddik, this husband-to-be had also been hit several times by Mr. Tabrani. When he asked permission to marry, Mr. Tabrani got angry, immediately hit him, and kicked him out of his office, all witnessed by a crowd of people. Your Honor, he usually insulted people like that, in public in front of lots of people.

ATMA: You've been talking about the villagers. Villagers were humiliated. But how about you?

(TUK SYAM *is silent.*)

Were you ever asked for payment in return for dealings with Mr. Tabrani's office?

TUK SYAM: Never.

ATMA: Well then! Did you ever experience the slapping, hitting, or kicking yourself?

TUK SYAM: (*Offended*) That would be unlawful if it were to happen to me, Your Honor!

(TUK SYAM *pounds the table as he says these last words,*

startling ATMA.)

KAROMAN: So… Tuk Syam was never slapped?

(TUK SYAM *furiously turns his back on everyone, facing upstage.* KAROMAN *crosses toward* TUK SYAM.)

Tuk Syam…?

MATASIK: Sorry, to interrupt. You see, Mr. Tabrani didn't dare when it came to Tuk Syam.

KAROMAN: Why?

MATASIK: Because Tuk Syam is also formidable, as formidable as Mr. Tabrani.

KAROMAN: Does Tuk Syam also have a gun, like Mr. Tabrani?

MATASIK: Obviously not.

ATMA: In other words, Tuk Syam is the village hero, a respected champion, right?

MATASIK: The villagers see it that way, Your Honor. He's our leader, and because of him we had the courage to end Mr. Tabrani's tyrannical rule.

SIDDIK: Yes! Our leader!

TUK SYAM: Because our villagers were humiliated, Your Honor. My nephews among them, and my own family. Even Siddik here, Your Honor, is distantly related to me.

(*Beat.*)

Perhaps Your Honor knows about the masculine culture in our fishing village. Our male villagers have a custom of being macho. It's taboo for us to be insulted like that, especially if the insults are carried out again and again, and in public. Such humiliation must not only be stopped, but must be countered in kind, by risking one's life if necessary. That's manly! That's human! Death is a challenge we must face when insults keep piling up over the years. If he doesn't die, we die. If it didn't happen yesterday, it must happen today. If it doesn't happen today, then it must happen tomorrow. The point is, it must happen!

VILLAGERS: It must! Must! Must!

TUK SYAM: I don't even have to be slapped, Your Honor. Touching my head, just touching it, is an insult. If it's done on purpose to insult me, in public, even by Your Honor, rest assured you would die at my hands!

(*Beat.*)

We are men of the sea, Your Honor. To be able to live on dry land, we have to brave the waves, wrestle the sea, often with fierce winds as our enemy... our lives are full of danger... death...

(*Beat.*)

Our souls are green, black and red.

SIDDIK: Green, black, and red are the basic colors of our fishing boats.

MATASIK: Green is the color of fertile agricultural fields, our dream for generations.

SIDDIK: The deep sea is also green, the source of our sustenance.

MATASIK and SIDDIK: Green means courage.

(*Beat.*)

TUK SYAM: Black is the night sky, where the stars reside that guide us how to live wisely. It's also where the fierce winds dwell that test the faithful and our beliefs. Black means persistence.

MATASIK, SIDDIK and KAROMAN: Red is the color of our blood, meaning bravery.

(*Beat.*)

KAROMAN: I would like to ask a question. How did it happen that Mr. Tabrani could become the Village Head?

(*The* VILLAGERS *do not answer.*)

Was it because he made grandiose campaign promises that tickled your fancy, so that he was elected?

(*The* VILLAGERS *do not answer.*)

Or was he once good, but after elected as Village Head, he changed?

(*Silence for a moment.*)

TUK SYAM: There were no promises because there was no campaign.

MATASIK: There was no campaign because there were no other candidates.

SIDDIK: Mr. Tabrani was the only candidate sent by the city.

TUK SYAM: That's what happened in our village. I don't know about any issues in other villages.

(*Silence returns.*)

KAROMAN: Finally, we arrive at the crux of the matter.

(*Beat.*)

ATMA: But all of that is irrelevant! There is a thing called crime, there are those who fall victim to it, there are those who commit it, and for all, that there are laws and regulations.

(ATMA *knocks the gavel on the table three times.*)

There are officers of the court responsible for upholding law and justice. I'm one of those officers. I'm the law!

(ATMA *knocks the gavel on the table three times.*)

And you, Karoman, are not one of those officers!

KAROMAN: But what you're judging are human beings, living human beings, in specific circumstances, who hold honorable values, who experience the sweetness and bitterness of life, who are rightfully angry when they are constantly trampled upon, insulted for years, spit on, blackmailed, dishonored, their male dignity destroyed, as human beings! All of it! Yes, it's relevant and must be considered, and it's not impossible for there to be some truth in it, Atma!

ATMA: Proceed with care, Karoman!

KAROMAN: No! No need! I just want you to open your eyes wide, Your Honor! You're not dealing with machines or robots, but human beings! Open your eyes! Look! Take a look at who Mr. Tabrani was! Mr. Tabrani, who became the Village Head! Look! He was a person born into a time when pleasures of the material world are worshipped; the result of an excess of the progress of modern times. He was a man who had been deliberately programed by increasingly sophisticated modern systems of communication and advertising to become a voracious consumer of the overabundance of goods! He never wasted any potential opportunity to dominate others. He used any available way, legal or illegal. He was a soul possessed by those corrupt devils, no longer able to distinguish between good and evil. Whether he was aware of it or not, he destroyed a healthy and virtuous society. He never acknowledged his sins, let alone concern for his fellow human beings. He became ever more adept at walking with his head held high while his feet trampled on victim after victim left scattered and wailing in his wake. His life did not bring blessings, but catastrophe to others! Should such a creature be left to roam the earth, along with our way of life, Atma?

VILLAGERS: It must end! Kill! Kill! Kill!

(*Silence.*)

ATMA: Karoman, your position can be considered dangerous and a threat to national security interests.

KAROMAN: This is a matter of human dignity ravaged by an oppressive power, insulting lives through exploitation.

(*Beat.*)

KAROMAN: (*Quietly in low voice*) And that's what they are dealing with here.

(*Heartbreaking sounds of people wailing and moaning in pain.* ATMA *nervously swallows a pill and drinks. He's tired and has a headache.*

Time passes.)

4.

ATMA *droops in his chair, exhausted, his head reeling. The* NARRATOR, *as the old man, enters. He massages* ATMA's *shoulders and head and comforts him with a song.*

Time passes.

ATMA: Stop that! I may be a bit lightheaded, but I'm still strong!

(*The* NARRATOR *exits.* ATMA *knocks the gavel on the table three times.*)

Let's not keep circling around the problem! It's redundant and abusing the opportunity that you've been given to speak. You've just circled around without getting to the heart of the matter, which is real and proven and acknowledged!

KAROMAN: Objection!

(*The* NARRATOR *hurriedly reenters.*)

NARRATOR: Oh boy, oh boy, ooooh noooo… starting again… starting again… what a mess, headache-inducing, dizzy, throbbing! Patience, be patient, wait your turn to speak, one at a time. (*To* KAROMAN) Got it? (*To* ATMA) Now whose turn is it?

ATMA: Now it's my turn to interrogate the defendants. (*To* KAROMAN) It will be your turn next. You will have a turn, don't worry.

KAROMAN: Fine! Please! You go!

NARRATOR: Now, that's it. Okay?

(*The* NARRATOR *exits.*)

ATMA: Who killed Mr. Tabrani, the official Village Head of your fishing village? Answer!

VILLAGERS: We did!

ATMA: (*To* KAROMAN) See! You heard it yourself! This is a case of homicide, clear-cut, proven, with confessions!

KAROMAN: Yes, clear-cut, of course, but—

ATMA: There are no buts! Clear-cut is clear-cut! Period! Or is there something that doesn't match what you know?

KAROMAN: No.

ATMA: Well! Then that's enough!

KAROMAN: But what happened next, Atma, what happened next...

ATMA: Listen listen listen! Look, Karoman, I can tell you what happened next. Listen, Karoman!

(*Beat.*)

ATMA: After the forty men took Mr. Tabrani,'s life, the life of the Village Head, the life of a legitimate government official, they sat in a circle around the body of their victim with their heads bowed, silent.

VILLAGERS: We did it, we are ready to take responsibility, to accept the punishment that will be handed down by Your Honor's court.

ATMA: (*Almost whispering*) You hear, Karoman?

KAROMAN: (*Slow to answer*) Yes.

ATMA: See!

KAROMAN: But—

ATMA: (*Interrupts*) Has there been anything incorrect?

KAROMAN: No, nothing wrong. Of course.

ATMA: So it's no different from what you know?

KAROMAN: Nothing different. Evidently. But, Atma—

ATMA: (*Interrupts*) Enough! Enough enough enough enough! I don't need any more discussion to decide on a verdict in accordance with law and justice, I'm the judge! I've held this post for years. You don't need to teach me on this one. I know my duty, I know how to handle it, I know how to do it, Karoman. That's enough!

KAROMAN: But these men also knew their duty!

ATMA: (*Taken aback*) Du... dut... what?!

KAROMAN: These men also knew how to do their duty.

ATMA: Duty?!

KAROMAN: (*To the villagers*) Was Mr. Tabrani a beloved figure in your fishing village?

VILLAGERS: No, he was disliked!

ATMA: Stop stop stop!

KAROMAN: Stop yourself, Atma! Now it's my turn to interrogate them!

(ATMA *can't prevent him.*)

When there was an election, would you have chosen Mr. Tabrani as Village Head for your village?

VILLAGERS: No!

KAROMAN: Who would you have chosen?

VILLAGERS: Musa or Ma'ruf depending on who got the majority of the villagers' votes.

ATMA: This is all irrelevant!

KAROMAN: (*Ignores* ATMA) Was Mr. Tabrani known for performing good deeds or evil deeds?

VILLAGERS: Evil! He was evil! He was despotic!

ATMA: Everyone is considered innocent, not evil, before the court renders a verdict.

KAROMAN: (*Ignores* ATMA) Did you ever report Mr. Tabrani's actions to the city government?

VILLAGER: Yes, we did!

TUK SYAM: Two of our villagers did that.

MATASIK: Exactly three years ago.

SIDDIK: But instead they were accused of causing trouble in the village.

MATASIK: Both were terrified and ultimately sailed away with the salt boats.

SIDDIK: Their wives and children left with them.

MATASIK: They never came back to the village.

SIDDIK: They live overseas, afraid of Mr. Tabrani.

MATASIK: One is called Musa.

TUK SYAM: The other is Ma'ruf. A soup seller.

KAROMAN: So, what was the purpose of your actions against Mr. Tabrani?

VILLAGERS: To stop Mr. Tabrani's evil doings for good.

KAROMAN: If I'm not mistaken, ending cruel behavior could be considered a noble act. Do you agree with that?

VILLAGERS: Agreed!

KAROMAN: But you've also been accused of being criminals, just like Mr. Tabrani. What about that?

VILLAGERS: We aren't criminals! Mr. Tabrani was the criminal! Evil! He was cruel!

KAROMAN: (*To* ATMA) There! It's evident they're not criminals; on the contrary, they eliminated evil from the face of the earth.

ATMA: Not criminals? They're murderers! Karoman! Clear-cut, proven, with confessions!

KAROMAN: The people who opposed colonialism also committed murders, but they weren't all bad people. Not all killers are criminals. You know this very well, Atma!

ATMA: Wrong wrong wrong! They cannot be equated with our

revolutionary heroes! Wrong! The colonial government was an illegitimate government, but Mr. Tabrani was legally appointed as the Village Head by a legitimate government! Be careful what you say, Karoman. Instead of vindicating these defendants, they could instead be accused of being rebels or subversives. Wrong wrong wrong! I've already said that your circuitous babble is irrelevant. This is a case of murder! Period!

(ATMA *knocks his gavel on the table several times.*)

KAROMAN: Knock knock knock! Bang your gavel a thousand more times! Knock, knock, knock! But I believe your heart is full of genuine justice, a righteous voice that cannot be silenced even with a million whack, whack, whacks of a sledgehammer!

(*Beat.*)

And more importantly, a million knock, knock, knocks of your gavel won't prevent your real guest from entering. We're in this space, with all the complications of court debates, all the nostalgia from our high school days. All… yes, all this is meant to buy time so the real guest can't enter.

(*Heartbreaking sounds of people wailing and moaning in pain fill the space.* TUK SYAM *walks upstage. The* NARRATOR *enters from backstage carrying the folded the white cloth from earlier and gives to* TUK SYAM. TUK SYAM *spreads the cloth out like* KAROMAN *had done. The same image appears on the cloth.*)

TUK SYAM: Your real guest left this.

KAROMAN: The same cloth with the image on it.

ATMA: Give it to me!

(TUK SYAM *dodges* ATMA *as he lunges to grab the white cloth.* MATASIK *and* SIDDIK *trap* ATMA *so he cannot move.* TUK SYAM *throws the cloth downstage where it lands on the ground in a pile.* MA OLONG *and* MORNI *re-enter from stage right, trudging with painful, heavy steps. The first of the two women carries a bamboo pole with a lighted lantern on one end.*)

KAROMAN: Are you still trying to avoid meeting your real guest, Atma?

ATMA: I have the right to control the space in my head!

(KAROMAN *and* VILLAGERS *laugh at* ATMA.)

KAROMAN: For the time being.

NARRATOR: It is the space in our heads that is the most difficult to control!

(*The* NARRATOR*'s words are greeted by laughter from* KAROMAN *and the* VILLAGERS. *Meanwhile,* MA OLONG *and* MORNI *have picked up the white cloth and carried it across the stage. They exit stage left.* MATASIK *and* SIDDIK *are thrown to the ground as* ATMA *uses the last of his strength to free himself from their grasp.* ATMA *trudges to the table and immediately reaches for the bottle of sedatives, but the* NARRATOR *grabs it first.*)

NARRATOR: These are useless! Sedatives won't help you!

KAROMAN: (*To the* VILLAGERS) Friends, friends! Now is the time!

ATMA: No! Don't let him in here!

KAROMAN: Come on, my friends! Let's go!

ATMA: Don't! I don't want a corpse in my head space! Don't! Don't!

(*But the* VILLAGERS *and* KAROMAN *exit.*)

ATMA: (*Delirious*) Don't… don't… don't…

NARRATOR: Shush! Be patient.

ATMA: Give me a pill… thirsty… water…

(*The* NARRATOR *doesn't give him a pill, just some water. Then, the* NARRATOR *massages ATMA's back, neck, and head.*)

NARRATOR: I feel sorry for you, bucko. If you take all the sedatives, you won't have enough strength to stop your real guest from showing up. The guest who has been waiting for the opportunity to enter your head space.

ATMA: But I am tired… sleepy… I need some serious sleep…

NARRATOR: Sooner or later your guest will come anyway, whether you're sleeping or awake.

ATMA: I don't want… a corpse… inside my head… don't… don't… I want to sleep… so tired…

NARRATOR: Yes, you will sleep eventually. You're exhausted from your inner struggle. And when you are asleep, son, don't be surprised when access to your dream space is wide open. Your real guest will be able to freely enter.

ATMA: No…. No...

NARRATOR: And when you are in the space of dreams, your guest can change shape into a variety of forms. It could become a gruesome ghost and clutch you in its claws until you are crushed—

ATMA: No…!

NARRATOR: You'll be delusional, screaming—

ATMA: No…!

NARRATOR: Nightmares—

ATMA: (*Crying hysterically*) No…! I don't want a ghost corpse in my dreams! Go away! Go away! Go away!

(Stage lights fade to black. Heartbreaking sounds of people wailing and moaning in pain are accompanied by a menacing scream, deafening and fierce.

Time passes.)

Part Three
Atma Dreams

1.

ATMA *is alone onstage. He sits, reclining in the chair, asleep. Amber spotlight up on* ATMA, *casting a much larger shadow of his head and upper body on the shadow screen.*

Silence.

ATMA: (*In a delirium*) Karoman… are you still there?

(*A loud "knock-knock-knock!" of a judge's gavel is heard as lights up behind the screen. The shadows cast on the screen are not of* KAROMAN, *but of* MA OLONG *and* MORNI.

Silence returns.

Time passes.)

Who are they?

(*"Knock, knock, knock!" Then silence.*)

When are we now?

(*The "knock-knock-knock!" becomes louder and lasts longer. Each repeated "knock" is like an invisible gavel or fist hitting* ATMA *so that he noticeably staggers as he gets up from the chair. Lights out behind the shadow screen,* MA OLONG *and* MORNI *enter in front of the shadow screen.* ATMA *tries to drive them away, but he walks if he were reeling from the blows of an imaginary gavel or imaginary fists.*

Time passes quickly.)

ATMA: (*To* MA OLONG *and* MORNI) Get out! Go awaaaay! Don't come into my dream space!

(ATMA *falls helplessly to the ground. The "knock-knock-knock!" fades out.*)

MA OLONG and MORNI: There is a thing called crime, some who commit crimes, some who become victims of crime, some who must be punished.

(*Loud continuous "knock-knock-knock!"*

Time passes.

Silence returns.)

MA OLONG: My son is the corpse. My only child in the world.

(*A single "knock!"*)

I never thought this would be my fate as a mother. I never imagined a fate like this. I always believed that I would go first, not him, because he was my child and I, Ma Olong, his mother. That's how fate is naturally meant to be, the old go first, not the young.

(*A single "knock!"*)

My fate is unnatural. It shouldn't be like this. It's outside the norms of destiny. It's abnormal. It's wrong. I should have been the one who died, not him, not my child. No, no, no!

(*A single "knock!"*)

MORNI: My husband is the corpse. My only husband in the world.

(*A single "knock!"*)

Yes. Now, he's no longer alive. But he was alive. He breathed. He whispered the most intimate words in my ear. His breath was sweet. You could see his heart beating in his chest. His sparkling eyes flashed a zest for life… life… he was alive.

MA OLONG: He was in my womb for nine months. His father couldn't be there when he was born to witness the extraordinary event, the only extraordinary event I've experienced in my life. It was amazing to witness a new baby… come from my womb! Amazing! I will never forget that miraculous experience! Yes! Miraculous! His first cry… tiny feet kicking… tiny hands waving… such a tiny creature… then a rooster crowed, a sign it was dawn.

(*Beat.*)

Taking care of him, raising him, made me happy. I washed him in sea water. I dried him in the sun. I taught him to walk on the beach, making tiny footprints in the sand, wet with seafoam from the waves. He was a healthy child! He was never fat, but a good eater. Cooking for him was a pleasure. Watching him eat heartily gave me joy. Especially when I cooked his favorite… grilled spicy fish wrapped in banana leaf. Watching his fingers open the grilled banana leaf wrapped around the fish, watching him chew, swallow, and his nose run when it was too spicy… all of it made me happy. He was the reason I liked to grill spicy fish in banana leaf. If he was upset, if he wasn't feeling well, the only thing that would calm him was my grilled spicy fish in banana leaf.

MORNI: My husband was a hard-working fisherman. Every time he returned from fishing, he always brought me giant prawns he had caught as a special gift. Always. He cleaned them and grilled them himself, and then he gave them to me, Morni, his wife… whom he loved… me.

(MORNi *fights back tears.*)

MA OLONG: But it all just disappeared… he no longer eats…

MORNI: He no longer breathes…

MA OLONG: He no longer leaves his footprints on the beach…

MORNI: He no longer speaks… the sun no longer warms his sturdy shoulders…

MA OLONG: He's alone in a dark hole…

MORNI: He's a corpse now…

(MORNI *can no longer stop herself from crying. Neither can* MA OLONG.

Time passes.)

MA OLONG: Never mind grilling fish in banana leaf now… I can't even stand to see it served on the dinner table… cruel! They're cruel! The men who came by truck were cruel! They took the life of my innocent son, my son who had nothing to do with the Village Head's murder. Cruel! My heart is broken, Your Honor. My spirit has been deeply wounded, a gaping wound that will remain open until my death, Your Honor. It's so painful… so painful...

(MA OLONG *and* MORNI *can't stop crying.* KAROMAN *and the* VILLAGERS *enter.*)

MA OLONG: (*Vengefully*) This gaping wound in my spirit can only be patched with a living soul! Give me one soul in exchange for my child, give me just one life, so I have strength to continue my life's journey into my old age! So I have strength to face fish wrapped in banana leaf! To grill spicy fish wrapped in banana leaf in my kitchen, Your Honor.

VILLAGERS: There is a thing called crime, some who commit crimes, some who become victims of crime, some who must be punished.

(*Loud continuous "knock-knock-knock!"*

Time passes.)

MORNI: Why did my husband have to be killed? Why not someone else? Why not those who were actually involved in the Village Head's murder? My husband was innocent, he didn't participate in the killing of Mr. Tabrani. He was innocent, not guilty...! Give me a gun! I will avenge my husband's death! I will avenge my husband's death! Give me a weapon! Give me... a life!

(MORNI *faints.* MA OLONG *supports her so she doesn't fall down.*)

MA OLONG: Morni!

(ATMA *tries to get near* MORNI.)

ATMA: Oh Lord! Don't call this unfortunate woman yet! Don't!

(ATMA *is blocked by the* VILLAGERS. *They push* ATMA *until he finally falls downstage left.* MORNI *is on* MA OLONG*'s lap.*

Time passes.)

KAROMAN: They don't need your sympathy. Sympathy alone is not enough, Atma. You're a judge, you should be able to do more than just express sympathy.

ATMA: But she fainted, Karoman, and I am a human being, a human watching another faint. Isn't that a normal reaction?

KAROMAN: She fainted, not only from grief, but more than that, she fainted from the loss of hope. And that lost hope is ... you! Her hope to get justice from you! Justice, Atma, not sympathy!

MA OLONG: My daughter-in-law asks for a life, Your Honor!

VILLAGERS: We took action, we're ready to accept the verdict, willing to give up our lives.

MA OLONG: Your lives must end! But that's to pay for the death of Mr.

Tabrani, the life of the Village Head, not for the life of my son, my daughter-in-law's husband.

(*"Knock!"*)

KAROMAN: Do you hear, Atma?

(ATMA *doesn't answer.*)

Now we need to address what happened after Mr. Tabrani's murder.

(*"Knock!"*)

MA OLONG: Explain what happened in the aftermath of Mr. Tabrani's death, so His Honor understands the issue.

ATMA: I already know!

VILLAGERS: Be quiet, Your Honor!

KAROMAN: Have you forgotten where you are now? In your dream space, you're the defendant!

(*"Knock-knock-knock!"*)

Now!

(KAROMAN *claps three times. The* NARRATOR *enters, still as an old man.*)

KAROMAN: (*To* ATMA) Atma, we've given you the opportunity to explain what happened next, but you keep avoiding it, putting it off. You limit the discussion by ending with the murder.

(KAROMAN *motions to the* NARRATOR *to speak.*)

NARRATOR: Yes! It's true, at the end of the incident, the forty villagers sat in a circle around the victim's corpse, Mr. Tabrani's corpse. They sat, heads bowed, resigned to the legal consequences. It's true! That's what they did while waiting for the messenger they sent to the city to report their actions to the police. But as a small town, the news spread quickly, reaching the ears of a certain group of people who were closely tied to Mr. Tabrani at the time. So, the first to arrive at the fishing village wasn't the police, but that gang! They came in trucks, rampaged the fishing village, and without any sort of investigation, they struck, punched, and brutally tormented the village men! Cruelly! They beat not only the forty men involved, but every man they met in the village, attacking wildly, beating all of them, even those not involved. They were also attacked and viciously tortured!

MA OLONG: Including beating my son to death!

NARRATOR: Even though Ma Olong's son was completely unaware of what had happened. He had only just returned from fishing and was putting away his catch and gear.

(*The* NARRATOR *is silent for a moment.*)

NARRATOR: Even Mr. Tabrani's adult son didn't escape the mob's rampage. No joke! Sadistic! Raging! Bunch of vigilantes! Many who fell died, left scattered on the streets in the village, in parks, yards, and on the beach and boats.

MA OLONG: My son was found dead on the beach.

(*Beat.*)

KAROMAN: You know all of this is true. You know who heartlessly rampaged that fishing village. You know who they are, Atma!

VILLAGERS: Under the rule of law, all actions and behavior of our citizens must be measured and judged by the prevailing norms of law and justice!

KAROMAN: There are officers of the court responsible for upholding law and justice. And you are one of those officers.

(*Beat.*)

NARRATOR: Those are the words you said. Words you kept repeating.

KAROMAN: Now, Atma, where are your actions to match those words?

VILLAGERS: Poser!

TUK SYAM: Don't just get tough with those like us, the weak, powerless, and unarmed!

MA OLONG: Give me one life!

(ATMA *remains quiet.*

Time passes.)

KAROMAN: Now you are silent!

(*Time passes.*)

2.

MORNI *has recovered consciousness.* ATMA *still sits on the ground. Helpless.* KAROMAN *signals to the* NARRATOR. *They force* ATMA *to stand up and face the villagers.* ATMA *and the villagers stare at each other.*

KAROMAN: Familiar faces, Atma.

ATMA: (*Turns his head away from the* VILLAGERS) That's enough, Karoman.

KAROMAN: (*Forces* ATMA *to look at the* VILLAGERS) Faces awaiting your verdict.

ATMA: I know, but be quiet, don't disturb my sleep. Stop pressuring me, Karoman.

KAROMAN: The death penalty, Atma?

ATMA: (*Sits down*) Shut up!

KAROMAN: By firing squad, Atma?

ATMA: (*Raises head to look at* KAROMAN) Shut up, I said!

KAROMAN: (*Challenges* ATMA*'s gaze*) Now that everything is clear, are you still able to render a verdict on these villagers, Atma?

(ATMA *frees himself from* KAROMAN *and the* NARRATOR.)

ATMA: Shut up! Don't keep stirring up my state of mind! You really are heartless, Karoman! Just quit disturbing my sleep. All of this has upset my stomach, given me a throbbing headache, shaken my nerves, and made me anxious and uncomfortable.

(ATMA *moves away from* KAROMAN, *the* NARRATOR, *and the* VILLAGERS.)

ATMA: A judge's mental state is always like this. At least if that judge is me when I take on a murder case carried out unimpeded and without resistance from the victims!

(*Beat.*)

My head feels like it's spitting! My chest is about to explode! My stomach is queasy… nauseous, Karoman! That's enough, leave me alone in my sleep. Quit bothering me with this nightmare.

(*Beat.*)

Look! You see the faces of these forty men! See! Their faces, their ordinary faces, faces that can be affable, can exude the joy of living as human beings, normal human faces… human beings, Karoman! They are human beings! But what have they done with their own hands? Hands rough from the oars and rigging of life, hard from the sea salt of experience, and the scorching sun of work. Look! Observe these creatures called human beings, creatures none other than ourselves, me, you… us! Yes, we are all human beings! Human beings, Karoman!

(*Beat.*)

Look! Pay close attention to this kind of creature, Karoman! Look at their hands, look at my hands, look at your hands, look carefully, Karoman!

(*Beat.*)

We inherit hands tarnished with blood!

(*Beat.*)

These hands of ours, these human hands, hands that, for who knows how long, have been recorded in history… stained by blood. Blood! And history? What is recorded on the eternal pages of history? Read the blood that has stained those ancient pages, the blood that flows on the pages of today, the blood spilling again and again soaking the pages of the future… continuing forever because no one can stop it. It's all because of hands, my kind of hands, your kind of hands, the kind of hands of these creatures called human beings! Us, ourselves! Hands that can turn into claws and strangle each other's throats! Flashes of sword blades, exploding bullets, battles, wars, invasions, scorched earth, screams, lingering wails forever filling the pages of newspapers and magazines, literature, philosophy, and even the holy books!

(*Beat.*)

No no no… no, Karoman, not wild beasts! No! But humans! Yes! Us!

(*While speaking,* ATMA *dismantles the pile of over-sized books, mixed with boxes, bundles, old typewriters and so on, revealing a pile of blood-stained stones.*)

Forty humans picked up these big stones, then used them to repeatedly strike the Village Head's skull! Again and again and again… until finally his head was crushed… and his brains splattered across his own yard… blood! Horrible… my God!

(*Beat.*)

Alright alright alright… enough, Karoman, I'm so tired…. Don't plague me with what fate befalls the victim's relatives. Don't plague me with what fate awaits the murderers' relatives… don't! Don't, Karoman. There have been so many cases like this one, with so many of the same kind of stories resulting from the handiwork of men like these… the burden and suffering that all involved will bear… heavy economic toll, crushing mental anguish! It will be tough for the village and villagers to move on. It will remain deep-rooted for years, haunting their children and grandchildren for generations! An age-old curse!

(*Beat.*)

But not a single person seems to notice! All of this done for the sake of a male custom of manliness, for a whole variety of reasons, depending on the time and place. The reasons, from the most primitive to the most modern, have remained essentially the same. I don't know where this kind of savagery and inhumanity came from or how it has been passed down for generations, ingrained in the human psyche that turns hands into claws! Firmly embedded in the human psyche like a wild lion that pounces immediately when disturbed! Attack first, figure it out later! What is this? Why is it that all the punishments dictated by law, imposed by the scriptures, or even the philosophical and scientific wisdom of geniuses, are unable to tame the wild lion in the human psyche? Why aren't examples of suffering prisoners locked up in iron cages, or examples of being thrown into hell by God, convincing enough to be an effective deterrent?

(*Beat.*)

Idiots! What kind of idiocy is this, Karoman?!

(*Beat.*)

These forty men, or the gang that came with the trucks, or men who make the newspapers and magazines headlines, news from trenches, criminal events in the family or community, are all ordinary human faces that can be friendly and radiate the joy of life, regular human faces, faces we know well, Asian faces, Japanese faces, Chinese faces, Malay faces, Indian faces, Filipino faces, Korean faces, Russian faces, Afghan faces, Pakistani faces, Arab faces, African faces, European faces, American faces, Cuban faces, Latin American faces, Native-American faces, Pacific Islander faces, Australian faces, Papuan faces, faces we know, our own faces, my face, your face, all are no different. Identical! Could it be that our everyday faces, our human faces, are only masks, and behind our faces there is a real face, and that face behind this face is the face of that ferocious, wild lion? A face that is both primitive and modern, ancient and eternal!

(*Beat.*)

And those of us who have that kind of face behind our everyday face, call ourselves human beings, proudly and resolutely, without hesitation. Superior beings on this earth, as recorded in our holy books, scientific manuscripts, literature, and children's bedtime stories, etched on our hearts and beliefs. But behind that mask-like ordinary face hides a force that glorifies violence and that, in a flash, can transform our hands into fists with nuclear warheads!

(*Pauses for a moment, surprising himself by what he has just said.*)

Nuclear?! Look, Karoman, our hands are not only covered with blood, but dirty with radioactive dust.... We'll eventually become dust dust dust dust all dust! (*Mesmerized by the terrible threat*)... dust... and all the rest will be a long silence... desolate like on the plains of the moon... stark... monotonous... flat.

(*Beat.*)

Hush! I don't need an answer. Don't say anything or I'll despair and lose my faith in God. Hush! Don't say anything or I'll no longer believe in the significance of human beings and the civilizations we have cultivated for centuries on this earth. Hush! Be quiet, Karoman!

(*Time passes.*)

3.

Spotlight up on the CORPSE'*s head, as pale as chalk, on the back wall, stage left of the shadow screen, followed by the appearance of two hands, also white as chalk. Visible on the head and hands are images of skeletons and skulls. The rest of the* CORPSE'*s body is not visible.*

Sounds of groaning and heart-wrenching wailing.

ATMA *is shaken and alarmed by the emergence of the* CORPSE. *Everyone looks at the* CORPSE.

MA OLONG: This is his body. My son's corpse. My only son in the world.

ATMA: (*Covers his eyes*) Don't... don't... don't come in!

NARRATOR: (*To* ATMA) I told you, son, sooner or later your real guest would show up too.

ATMA: I don't want a corpse in my dream...!

(KAROMAN *walks to the table and sits in* ATMA*'s chair.* KAROMAN *picks up the judge's gavel and knocks it three times on the table.*)

KAROMAN: Now it's your turn to make this defendant speak!

(KAROMAN *knocks the gavel on the table three times.*

The VILLAGERS *ensnare* ATMA *in a large net.*)

TUK SYAM: (*To* ATMA) You just circle around without getting to the heart of the matter, which is clear, real, and proven!

VILLAGERS: Open your eyes! Take a good look! That's the victim who was killed! An innocent victim! Open your eyes wide!

ATMA: (*Helpless*) Okay okay okay... okay!

VILLAGERS: Who killed this unlucky husband? Answer!

ATMA: Them!

VILLAGERS: Who are they?

ATMA: A gang of men.

VILLAGERS: What gang?

ATMA: Them.

VILLAGERS: Who are they?

ATMA: Them.

VILLAGERS: Who?

ATMA: Them... yes... them...

VILLAGERS: Come on, defendant, repeat after us!

ATMA: Okay okay okay... okay!

VILLAGERS: They…

ATMA: They…

VILLAGERS: A gang of men…

ATMA: A gang of men…

VILLAGERS: Came in trucks…

ATMA: Came in trucks…

VILLAGERS: Wearing military belts…

ATMA: Wearing military belts…

VILLAGERS: Wearing boots…

ATMA: Wearing boots…

VILLAGERS: And carrying weapons.

(*With great difficulty,* ATMA*'s mouth tries to repeat the final three words, but no sound or words come out. Silence. Stage lights dim, but the spotlight on the* CORPSE *remains bright.*)

NARRATOR: As far as we know, those boots were most likely meant for protection.

(*The villagers take out flashlights and shine them on a pair of large black boots mixed in with the scattered books and blood-stained stones. Silence.*)

NARRATOR: At the same time, from the junction where the land meets the sea, amidst the evidence, with lengthy exhausted grievances, we beam news to the world that there are people on their knees, bowing their heads, begging for protection from a bloody threat, for the boots to stop kicking, stomping, stamping on their calves, arms, crotches, bellies, chests, skulls, heads, mouths, tongues, brains… hearts.

(*Beat.*)

But it feels like grievances will continue filling the pages of world history for a long time.

(*Beat.*)

It feels certain, from this dim corner, that our turn will come to add our grievances about a pair of boots that relentlessly stalks us with the threat of death.

(*Stage lights up.*)

VILLAGERS: Do you intend to toss this innocent husband's case into the trash?

MA OLONG: That can't happen! It can't! There has been a crime! People committed this crime! People have done something cruel. Some have fallen victim to that cruelty! Someone must be punished!

VILLAGERS: Death! The death penalty! Death! Death!

MORNI: Give us weapons! Weapons! We're ready to shoot the killer! Give us weapons!

MA OLONG: Give us weapons!

VILLAGERS: They did it! Come on! What do you call their conduct?

(KAROMAN *waits a moment for* ATMA*'s answer.*)

KAROMAN: Answer, Atma!

(KAROMAN *knocks the gavel on the table three times, then waits again for* ATMA*'s answer.* ATMA *doesn't answer. Fed up,* KAROMAN *leaves the judge's table and walks toward* ATMA.)

Now you're mute. Earlier, you spoke so fluently about the law, justice, regulations, and rules.

(*He gestures to the* VILLAGERS *to drag* ATMA *to his chair. After they seat* ATMA *on the judge's chair, they put the gavel in his hand. They lift the gavel up high, ready to knock it against the table.* ATMA *is limp, giving the impression that the* VILLAGERS *are lifting the gavel with no help from him.*)

VILLAGERS: Come on, Judge, answer! What do you call what that gang did?

ATMA: What they did, what that gang did, was vigilantism, taking the law into their own hands!

(*The* VILLAGERS *move* ATMA'*s hand so the gavel knocks on the table three times. The* VILLAGERS *then release* ATMA *from their grip and leave him sitting alone in his chair. They join* KAROMAN, *who has been watching from in front of the judge's table. They shine their flashlights on* ATMA, *who leans face down on the table.*)

KAROMAN: You're a judge, Atma. You are a pillar of justice.

(KAROMAN *and the* VILLAGERS *exit.*

Lights up behind the shadow screen revealing KAROMAN *and the* VILLAGERS *as shadows on the screen.*

Silence.)

4.

The NARRATOR *frees* ATMA *from the net.*

Time passes.

NARRATOR: Karoman is right, son. You're a judge. You're a pillar of justice.

ATMA: (*Laughs bitterly and grimaces*) Indeed! Yes. I should be. But I am just… a judge, only one. And this one is not a pillar.

(*Time passes.*)

When people talk about law and justice, they're usually speaking about a type of broom, a clean sweep, to keep our existence as a country and a people free from all kinds of muck.

NARRATOR: You're that broom!

ATMA: You're looking at it the wrong way! I am only one bristle. To be a broom, all the bristles must be gathered together and tied. Then it becomes a broom. And a broom? What's the meaning of a broom? Because, in the end, it's the hand that holds and moves the broom that is far more important; namely a strong, powerful, and official hand.

(*Time passes.*)

There! Now you see! This is my reality as a judge. I am only one bristle. What can one bristle do against the hand that holds the broom? A single bristle can be pulled out of the broom, broken into tiny pieces, and end up dumped in the trash!

(*Beat.*)

This is the scourge of our era.

(*Beat.*)

Hopeless…

(*Again,* ATMA *slumps face down on the table.* KAROMAN *quickly reappears onstage from behind the shadow screen. The light behind the screen goes out. The shadows of the* VILLAGERS *disappear.*)

KAROMAN: No, no, you can't! You can't give up! You're a judge! You're our hope! This time we move in harmony and together! We will win! We're strong!

NARRATOR: We will succeed this time and in the future we'll be role models!

(*Beat.*)

ATMA: Words are certainly easy to send soaring, just as wings make it easy for butterflies to fly. But like butterfly wings, however beautiful they may be, words are nothing compared to the brutality of bullets.

(*Beat.*)

Each year demands more trust in weapons. Our faith in the universe's everlasting mercy is crushed by their deafening noise. Year after year, we are increasingly incapable of doing anything but to surrender…

KAROMAN: Atma! You're a judge!

ATMA: Me?!

KAROMAN: You! Yes! You!

ATMA: A judge?!

KAROMAN: A pillar of justice!

ATMA: I'm only a single bristle. What is one bristle, if we are to tame the wild lion embedded in our psyche?

(KAROMAN *is silent.*)

And you? Who are you?

KAROMAN: I am Karoman, a poet.

ATMA: A poet? Ah, as far as I know you're just a butterfly whose wings have been shredded by the talon's grip.

(*Suddenly the* CORPSE *wails and moans, followed by the sounds of violent clashing. Shabby, ripped, and blood-stained white clothing falls from above.* ATMA *becomes flustered.*

KAROMAN *and the* NARRATOR *search for an exit, but* ATMA *stops them.*)

No! Don't leave me alone here! Don't! Stay with me! Don't go!

(*The sounds of battle becomes deafening. Sirens. Explosions. The whoosh of an airplane taking off. Bombs. Barrage of gunfire. Along with the white pieces of clothing falling from above, objects are thrown in from the wings. These objects and clothing pile up on* ATMA, KAROMAN, *and the* NARRATOR.

Time passes.

Everything stops. The CORPSE *disappears. Silence!*

The NARRATOR *is nowhere to be seen onstage.* ATMA *and* KAROMAN *fight their way out of the pile of stuff under which they are buried. They stand up.*)

ATMA: (*To* KAROMAN) Who are you actually?

KAROMAN: You call me Karoman.

ATMA: But that's not your name.

KAROMAN: Karoman is a poet.

ATMA: But I've never known poet named Karoman.

KAROMAN: Karoman was your friend when you were teenagers.

ATMA: But I never had a teenage friend named Karoman.

(*Beat.*)

Who am I?

(*Quiet.*)

Who are you?

(*Quiet.*)

Who are they?

(ATMA *points to the screen and the upstage left wall.*

Beat.)

Who are we?

(*Beat*

ATMA *crosses to* KAROMAN *and shakes his shoulder.*)

ATMA: Who are you really?

(*Beat.*)

ATMA: (*Impatient*) Answer!

KAROMAN: Shhh!

(*The table begins to move because something is pushing it from underneath. Everything falls onto the ground. The table falls apart. In a burst of smoke,* MOMOK OBLONGACHAK, *a gigantic, part-living, part-machine/robot creature, emerges from under the table, growling loudly. Its body is covered with an assortment of deadly weapons, including daggers, long swords, pistols, automatic rifles, cannons, grenades, mines, bombs etc. It also has fangs, talons, and a number of open threatening eyes.*)

MOMOK OBLONGACHAK: (*In a monstrous voice*) I exist in the minds of every living creature, including the minds of every human being. I am primitive thinking and also modern, ancient, and eternal, always ready, at any time through the ages, to destroy fellow living creatures, including human beings. I'm Momok Oblongachak-chak-chak-chak…

(*Offstage, the* VILLAGERS *chant "Momok Oblongachak-chak-chak-chak" solemnly in a low but clear tone. They enter carrying the* CORPSE *in a holy ceremonial procession. The* VILLAGERS *continue to chant.* MA OLONG, MORNI *and the* NARRATOR *accompany them.*

The VILLAGERS *come to a stop. They carefully lower the CORPSE. The burial ceremony begins.*

TUK SYAM *takes a number of guns from* MOMOK OBLONGACHAK *and distributes them to the* VILLAGERS. *Silence!*

KAROMAN *oversees the ceremony. He gives instructions, but only his mouth moves while no sound comes out. As if they had heard, the* VILLAGERS *carry out his instructions in an orderly fashion.* KAROMAN *conducts a ceremonial requiem. Only mouths move while no sound is heard. Silence!*

Time passes.

KAROMAN *presides over the final rites of honor for the* CORPSE, *giving silent instructions to the* VILLAGERS *to fire a salvo of shots. Silence! And then the salvo is fired!*

Time passes.

The VILLAGERS *rush to bury the* CORPSE.)

ATMA: Don't.... Don't.... Don't bury him in my head.... Don't.... Don't.... Don't.... Don't.... Don't.... Don't.

(*Meanwhile the* VILLAGERS *recite prayers near the* CORPSE*'s grave, still without making a sound.*

Time passes.

In slow motion, the VILLAGERS *stand up, raise their rifles, and aim them at* ATMA.

Lights slowly dim. Blackout.

Silence.)

THE END

How Could You Burn Down the Rainforest?

Production Notes

Ikranagara wrote *Kok Bisa-bisanya Sih Kau Bakar Hutan Itu?* (*How Could You Burn Down The Rainforest?*) in 1977. The first production was directed by Amoroso Katamsi, and performed by Teater Saja in Teater Tertutup, at Taman Ismail Marzuki, November 1–12, 1997 as part of a festival celebrating the 29th anniversary of the founding of Taman Ismail Marzuki in Jakarta.

Characters

ATMA, a playwright

CHAK BINJUN 1, a man

CHAK BINJUN 2, a man

SITI KUALA TAMASIK, a woman

VOICE

THE DIRECTOR

STAGEHANDS

Setting

Some place somewhere. In this place, there is a desk on which is placed piles of books and stacks of papers, as well as various stationery items such as pencils, pens, erasers, rulers, and the like. There is no typewriter, let alone a computer. In this place, there is also an easel with a canvas on it. Upstage, there is a door in a frame that can be reached by a short staircase. There are no walls. The background is black. The floor is black. Thus, the impression is that this place is floating in space.

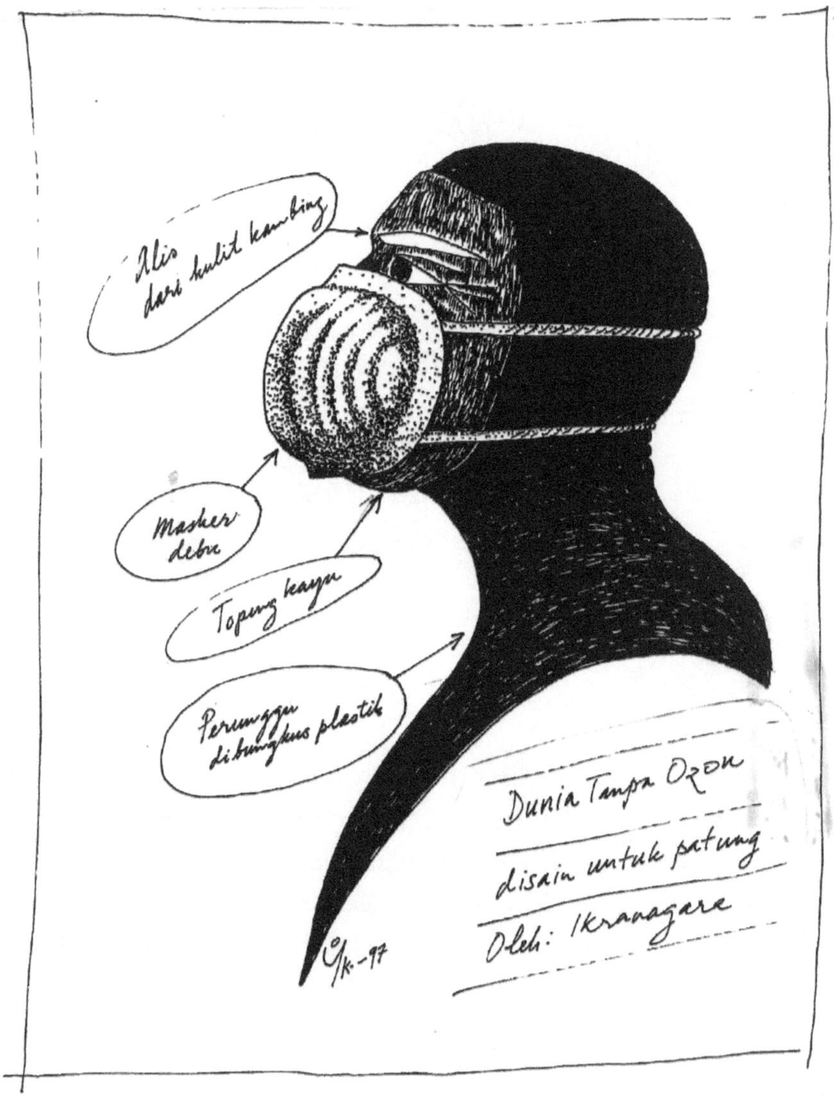
Alis
dari kulit kambing
Masker
debu
Topeng kayu
Perunggu
dibungkus plastik
Dunia Tanpa Ozon
disain untuk patung
Oleh: Ikranagara
IK.-97

1.

ATMA *sits on a chair facing the canvas on the easel. He's hidden from the audience by the canvas, which faces upstage so the audience can't see what's painted on it. Is it a painting in progress? Or perhaps there's no painting on the canvas at all? What's clearly seen are the easel,* ATMA's *feet, and the legs of the chair on which he sits, that's all.* ATMA *is barefoot. His sandals are nearby.*

Books and papers and stationery are stacked on the desk. Nothing moves. It is silent.

Time passes.

There's a knock at the door. ATMA's *feet search for his sandals. They find them and slip them on. Again, nothing moves. It is silent. There's another knock at the door. It's followed by a voice calling, "Atma...! Atma...!"*

ATMA *rises from his chair. Another knock at the door.*

ATMA: Hold on!

(*More knocking, louder.*)

ATMA: Yes! Just a minute! Oof!

(ATMA *walks toward the door and opens it.* CHAK BINJUN 1 *enters.*)

CHAK BINJUN 1: (*Hurriedly*) Well? Ready? Ready, ready, ready?

ATMA: (*Calmly*) Ready for what?

CHAK BINJUN 1: What do you mean? It should be ready, right?

ATMA: Okay, which one?

CHAK BINJUN 1: The play! Play, play, play!

ATMA: Which one? The translation? The adaptation? The revision?

CHAK BINJUN 1: The Ionesco! Ionesco, Ionesco, Ionesco!

ATMA: Yes! But translation takes a long time.

CHAK BINJUN 1: What? Didn't you say the other day that it was a short play?

ATMA: I was wrong.

CHAK BINJUN 1: So, it's long?

ATMA: It's not really long. But it can't be classified as a short play.

CHAK BINJUN 1: Well, then it's not right for the Short Play Festival! Can it be shortened? Can it? Can it, can it, can it?

ATMA: Well, it could, but it would lose a lot, even though it can't be classified as a long play.

CHAK BINJUN 1: It's not a long play? Then it's a short play!

ATMA: It's not truly long! But it can't be classified as a short play! Ah!

CHAK BINJUN 1: Can an adaptation be done faster, or not?

ATMA: Not! That takes longer than translating!

CHAK BINJUN 1: Well, then what? There's not much time left. When will we rehearse? When can we learn our lines?

ATMA: Patience, sit down.

CHAK BINJUN 1: (*Sits*) It won't be any good. Better to just drop out of the Festival!

ATMA: (*Searches for the right words*) Uh...

(ATMA *looks for the script in the pile of papers.*)

CHAK BINJUN 1: Um... by the way, have you worked on it or not?

(ATMA *finds the script.*)

ATMA: Okay, done!

CHAK BINJUN 1: Oh... if so, all is okay! We can start rehearsals right away!

ATMA: (*Searches for the right words*) Uh… it's not that easy.

CHAK BINJUN 1: Well, if the script is done, then—

ATMA: (*Interrupts*) It's done!

CHAK BINJUN 1: Then we can begin rehearsing, right?

ATMA: (*Searches for the right words*) Mmm… uh…

CHAK BINJUN 1: Um… by the way, about the script, which script is it? The translation? No? The adaptation? No? That other one, what did you call it?

ATMA: Uh, this is the revision. It isn't exactly Ionesco, but… mmm… uh… it's Ionesco! Only if you call it Ionesco… mmm… uh… it's not really!

CHAK BINJUN 1: Semi-Ionesco? Is that it?

ATMA: (*Stands up, searches for the right words*) Mmm… uh….

(ATMA *shakes his head.*)

CHAK BINJUN 1: Let me read it, please!

ATMA: Not yet! It still needs some fixing here and there.

CHAK BINJUN 1: Really? So how's that issue going?

ATMA: How's what going?

CHAK BINJUN 1: (*Searches the right words*) Uh…

ATMA: The title? Uh… here you go: "How Could You Burn Down The Rainforest?"

CHAK BINJUN 1: Which rainforest? When? Why the accusation? What business do I have with the rainforest?

ATMA: (*Laughs*) No! That is the title of my script! Here! Read this!

(ATMA *shows him the script.* CHAK BINJUN 1 *reads the title on the front page.*)

CHAK BINJUN 1:	But before you said the title was.... (*Tries to remember*) What was it?
ATMA:	"Improvisation or the Shepherd's Chameleon."
CHAK BINJUN 1:	Yes yes yes! Ionesco's work, right?
ATMA:	Exactly!
CHAK BINJUN 1:	But why… is the title different?
ATMA:	(*Points to the script*) Er, this is the revision.
CHAK BINJUN 1:	Let me read it!
ATMA:	Not yet. I still need to fix some things here and there!
CHAK BINJUN 1:	Oh, then it's not done yet! Will it take a long time?
ATMA:	No! Everything's fine. But I need to read it over again and make a few corrections here and there. Some of it is okay. I'll read the part that's already okay, okay? Listen carefully. This is the opening scene.
	(ATMA *gargles some water, swallows it, and begins to read from his play.*)
	Atma sits on a chair facing the canvas on the easel. He's hidden from the audience by the canvas, which faces upstage so the audience can't see what's painted on it. Is it a painting in progress? Or perhaps there's no painting on the canvas at all? What's clearly seen are the easel, Atma's feet, and the legs of the chair on which he sits, that's all. Atma is barefoot. His sandals are nearby.
	(*Beat.*)
	Books and papers and stationery are stacked on the desk.
	(*Beat.*)
	Nothing moves. It is silent. Time passes.

(*Beat.*)

There's a knock at the door.

(ATMA *mimes knocking on a door.*)

Atma's feet search for his sandals. They find them and slip them on.

(*Beat.*)

Again, nothing moves. It is silent.

2.

There's another knock at the door. It's followed by a voice calling, "Atma…! Atma…!"

ATMA *rises from his chair.*

Another knock at the door.

ATMA: Hold on!

(*More knocking, louder.*)

ATMA: Yes! Just a minute! Oof!

(ATMA *walks toward the door and opens it.* CHAK BINJUN 2 *enters.*)

CHAK BINJUN 2: (*Hurriedly*) Well? Ready? Ready, ready, ready?

ATMA: (*Calmly*) Ready for what?

CHAK BINJUN 2: What do you mean? It should be ready, right?

ATMA: Ok, which one?

CHAK BINJUN 2: The play! Play, play, play!

ATMA: Which one? The translation? The adaptation? The revision?

CHAK BINJUN 2: The Ionesco! Ionesco, Ionesco, Ionesco!

ATMA: Yes! But translation takes a long time.

CHAK BINJUN 2: What? Didn't you say the other day that it was a short play?

ATMA: I was wrong.

CHAK BINJUN 2: So, it's long?

ATMA: It's not really long. But it can't be classified as a short play.

CHAK BINJUN 2: Well, then it's not right for the Short Play Festival! Can it be shortened? Can it? Can it, can it, can it?

ATMA: Well, it could, but it would lose a lot, even though it can't be classified as a long play.

CHAK BINJUN 2: It's not a long play? Then it's a short play!

ATMA: It's not truly long! But it can't be classified as a short play! Ah!

CHAK BINJUN 2: Can an adaptation be done faster, or not?

ATMA: Not! That takes longer than translating!

CHAK BINJUN 2: Well, then what? There's not much time left. When will we rehearse? When can we learn our lines?

ATMA: Patience, sit down.

CHAK BINJUN 2: (*Sits*) It won't be any good. Better to just drop out of the Festival!

ATMA: (*Searches for the right words*) Uh…

(ATMA *looks for the script in the pile of papers.*)

CHAK BINJUN 2: Um… by the way, have you worked on it or not?

(ATMA *finds the script.*)

ATMA: Okay, done!

CHAK BINJUN 2: Oh… if so, all is okay! We can start rehearsals right away!

ATMA: (*Searches for the right words*) Uh… it's not that easy.

CHAK BINJUN 2: Well, if the script is done, then—

ATMA: (*Interrupts*) It's done!

CHAK BINJUN 2: Then we can begin rehearsing, right?

ATMA: (*Searches for the right words*) Mmm… uh…

CHAK BINJUN 2: Um… by the way, about the script, which script is it? The translation? No? The adaptation? No? That other one, what did you call it?

ATMA: Uh, this is the revision. It isn't exactly Ionesco, but… mmm… uh… it's Ionesco! Only if you call it Ionesco… mmm… uh… it's not really!

CHAK BINJUN 2: Semi-Ionesco? Is that it?

ATMA: (*Stands up, searches for the right words*) Mmm… uh…

(ATMA *shakes his head.*)

CHAK BINJUN 2: Let me read it, please!

ATMA: Not yet! It still needs some fixing here and there.

CHAK BINJUN 2: Really? So how's that issue going?

ATMA: How's what going?

CHAK BINJUN 2: (*Searches the right words*) Uh…

ATMA: The title? Uh… here you go: "How Could You Burn Down The Rainforest?"

CHAK BINJUN 2: Which rainforest? When? Why the accusation? What business do I have with the rainforest?

ATMA: (*Laughs*) No! That is the title of my script! Here! Read this!

(ATMA *shows him the script.* CHAK BINJUN 2 *reads the title on the front page.*)

CHAK BINJUN 2: But before you said the title was.... (*Tries to remember*) What was it?

ATMA: "Improvisation or the Shepherd's Chameleon."

CHAK BINJUN 2: Yes yes yes! Ionesco's work, right?

ATMA: Exactly!

CHAK BINJUN 2: But why... is the title different?

ATMA: (*Points to the script*) Er, this is the revision.

CHAK BINJUN 2: Let me read it!

ATMA: Not yet. I still need to fix some things here and there!

CHAK BINJUN 2: Oh, then it's not done yet! Will it take a long time?

ATMA: No! Everything's fine. But I need to read it over again, and make a few corrections here and there. Some of it is okay. I'll read the part that's already okay, okay? Listen carefully. This is the opening scene.

(ATMA *gargles some water and swallows it. He prepares to read from his play.*)

3.

A VOICE *is heard over a microphone.*

VOICE: Members of the audience, please remain in your seats. The performance will continue in a moment after these brief announcements.

(*Music plays to accompany the announcements. A banner flies in from above. It spans the stage from left to right and reads: "Everlast—No Fire Like It!"*)[10]

VOICE: "Everlast"! Essential tool for every corporate jungle prospector! Powered by sophisticated computer systems! Equipped with remote control! "Everlast" is our latest state-of-the art product to burn down the rainforest! Our motto is: "Use once, two to three forests gone!" "Everlast," the epitome of efficiency, modernization! "Everlast"—no fire like it!

(*More announcement music. Another banner flies in, spanning the stage from left to right with the message: "Haze—No Narcotic Like It."*)[11]

VOICE: "Haze." The latest national product. Smoke mixed with dust mixed with germs! Pure, made by burning virgin rainforest! "Haze!" Try it! Breathe deeply, a replacement for "Ecstasy!" "Haze!" Suck it in deep before hitting the dance floor! Guaranteed to retire your lungs in the near future! "Haze"—no narcotic like it!

(*Haze announcement music ends. The promotional ad program has ended.*

Time passes.)

4.

ATMA: (*Reading*) Atma sits on a chair facing the canvas on the easel. He's hidden from the audience by the canvas, which faces upstage so the audience can't see what's painted on it. Is it a painting in progress? Or perhaps there's no painting on the canvas at all? What's clearly seen are the easel, Atma's feet, and the legs of the chair on which he sits, that's all. Atma is barefoot. His sandals are nearby.

(*Beat.*)

Books and papers and stationery are stacked on the desk.

(*Beat.*)

Nothing moves. It is silent. Time passes.

(*Beat.*)

There's a knock at the door.

(ATMA *mimes knocking on a door.*)

Atma's feet search for his sandals. They find them and slip them on.

(*Beat.*)

Again, nothing moves. It is silent.

(*There is a knock on the door. It's followed by a voice calling, "Atma…! Atma…!"* ATMA *rises from his chair.* CHAK BINJUN 1 *blocks* ATMA *from moving.*)

CHAK BINJUN 1: Don't! Don't open that door! No! no, no, no!

ATMA: What? What's the matter?

CHAK BINJUN 2: (*To* CHAK BINJUN 1) Sorry, we haven't met yet.

CHAK BINJUN 1: Don't! Don't tell me who you are! I've already guessed! Don't, don't, don't!

CHAK BINJUN 2: What? What's wrong with my name? You think it's fake? (*Takes out his wallet, and shows his I.D.*) Here! It's the one on my ID! (*Takes out his driver's license*) And my driver's license! Passport! (*Looks in his jacket pocket*) Passport, passport, passport! (*To the audience*) Wait, who carries their passport in their own country? But it's the same name as on my passport. *(Takes out his credit card*) Here! Credit card! Look! (*To* CHAK BINJUN 1) Read it! Read it, read it, read it.

(*There's knock at the door.*)

ATMA: What about the door? Can we open it now or not?

CHAK BINJUN 1: (*To* ATMA) Don't! Don't open that door! (*To* CHAK BINJUN 2) I believe you! Put your cards back in your wallet! I believe you! You don't need to show proof! But I don't want to know your name! Don't tell me! This is crazy! Totally nuts!

CHAK BINJUN 2: Hey! Okay, you don't want to get acquainted, so instead you sling insults, saying it's all crazy, even though you don't even know me yet.

ATMA: Patience, patience, patience. God loves patient people, as elementary school children are taught to say by their religion teachers. Be patient!

CHAK BINJUN 1: (*To* CHAK BINJUN 2) You're not what's crazy! But this situation we're in! This crazy loop! I know your name without you telling me.

CHAK BINJUN 2: How?

ATMA: (*To the audience*) This is interesting! He's never met him, but he claims he's guessed his name! Interesting!

And even more interesting, he doesn't want to be told what his name is, and doesn't want to see his ID! That means he is sure, completely convinced! Interesting! But the most interesting thing is, he…

(ATMA *closely observes* CHAK BINJUN 1*'s face.*)

Why are you so scared, afraid of him?

(ATMA *points to* CHAK BINJUN 2.)

Is he…?

CHAK BINJUN 2: Afraid? Am I scary? (*Laughs, then to the audience*) This is the first time, in my entire life, that someone has been scared of me! Me?!! (*Laughs*) Besides, I've been mugged several times in my life, so I'm usually the one who's scared. (*To* CHAK BINJUN 1) Am I scary? Me? (*Laughs, then to the audience*) Bah! Acting like he can guess anything!

CHAK BINJUN 1: Your name is

(*Beat.*)

Chak Binjun!

(CHAK BINJUN 2 *is dumbfounded.*)

ATMA: (*To* CHAK BINJUN 2) What? Is that correct? Is your name really Chak Binjun?

(CHAK BINJUN 2 *is so stunned that he can't move. Even his breath is out of breath.*)

CHAK BINJUN 2: You… you...

(*He sits on the ground.* ATMA *quickly takes a glass of water from the table and gives it to* CHAK BINJUN 2. *His breathing calms after drinking the water.*)

CHAK BINJUN 2: Is this a holdup?

(*There's a knock at the door.* ATMA *turns to* CHAK BINJUN 1 *and gestures questions using his hands, face, and body.* CHAK BINJUN 1 *motions to* ATMA *not to open the door.* ATMA *doesn't open the door.*)

CHAK BINJUN 1: Me? A mugger? What! That's crazy! Nutso, nutso, nutso!

CHAK BINJUN 2: But everyone who has ever held me up knew my name even before I told them.

CHAK BINJUN 1: What the…?!

ATMA: (*To the audience*) This is very interesting! Especially if he's a real mugger, and this is a holdup! Ooh! Fun! (*Laughs*) But we're both screwed! Ugh. Now what? I just let him in, even though I didn't know him, I just let him in because he knocked on my door, called my name, and I opened it so he could come in. (*Looks at* CHAK BINJUN 1) Why did I do that?

CHAK BINJUN 1: (*Points at* ATMA) This is nuts! I'm being forced to explain a lot of stuff here! As I said before, this is crazy, it's a vicious cycle. You, me and him, all of us, are being controlled by an external mechanical force! And now, I'm even suspected of being a mugger! Nuts, nuts, nuts!

CHAK BINJUN 2: But, you're not a thief, are you?

CHAK BINJUN 1: Man! Why ask like that? Why begin with the word "but"! That means you're still suspicious! Damn it! (*Tries to control his breathing*) Want to know my name?

ATMA and CHAK BINJUN 2: Yes!

CHAK BINJUN 1: My name.... (*He pauses a moment, but doesn't continue. He turns to address the audience.*) It's important to pause for a moment. (*Points to* ATMA) Now you, the playwright, are definitely aware of this. (*Turns back to the audience*) The momentary pause heightens dramatic tension! The audience is forced to wait. And the wait puts the audience on edge! (*Laughs*) My name is...

(*Beat.*)

Chak Binjun!

(ATMA *and* CHAK BINJUN 2 *are dumbfounded.* CHAK BINJUN 1 *laughs in surprise.*)

ATMA and CHAK BINJUN 2: (*Let out sighs of relief*) Oh my God! (*Laugh.*)

ATMA: The problem is, if I've made a mistake and he really is an armed robber, uh, one of our scenes will turn out to be like a scene from one of those savage soap operas!

(ATMA *and* CHAK BINJUN 2 *laugh out loud.*)

CHAK BINJUN 1: (*Snaps*) That's not what is going on here!

(ATMA *and* CHAK BINJUN 2 *are silent.*)

But, your name (*points to* CHAK BINJUN 2) is the same as mine, that's what scares me. Because that means we're caught in a vicious cycle! What you've done, what you've said since you knocked on the door, until he (*points to* ATMA) read the opening scene of his play, is exactly what I did and said. He also (*points to* ATMA) did and said exactly the same words! That means everything from the beginning has been repeated, it means... (*feels horrified*) it's cycling! And we've done it all without being aware of it! (*More horrified*) We've become part of a machine driven by an outside force! (*Full of dread*) A vicious cycle! This is a vicious cycle! (*Gasps*) Do you get it?

ATMA and CHAK BINJUN 2: Got it!

CHAK BINJUN 1: (*Irritated*) You say you get it! You get it! But do you two feel what I feel?

ATMA: (*Not quite understanding*) What do you feel?

CHAK BINJUN 2: Yes! What?

CHAK BINJUN 1: This!

(*He expresses his feelings of horror wordlessly with hand gestures, body and facial tension with his mouth stretched wide and eyes bugging out.* ATMA *and* CHAK BINJUN 2 *look at each other, confused.*)

Well?

CHAK BINJUN 2: (*To* ATMA) Well?

ATMA: (*To* CHAK BINJUN 1) Honestly, it's hard to understand what you're saying!

CHAK BINJUN 2: (*Adds*) It would be better to use words.

ATMA: (*Adds*) So it would be easier to understand.

CHAK BINJUN 2: (*Adds*) Even though words have a limited ability to express feelings.

ATMA: (*Adds*) Correct! In fact, many things are better communicated without words.

CHAK BINJUN 2: (*Adds*) That's why there are painters!

ATMA: (*Adds*) There are dancers!

CHAK BINJUN 2: (*Adds*) There are mimes!

ATMA: (*Adds*) There are faces!

CHAK BINJUN 2: (*Adds*) There are hands!

ATMA: (*Adds*) There are bodies—

CHAK BINJUN 1: (*Interrupts*) Correct! Exactly, exactly, exactly! Isn't that what I was doing, using my face, as well as my mouth, hands, and body? Get it?

(ATMA *and* CHAK BINJUN 2 *look at each other.*)

Well?

ATMA: No change!

CHAK BINJUN 2: Same here, no change!

CHAK BINJUN 1: You're both still the same, but why no change?

ATMA: Uh...

(ATMA *walks while searching for the right words.*)

CHAK BINJUN 2: Mmm...

(CHAK BINJUN 2 *walks while searching for the right words. Another knock at the door. All eyes turn toward the door. Nothing moves. There is no sound.*

Time passes.

The three of them look at each other.)

CHAK BINJUN 1: (*Anxious from the mystery*) If you open it, the vicious cycle will repeat itself. The one who enters will also be named… Chak Binjun! Once he's here, there will be another knock, and new Chak Binjun will enter again, again, and again, and on, and on! Their numbers will steadily increase. The forward momentum will be unstoppable! This place will be packed with Chak Binjun 1, Chak Binjun 2, Chak Binjun 3, Chak Binjun 4, Chak Binjun 10, Chak Binjun the 100th, Chak Binjun the 500th, Chak Binjun the 1000th, Chak Chak Chak Chak Chak…![12]

ATMA, CHAK BINJUN 1 and 2: Chak Chak Chak Chak…Chak Binjun Chak Chak Chak Binjun Binjun Binjun Chak Chak Chak…

(*The chorus "Chak Chak Chak. Chak…Chak Binjun Chak Chak Chak Binjun Binjun Binjun Chak Chak Chak…" echoes and reverberates repeatedly from all directions.*)

CHAK BINJUN 1: (*Interlocks with the "Chak Chak Chak Chak…" chorus as it continues*) Imagine! You should feel it now, if all that happens.

(*Beat.*)

We won't be able to escape the vicious cycle if you open that door! We'll live jostling each other, elbowing each other, up against each other, squeezing each other, grabbing each other… chaos, chaos, chaos! Where will we get food and shelter for millions of Chak Binjuns? Where will they piss and shit? Not to mention, how to handle it when millions of Chak Binjuns fart? Can you imagine the global catastrophe that will befall our room? Can you feel all that now?

(*There is a knock at the door.*)

CHAK BINJUN 2: (*To* ATMA) I can feel it now! This is it! This!

(*He expresses his feelings with hand gestures, body tension, and an expression of horror on his face, without sound, even though his mouth is agape.*

There is a knock at the door.)

ATMA: Yes! Yes, yes, yes! I feel it too, just like that. Like this! This!

(*He expresses his feelings with hand gestures, body tension, and an expression of horror on his face, without sound, even though his mouth is agape.*

There is knocking at the door, loud and insistent.

ATMA, CHAK BINJUN 1, *and* CHAK BINJUN 2 *each express their feelings with hand gestures, body tension, and expressions of horror on their faces, without sound, even though their mouths are agape.*)

5.

Lights out, except for one focused on ATMA, CHAK BINJUN 1, *and* CHAK BINJUN 2, *and one focused on the doorway. Passing sounds of an airplane, a ship, a train, and a speeding, out-of-control car. Then the door is violently smashed open, followed by the deafening sounds of a plane crash, ships colliding, a train wreck, a car crash, and the victims' screams! The thunderous sounds not only fill the stage, but envelop the entire audience. Meanwhile,* ATMA, CHAK BINJUN 1, *and* CHAK BINJUN 2 *become more intensely focused on physically expressing their feelings.*

At last, the door has been forced open! Thick smoke fills the doorway. A strobe light illuminates the upstage area giving the impression of a raging fire. All sounds subside except for the sound of crackling flames. A woman, SITI KUALA TAMASIK, *stands boldly in the doorway between the smoke and the licking flames behind. She holds a large flashlight in each hand. She focuses her flashlights on* ATMA, CHAK BINJUN 1 *and* CHAK BINJUN 2. *They immediately freeze facing the door.*

Time passes.

ATMA: (*Anxious*) Is your name also…

CHAK BINJUN 1: (*Puts his hand on* ATMA*'s shoulder*) Don't ask about names!

CHAK BINJUN 2: (*Puts his hand on* CHAK BINJUN 1*'s shoulder*) It won't change anything! Whether you ask or not, their name is their name. It would be better to know than not.

(*Gestures to* ATMA *to continue.*)

ATMA: Is your name also—

CHAK BINJUN 2: (*Interrupts impatiently*) Chak Binjun?

(SITI KUALA TAMASIK *doesn't immediately answer.*

Nothing moves. No sound.

Time passes.)

SITI KUALA TAMASIK: I don't know that name!

(ATMA, CHAK BINJUN 1 *and* CHAK BINJUN 2 *look at each other and then embrace happily.*)

ATMA, CHAK BINJUN 1, and CHAK BINJUN 2: We're free! We're free! The vicious cycle is over! Freedom! Independence!

(*They dance around the desk.*)

Come on! Three cheers for happiness!

(ATMA *climbs up on the chair and puts one foot on the desk.*)

ATMA: (*To* CHAK BINJUN 1) You were right! If I had opened the door, I would have repeated everything we did and said, like what happened between you and me (*To* CHAK BINJUN 2) and also between me and you! Accursed vicious cycle!

(ATMA *gets down and speaks directly to the audience.*)

Hey! But some say vicious cycles are what is called "the dialectic"! Damn you, "the dialectic"!

CHAK 1 and 2: Called the what?

ATMA: Ach, it's not important. Shakespeare once said, "What's in a name?" (*Laughs*) The point is, death to "the dialectic!"

CHAK 1 and 2: (*Follow along*) Death to "the dialectic"!

ATMA: "The dialectic" is a myth!

CHAK 1 and 2: "The dialectic" is a myth!

(*The three of them express their joy for a while by dancing and singing, laughing and hollering. Eventually, they become exhausted.*

Time passes.)

SITI KUALA TAMASIK: Who's the owner of this place?

ATMA: (*Holding up his index finger*) Me!

CHAK 1 and 2: Yes, him, he's the one.

SITI KUALA TAMASIK: Why didn't you answer my telegram?

ATMA: Oh! You're the one who sent the telegram? So you're Siti Kuala Tamasik? But you didn't include your address with the telegram.

SITI KUALA TAMASIK: My address isn't important! What's important is that you had to answer it!

ATMA: Why should I? Anyway, I think you sent your telegram to the wrong address.

SITI KUALA TAMASIK: The telegram is indeed for you, and you should have answered it!

ATMA: So, you're accusing me of something?

SITI KUALA TAMASIK: Stupid! Read the telegram again, carefully.

CHAK BINJUN 2: (*To* CHAK BINJUN 1) Yikes! She's fierce!

ATMA: I know your telegram by heart. Chak Binjun does too!

CHAK BINJUN 1: Huh? What telegram?

CHAK BINJUN 2: Uh-uh, don't involve me.

ATMA: That one, from earlier!

CHAK BINJUN 2: Which one? (*To* CHAK BINJUN 1) Did you see a telegram?

CHAK BINJUN 1: No, never!

ATMA: Ah, shush!

CHAK 1 and 2: Huh?!

ATMA: I told both of you the title of my play. Remember?

CHAK 1 and 2: Uh-huh! Yup!

ATMA: The title is the telegram!

CHAK 1 and 2: "How could you burn down the rainforest?"

ATMA: Hey! Don't you two accuse me as well! Damn!

CHAT BINJUN 1: I mean, that's the title of your play, right?

ATMA: (*Annoyed*) Yes! But be careful how you say it. Don't make it seem like I'm the person who burned down the rainforest! Ah, this is messed up!

CHAK BINJUN 2: It's not like that, man! It's just the title!

SITI KUALA TAMASIK: (*Curtly*) That's what my telegram said!

CHAK 1 and 2: Ooh…!

SITI KUALA TAMASIK: (*Assertively*) Yes!

ATMA: There! It's obvious, right? This telegram came to the wrong address! Why should it be sent to me? Did I burn down the rainforest? Come on! I've never even been to a rainforest, unless you mean the urban concrete jungle, that's different! But you don't mean the concrete jungle, do you?

SITI KUALA TAMASIK: No!

CHAK BINJUN 2: The urban concrete jungle was burned down by the White Monkey King Hanoman!

CHAK BINJUN 1: That was the Kingdom of Alengka!

SRI KUALA TAMASIK: That's part of the *Ramayana* epic! A legend! The forests I'm talking about are real wild rainforests, the lungs of life on our earth, where fewer animals and trees now live!

CHAK BINJUN 1: Oh, that's Hanoman's jungle.

CHAK BINJUN 2: (*Speaks as if a puppeteer performing a shadow puppet show, including the sound of a hammer hitting a wooden box*) Tok, tok-tok-tok-tok tok! Because his rainforests were burned down, Hanoman came to the city of Alengka.

(CHAK BINJUN 1 *dances or mimes the role of Hanoman. His movements follow the rhythm of* CHAK BINJUN 2*'s shadow play narration and the "tok-tok-toks."*)

CHAK BINJUN 2: Tok, tok-tok-tok-tok, tok! Beware, beware, beware, beware! Hanoman has taken a torch from the municipal stadium! With this torch, he burns down the entire city! It is said he's aided by hooligans and street punks, frustrated because their soccer club lost the competition! Tok, tok-tok-tok-tok, tok!

CHAK BINJUN 1: (*Stops miming Hanoman*) Wait! Mr. Puppeteer, Mr. Puppeteer! Why did Hanoman burn down the city? Were the ones who burned down Hanoman's rainforest from Alengka? I heard it was burned down by trespassers to create new fields for farming.

CHAK BINJUN 2: (*As puppeteer*) Know this... eee... know this, you in the audience! According to the teller of this story, those encroaching on the rainforest these days are ordinary urban dwellers wearing ties and carrying cell phones! Tok, tok-tok-tok-tok, tok!

(CHAK BINJUN 2 *mimes someone putting on a tie and carrying a cell phone.*)

The people wearing ties and carrying cell phones come from the city of Alengka! Tok, tok-tok-tok-tok, tok!

(CHAK 1 *and* 2 *dance to the "Tok, tok-tok-tok-tok, tok" rhythm with much merriment.* SITI KUALA TAMASIK *strides up to them.*)

SITI KUALA TAMASIK: (*Offended*) You think the burning forests are just a myth like the *Ramayana*? Don't you smell the smoke?

CHAK BINJUN 1: Well, I don't smell smoke. I only see the fires on TV.

CHAK BINJUN 2: How can we smell smoke on TV?

CHAK BINJUN 1: It's possible!

CHAK BINJUN 2: Oh please!

CHAK BINJUN 1: Well, if the television catches on fire, the flames will produce smoke, right?

(CHAK 1 *and* 2 *laugh and high five each other.* SITI KUALA TAMASIK *moves in closer.*)

SITI KUALA TAMASIK: (*Offended*) Stupid! Stupid! Stupid! Stupid![13] Not funny. This is a serious issue. The smoke from the burning rainforests is not only eroding the ozone, but it's also eroding our lungs breathing that smoke! Everyday life has been destroyed! Our children have lost their smiles and joyful laughter! This is a national disaster in our country! So, you must answer that telegram!

ATMA: But as I said, the contents of your telegram accuses me of burning down the rainforests.

(*He sits on the chair near the desk.*)

And that's not true!

CHAK BINJUN 1: Not true at all!

CHAK BINJUN 2: We are witnesses!

SITI KUALA TAMASIK: You all misunderstand the meaning of my telegram! Actually the telegram was inspired by the title of a poem by Agus R. Sardjono, one of our national poets. Since you are an artist, you are responsible for answering, "How could you burn down the rainforest?" Of course, those responsible for the forest fires aren't artists, not you, nobody except for the ones who actually set fire to the rainforest! The sentence, "How could you burn down the rainforest?" is directed at whomever burned them down. They're the first. Secondly, it's directed at anyone who's benefitted from the rainforest business. But… artists?

(*Beat.*)

Artists must answer, not by answering my telegram with a telegram, but with creative works! (*Takes a step*) Art! (*Points her finger at* ATMA) If you aren't willing to answer it, then where is your moral commitment as an artist? (*Turns to the audience*) I'm not recommending artists create works of *normative functionalism* that include instructions for this or that, or try to teach this or that, let alone involve protest or propaganda for this or that. And I don't mean artists should create their work as *craft*, no. But they could be works of *descriptive functionalism*, so that in addition to maintaining their artistic value, they could be meaningful with a depth of vision, taking a complex approach to issues rather than being black and white and simplistic. (*To* ATMA) I know it isn't easy to create such works! (*Approaches the desk*) But do you, as an artist, just want to write easy things, like most of the soap operas broadcast on thousands of tv channels around the world? (*To the audience*) Being an artist is indeed a heavy burden. What can we do? Artists are God's chosen ones, they are given special talents. It's up to the will and readiness of artists like you to carry out the holy mandate given to you by God! (*To* ATMA*)* See? (*Moves closer to the desk*) Is the telegram's request too weighty? Was it sent to the wrong address? (*Quiet for a moment, then hits the desk*) Well? (*Trying to control her heavy breathing*) Sorry, I'm getting emotional.

(CHAK BINJUN 1 *gives a glass of water to* SITI KUALA TAMASIK. *She drinks.*

Time passes.)

SITI KUALA TAMASIK: I can't stay here for long.

(SITI KUALA TAMASIK *walks toward the door.* ATMA, CHAK BINJUN 1 *and* CHAK BINJUN 2 *follow her.* SITI KUALA TAMASIK *stops and turns to face the others because she has something more to say.*)

I have to meet my son and husband who have been forced to flee abroad because of the thick smoke covering our city for the past several weeks. They've both developed asthma. Several years ago, my husband's late parents, my in-laws, died from complications due to asthma. My husband was traumatized by what happened. That's why he's leaving so quickly, to get away from the smoke! My apologies if this feels very personal. (*Beat*) The two of them are now on board a ship in your city harbor. The three of us are on our way south, by ship, because we're worried the plane may get into an accident because of the heavy smoke. We don't want to be victims! (*Beat*) I actually didn't want to tell you all this, but my husband and son are now in the care of the ship's doctor because, besides asthma, they have eye infections and itchy skin rashes from the smoke. Polluted smoke! We have a special name for this kind of smoke: haze!

CHAK BINJUN 2: What's it called?

SITI KUALA TAMASIK: Haze!

CHAK BINJUN 2: Haze.

SITI KUALA TAMASIK: Our ship sails tomorrow, so I took the opportunity to come to your city and meet you, and to specifically ask you about the telegram. Why hadn't you answered? But it's up to you, it's your right, and I don't mean to force you! I apologize if it seems like I was lecturing you. I only intended to explain the meaning of my telegram that you chose not to answer. That's all, nothing more! I'm not an artist. I am an ordinary person who loves art and reads literary theory as a hobby. My apologies.

(SITI KUALA TAMASIK *exits through the door.* ATMA *moves closer to the painting.*)

6.

CHAK BINJUN 1: (*Holds back tears*) I'm sorry for her... and sorry for her husband... sorry for her son... the children... sorry for them... all of them. I can feel... still.... We... all of us... how could... we... how... we as a nation... how... and I... I... oh... how could...

(CHAK BINJUN 2 *begins to cross toward* CHAK BINJUN 1. ATMA *continues to stare at the painting.* CHAK BINJUN 1 *pulls a gun out from under his jacket.* CHAK BINJUN 2 *sees the gun and is startled and frightened. He keeps on moving to distance himself.* ATMA *does the same.*)

CHAK BINJUN 2: (*Afraid*) So… it's true… you…

CHAK BINJUN 1: Yes, I'm a mugger.

(*Shows his gun.*)

I came here to use this to rob you.

(CHAK BINJUN 2 *moves away from* CHAK BINJUN 1.)

CHAK BINJUN 2: Don't! Don't shoot me! Here! Take my money! (*He hands over his wallet. He is panting.*) Take my money. It's not much.

(ATMA *gives a glass of water to* CHAK BINJUN 2.)

ATMA: Don't shoot us!

CHAK BINJUN 2: (*To* ATMA) Please give him what's in my wallet, so we don't get shot! Give it to him!

ATMA: (*Nervous and frightened*) Yes, yes, yes, give it to him, give it to him! Your money or your life!

CHAK BINJUN 2: We'll just give him money, not our lives!

ATMA: Yes, no, not life! Just money! Yes! Yes yes yes!

CHAK BINJUN 2: Hurry up! Oh, man! Give it to him!

ATMA: Yes! Yes yes yes!

(ATMA *puts the wallet near* CHAK BINJUN 1, *then moves away quickly.*)

Don't shoot us! I'm terrified of weapons! Allergic to them! But I… I don't have a wallet! Oh! Uh uh uh! I'm at a loss! The only valuable thing here… is just… just… I mean that you could sell… just… just… this glass… this chair… desk… uh, that! My painting! (*As he moves toward his painting*) But it's just the one painting. The only one I've ever made. Just one! I was planning to exhibit it in a solo show, a show with just one painting, this one painting of mine. But it's hard to find a sponsor to finance space rental and so on. The sponsors all asked for about thirty paintings or more for a single exhibition. To mount an exhibition, one has to find a cabinet minister, one that has rich business clients. That's so the minister can fleece the rich. The exhibition opening has to wow and be luxurious! It has to feel like the stock exchange, to have a commercial atmosphere, buying and selling. The painting will be guaranteed to sell for as much as possible. But I don't want to sell this painting. This painting is very personal to me besides being the result of my moral commitment to our shared humanity. Its theme is the burning of the rainforest and the haze. You'll be able to sell this painting, believe me.

CHAK BINJUN 2: Painting? The burning of the rainforest? Haze? (*Moves in front of painting*) That means you already answered Siti Kuala Tamasik's telegram! Why didn't you show her this painting?

ATMA: The problem is that I painted it long before I received her telegram! So it's not an answer to her telegram!

CHAK BINJUN 2: Meh, it's all the same! Don't be so hard and fast with logic!

(*Moves closer to* CHAK BINJUN 1.)

Please, don't take the painting. It's the answer to Siti Kuala Tamasik's telegram. Let the painting be exhibited. I'll give you more money later. I can get it from the bank.

ATMA: Yes! Yes yes yes! I'd also like to ask you to allow the painting to be exhibited, and after that you can sell it and keep the money for yourself.

CHAK BINJUN 1: (*Tears up*) I'm sorry, friends. I'm a wicked person. I'm a thug. I started out as a good person. I finished my studies. I graduated from college. But even with a degree, I was unemployed. I couldn't find a job. My circumstances made me do whatever I could for food. It was purely for my stomach! I was hungry! I did whatever I could to fill my empty stomach, including holding people up. (*Holds back tears*) But I've never fired a shot, let alone hurt or killed anyone. This gun is just a kid's toy!

ATMA: (*Taking the gun from* CHAK BINJUN 1*'s hand*) Damn it! A toy gun!

CHAK BINJUN 2: (*Taking the gun from* ATMA*'s hand*) Damn it! A toy gun! It's broken too.

ATMA: (*Giving the wallet back to* CHAK BINJUN 2) You don't need to give your wallet to this loser!

CHAK BINJUN 2: And you don't need to give your painting to this loser! Hey! I'll sponsor your solo painting exhibition. Agreed?

ATMA: (*Happily shaking* CHAK BINJUN 2*'s hand*) In total agreement! Thank you! (*To* CHAK BINJUN 1) Damn it!

CHAK BINJUN 2: So?

ATMA: So what?

CHAK BINJUN 2: What are we going to do with this loser?

ATMA: I write plays. Um… I can only answer from the point of view of a playwright. If this were a folk play from Jakarta, like *lenong*, there would be two ways to end this performance. This kind of person usually recognizes his wrong-doings, is forgiven, and then offered good advice. Second—

CHAK BINJUN 2: Hold on! Why did you use the phrase, "this kind of person"? Do mean he's a kind of symbol? Ah… I get it now. So, surely you're being sarcastic… right?

ATMA: (*Laughs*) Huh? You think there's some hidden meaning?

CHAK BINJUN 2: Judging from your word choice and arrangement, along with the way you spoke, it feels like you're making fun of us as a people, a nation that must atone, a nation humiliated by its own behavior, a doomed nation. So, uh… we have to undertake… a kind of national atonement! Is that it?

ATMA: Call it what you want! National atonement—

CHAK BINJUN 2: A nationalization of atonement?

ATMA: (*Joins*) Global atonement? (*Self-importantly*) A globalization of atonement to welcome the era of globalization in the twenty-first century.

CHAK BINJUN 2: Hey… watch out or someone will use it to their advantage! The era of globalization is the era of free trade, right? If not vigilant, atonement could become a commodity traded on the free market!

ATMA: (*Seriously*) Obviously, that would be immoral!

CHAK BINJUN 2: What do you mean? Sheesh! Since when has the free market ever been moral! (*Bellows*) The strong swallow the weak! (*Laughs*) Hard to believe? (*Bellows*) Ask Soros! Hey, uh, by the way, why did you make him (*Points at* CHAK BINJUN 1) a symbol of our nation?

ATMA: (*Laughs*) He's a kind of symbol! Clearly not a perfect one, but, more or less! So, even though he (*Points to* CHAK BINJUN 1) doesn't have a logging concession, he's a symbol of the motivation that gives rise to reprehensible behavior in our country, well… uh… it could work!

CHAK BINJUN 2: (*Teasingly*) I could go along with that idea! (*Laughs*) And, the second one?

ATMA: (*Laughing*) Well, the second one! To end this performance, we would hand over "this kind of person" to the police. The police would arrest him and send him to prison.

CHAK BINJUN 2: *Lenong* plays are usually like that?

ATMA: *Lenong* plays are usually like that.

CHAK BINJUN 2: Wait a minute! If we detained all these symbols, well… our prisons would be packed!

(*They both laugh. Suddenly,* CHAK BINJUN 1 *exits in a hurry.* ATMA *and* CHAK BINJUN 2 *can only stare after him. All lights go out onstage except for one spotlight on ATMA, focused on his face and shoulders.*)

ATMA: Huh! This is not what usually happens in a *lenong* play…

(CHAK BINJUN 2 *quickly exits in the darkness through the broken-down door.*)

7.

ATMA *is alone on the stage.*

ATMA: But can a play like this actually have an end?

(*The play's* DIRECTOR *enters.*)

DIRECTOR: (*As he enters*) Stop stop stop!

(ATMA *is stunned! At the same time, several* STAGEHANDS *also enter. Some begin to fix the broken door, others tidy up the stage so that it is back to the state it was at the beginning of the performance.*)

DIRECTOR: This performance is over.

ATMA: What! When?

DIRECTOR: Just then!

ATMA: Just then when?

DIRECTOR: When you said your line "Huh! This is not what usually happens in a *lenong* play…." That's the end of the play.

ATMA: How can you say that?

DIRECTOR: I'm the director!

ATMA: Yes, I know, you're the director. But don't just make arbitrary cuts like that! That's not okay in front of an audience! Really, what's going on?

DIRECTOR: I have nothing to do with whatever comes after that line! As far as I'm concerned, the performance is over! Period! The end!

(*The* DIRECTOR *starts to exit, chased by* ATMA.)

ATMA: Just a minute! Just a minute, just a minute, just a minute!

DIRECTOR: (*Stopping Briefly*) I don't need any argument from you! If you want to continue a performance that's already over, that's up to you! Just say it's an epilogue! Or whatever! Up to you! I have nothing more to do with it! Period!

(*The* DIRECTOR *briskly exits. The* STAGEHANDS *also exit.*)

ATMA: Hey hey hey… you're all…. Why? Hey! How come I've been left all alone here! Hey… don't go! (*Toward where the* DIRECTOR *exited*) Just because you're the director! Does he think he has the right to berate actors! Lowlife! All directors are the same! Don't bring your personal issues from home and take them out on the actors! Directors are human beings too, right. As a human being—

DIRECTOR: (*From offstage*) Stop, stop stop!

ATMA: (*Taken aback*) Huh? Now what? Stop stop to your heart's content!

DIRECTOR: (*Offstage, emotional*) Don't you bring my personal life into this! I know your babble will eventually describe me not just as a director, but as some kind of symbol. You really are a sly one! Smuggler! Rebel! Insurgent! This performance is over! Period! Period period period period!

ATMA: (*Grumbles to himself*) Why be afraid of symbols? What's wrong with this individual? Unseemly. What kind of a director acts like that?

(*Shrilly, toward the* DIRECTOR *offstage*) Yes, I am an actor! But, I'm also a spectator. As long as I'm acting onstage, then my double, me in my imagination, sits in the audience. Can you picture that or not? My double isn't just a spectator, but also controls my acting! Your job as director ended when the performance began, and that's when my double's job starts, taking your place! He acts as my puppeteer! Is that wrong? It's a fact! That's what happens and it's always like that! So don't think you're entitled to do or say whatever you want *just because.*

(*No longer toward offstage*) It's up to him if he wants to call it an epilogue, whatever! I'm going to keep going! This performance isn't over! Not yet! Not at all! He doesn't get that the performance isn't over for my double in the audience.

(*Toward the* DIRECTOR *offstage*) Obscene! I'm getting worked up! Don't you say just because, just because you're the director!

(*No longer toward offstage*) This performance has expanded! The stage has globalized!

(*Beat.*)

Yeah, sure, if you want to end it with that sentence, you can. But that's actively ending it. That means, it was wasn't really the actual end in the sense of a true ending. An engineered ending. Is everything to be engineered? What kind of culture is this? This is art, not technology! To *end*, we must get to *the end of the endpoint.* A point that's actually a point! To be concrete: the end of the endpoint is death. Death! And death on a global scale! The globalization of death! The terrible endpoint! I can feel it in my pores, pumping a cold sweat all over my body. Look at my hands, wet! My face, wet! Because this performance is continuing to the actual endpoint of the end! The endpoint is before us and the wheels of time drive us ever closer! We are now all acting out this *epilogue* together on the stage that we call the surface of our beloved earth! Don't forget that *we're all in this together*. It's not only performed by all humankind, but by all living creatures, animals and plants, seen and unseen, that exist on our earth. A colossal stage! (*Beat*) And the problem that *we all together* face is the *air* on which *we all together* depend. The *atmosphere*!

(*Changes position*) The atmosphere that has wrapped the earth in blue for who knows how long, that makes our planet, the light blue planet, beautiful in the eyes of all the planets and stars scattered throughout the universe! (*Awestruck*) How beautiful is this blue planet! Extraordinary! Almighty God! Your gifts are spectacularly beautiful! Glory be to God! Yaa… God The Most Merciful… aaa… aaa… aaa—

(*Breaks off*) But the light blue now appears to be disappearing little by little. It will eventually lose all its beautiful blue color. It's turning gray! More gray. The gray is getting thicker and thicker! Gray! (*Howls to the sky*) Gray!

(*Beat.*)

The Light Blue will end up as The Old Gray. Haze.

(*Bitterly*) Our cursed hands, hands that have become claws, claws in the form factory chimneys, in the form of exhaust spewed out of the asses of vehicles, claws that become the CFCs to keep refrigerators cold and to cool our rooms with air-conditioning, claws that become hairspray in beauty salons, claws that gush out from our nuclear reactors as brutal waste that can't be tamed. It is these hands of ours that not only spill the blood of our fellow creatures, but also destroy the earth, destroy the atmosphere, and ruin our environment! Our hands have also spread fires to burn down the rainforest, to set fire to the peatlands!

(*Bitterly*) It is us, with these hands morphed into formidable claws that tear the ozone, tear out the lungs of our fellow human-beings, tear apart everyday life, and rip the smiles off the tiny faces of our children, as well as from our grandchildren who will come to inhabit this earth. The damage we continue to inflict from day to day, from year to year, from decade to decade, will continuously stealthily accumulate until it reaches a point, the actual endpoint of this global stage performance entitled "Doomsday"!

(*Beat.*)

At that time, the sun will no longer be a friend and a blessing for our grandchildren—but their doom, a terrible fate that befalls them. Sunlight no longer as we know it, no longer a blessing, but instead something to be avoided because of the threat of UV radiation against which there's no protection because the ozone shield has been ripped to shreds and left powerless.

(*Bitterly*) Our children's lives will be deplorable. They won't be able to reside on the Earth's surface. To be safe, they'll have to live like worms, sheltering under the soil. We'll be no different than zombies living in an entombed city, even if we do possess sophisticated dwelling technology! (*Beat*) That is the stage upon which our collective descendants will act when they reach the end of the final endpoint, the point of global total haze! Horrendous!

(*Changes position*) Yes, yes, yes.... Some say humans are creative creatures! (*Smiles cynically*) Creativity? (*Laughs bitterly*) Have we forgotten the old saying, "No use crying over spilled milk"?

(ATMA *laughs uncontrollably, ending with a grimace full of pain.*)What creativity... in what field... can invent a time machine so we can turn back time? The milk has already been spilled... the milk has already been spilled... milk... not just any kind of milk, but the milk of last resort that brings disaster whether you drink it or not. Our grandchildren and great-grandchildren will need thousands of spacecraft, giant rockets to evacuate this galaxy and find a new planet where they can live. But as long as they are merely human... humans just like us, as we are... they will repeat the atrocity... the vicious cycle that will come knocking at their door... and... (*Walks over to the painting on the easel*) the milk has already been spilled... the milk of last resort... spilled milk... milk... milk...

(*When he arrives in front of the painting,* ATMA *examines it carefully. He still mouths the words, "the milk of last resort... spilled milk... spilled milk..." but no sound comes out. Nothing moves. It is silent.*

Time passes.

He lifts the canvas from the easel. He studies it. ATMA *stands so that he's hidden by the canvas, the back of which faces the spectators so they cannot see what, if anything, is painted on it. Nothing moves. It is silent.*

Time passes.

ATMA *returns the canvas to the easel.* ATMA *sits on a chair facing the canvas on the easel. He's hidden from the audience by the canvas, which faces upstage so the audience can't see what's painted on it. Is it a painting in progress? Or perhaps there's no painting on the canvas at all? What's clearly seen are the easel,* ATMA*'s feet, and the legs of the chair on which he sits, that's all.* ATMA *is barefoot. His sandals are nearby. Nothing moves. It is silent.*

Time passes.

There's a knock at the door. ATMA *does not get up from his chair. More knocking at the door, louder, repeatedly from all directions enveloping the stage as well as surrounding the audience! It's followed by roaring, thumping music, pounding everything apocalyptically! Lights slowly go to black. as the knocking gets louder, more insistent and the music becomes more terrifying!)*

(Not) THE END

Contextual Notes

1. "Out of the darkness comes light" is a reference to the collected letters of RA Kartini, titled, in Indonesian, *Habis Gelap Terbitlah Terang*. Kartini advocated for women's rights and is revered as a national Indonesian hero.
2. Indonesian pronouns are non-gendered. Therefore, PERSON could be male or female. Because the role was originally performed by the playwright Ikranagara, the pronouns he/his/him have been used in this translation, but that shouldn't preclude PERSON from being a woman or non-gendered in a different production of the play.
3. Child is not assigned a gender in the script. In the original production, the role was played by Innosanto Nagara, the playwright's son.
4. The reporter's gender isn't indicated in the script. Female pronouns are used in this translation because the role was originally performed by a woman, but either a woman or a man could perform this role.
5. The 1962 Indonesian National Theater Conference mandated that theater had to expressly support President Soekarno's 1959 Political Manifesto that decreed a new state ideology, Manipol-USDEK, based the Indonesian constitution, Indonesian socialism, guided democracy, guided economy, and Indonesian identity. Popular plays, such as *Bung Besar* (Big Brother) by Misbach Jusa Biran, which had won second prize in a national drama contest in 1958, and *Domba-Domba Revolusi* (Lambs of the Revolution, 1962) by Bambang Soelarto were banned and labeled as anti-revolutionary and anti-government. Both plays, staged at Indonesia's National Theater Academy (ATNI), depicted opportunistic negative characters; the former easily construed as an

indictment of Soekarno's totalitarian rule and the latter of so-called heroes of the revolutionary wars against the Dutch. Not only were the plays critical of the government, but they also did not adhere to the prescribed aesthetic principal that works of art should be optimistic leading the masses into a bright new future. While Manipol-USDEK was no longer the government ideology under President Soeharto's New Order regime when *SSST...!!!* (*Shhh...!!!*) was first performed in 1977, plays continued to be censored or banned for criticizing the government or depicting Indonesia in a negative light. One tactic used by playwrights to circumvent government oversight in the 1970s was to invoke or rely on traditional Indonesian performance genres, such as *wayang kulit* (shadow puppetry). These performance genres utilized their conventional and accepted repertoire of stories (*lakon*) to create an analogous critique of current day events or placed criticisms into the mouths of the clown characters as humorous interludes, which were considered less dangerous (to social stability) because they were just clowns, after all.

6. The translation included in this volume is a new translation of the rehearsal script for the original 1980 production at TIM in Jakarta.

7. An event like this took place at Taman Ismail Marzuki two years before Ikranagara wrote and performed this play. In 1978, the poet Rendra performed a reading of his protest poetry in the Open Theater on May 1, 1978 to a large audience, including former and current high government officials. Part way into the reading six plastic ammonia bombs were thrown into the audience from outside the theatre's walls. Rendra had received a threatening message in the mail warning of retribution if he read poetry in protest of the government, but had ignored it. He was arrested, jailed, and then released on house arrest for the next several months, charged with the Hatred Articles, a law that had remained on the books since Dutch colonial rule. The Articles allowed the government to charge and detain people on the grounds of inciting the masses and disturbing the peace. Although Rendra hadn't directly provoked the audience, it was argued that it was the "sound" of

the poetry that was dangerous. For example, Rendra's characterization of Jakarta as "chaotic" was perceived by the authorities as an "untruth" that contradicted the government's image of the capital city as secure, peaceful, and orderly. The government's struggle to portray Indonesia as a modernizing and progressive and tidy state was threatened.

8. "New Reality" here brings to mind President Soeharto's "New Order" regime.

9. I Chongek's mantra is derived from the Adi Mantra, or primary mantra, *ong namo guru dev namo,* from Kundalini Yoga. It's a way to open up to one's own inner wisdom and to connect with the infinite creative consciousness. The final lines of I Chongek's mantra are translated by him in the next bit of dialogue: "If dead, to the grave. If alive, be family." I Chongrek goes on to riff on the mantra throughout his following scenes depending on what he's thinking in the moment.

10. "No Fire Like It" is in English in the original script.

11. "No Narcotic Like it" is in English in the original script.

12. The repetition of the sound "chak" recreates the *cak* (pronounced "chahk") chorus traditionally performed by men as part of Balinese trance rituals. In the 1930s, a performance called *kecak* was developed to tell the narrative outline of the Hindu epic *The Ramayana.* In a *kecak* performance, the *cak* chorus portrays the Monkey King Hanuman's monkey army that helps Rama rescue Sinta from imprisonment by the evil ogre Ravana. *Kecak* has become one of the best known and most popular Balinese dance performance for tourists, featuring *cak* choruses of dozens of men who sit in concentric circles and chant "*cak*" in interlocking rhythms while performing synchronized head, arm, and upper body gestures.

13. "Stupid! Stupid! Stupid! Stupid!" is in English in the original script.

Biographical Information

Ikranagara (1943–2023) was born and raised in Negara, Bali. He attended Balinese schools in Negara through junior high school and then went to Singaraja, North Bali, for high school. Ikra was a classmate of playwright-director Putu Wijaya. After graduating from high school, the two of them wrote and performed several performances together in Bali.

Ikra was admitted to Gadjah Mada University in Yogyakarta, but he spent most of his time there with drama groups led by Rendra and Arifin C Noer. In the political chaos of the 1960s, he moved to Jakarta and wrote for Mochtar Lubis' *Indonesia Raya* newspaper. He also became a principal actor in Arifin C Noer's Teater Ketjil in Jakarta.

When Arifin C Noer left for studies in the US, Ikranagara became the director of Teater Ketjil. In 1975, he started his own theater group, Teater Saja, writing for and performing mainly at the Jakarta Art Center, Taman Ismail Marzuki. He also taught and performed with Teater Saja and local groups in the US, Taiwan, Singapore, Malaysia, and the UK. He received two Fulbright grants to teach and direct theater in the United States at University of California, Davis and Ohio State University..

Celebrated as an accomplished movie actor, in 2009, Ikranagara won the Best Actor award at The 3rd Annual Indonesian Movie Awards and the Best Actor in a Supporting Role award at the Bandung Film Festival for *Laskar Pelangi* (The Rainbow Troops). In 2013, he won the Best Male Lead Actor Award at the Bandung Film Festival and was nominated for the Best Actor award at Indonesian Film Festival the for his role as the titular character in *Sang Kiai* (The Cleric). He also published his poetry and frequently did readings throughout Indonesia.

Cobina Gillitt is a translator of Indonesian plays and production dramaturg located in New York City. Her translations of Indonesian plays can be found in *The Lontar Anthology of Indonesian Drama, Vol 3: New Directions 1965-1998* (University of Hawaii Press, 2017) and *Islands of Imagination I: Modern Indonesian Plays* (University of Hawaii Press, 2015) both of which she edited and for which she wrote the introductions. Other published translations are included in *New Indonesian Plays* (Aurora Metro Books, 2019), *Three Plays by Three Indonesian Playwrights* and *Playwriting Workshop: Three Selected Plays* (The Jakarta Arts Council, 2006). Her scholarship on contemporary Indonesian theater includes "How the Fish Swims in Dirty Water: *Antigone* in Indonesia" in *Antigone on the Contemporary World Stage* (Oxford University Press, 2011) and "Indonesian Theatre and its Double: Putu Wijaya Paints a Theatre of Mental Terror" in *Performance of the Senses* (Routledge, 2006). Since 1988, she has been a member of Jakarta-based Teater Mandiri, founded and headed by Putu Wijaya.

Kay Ikranagara was born and raised in the US until 1957–60 when her family moved to Jakarta, Indonesia as her father joined the joint University of California and University of Indonesia Economics Project. She returned to UC Berkeley where she did her MA in Linguistics. She later completed her PhD in Linguistics at the East-West Center, University of Hawaii after field work in Jakarta. She is the author of several papers and books on Indonesian linguistics.

She returned again to Indonesia in 1969. While working on the Stanford program on Language Planning in Jakarta, she met and married the Indonesian playwright and director Ikranagara. They have two sons. She worked mainly on programs in the fields of Education Development and Educational Exchange in Indonesia, most recently the USAID Program Higher Education Leadership and Management. They lived primarily in Indonesia for over 50 years, first in Jakarta, then Yogyakarta, and then Bali.

www.ingramcontent.com/pod-product-compliance
Lightning Source LLC
Chambersburg PA
CBHW031320230926
51848CB00001B/28